D0228227

SPORT PSYCHOLOGY

DATE DUE

28. SEP. 1998	23. NOV. 2000	-1. MAY 2002
-2. NOV. 1998	20 MAR 2001	2 JAN 2003 NV 2
-2 NOV. 1998	-9 MAY 2001	-7. JAN. 2003
-6. NOV. 1998	4. JUN 2000	0. MAR. 2004
-4. JAN. 1999		
-4. JAN. 1999	-8. JUN 2001	
19. OCT. 1999		-6. JUL. 2005
-5. NOV. 1999	22. JUN	26. MAY 2005
29. NOV. 1999	10. SEP 2001	19. JUN. 20
28. FEB 2000	18. OCT 2001	0. JUN. 2005
-13 MAR 2000	-1. NOV. 2001	13. SEP 20
		28h sep 06
30. MAR. 2000	28 NOV. 2001	17. OCT 2006
	20. FEB 2002	
		11. FEB 2008
-5. JUL 2000	-5. MAR 2002	13 OCT 2014
-2 NOV. 2000		
	-7. MAR 2002	
GAYLORD	18. MAR. 2002	PRINTED IN U.S.A.

86479

037712

THE HENLEY COLLEGE LIBRARY

SPORT PSYCHOLOGY
CONCEPTS AND APPLICATIONS

F. C. Bakker
Department of Psychology, Faculty of Human Movement Sciences, The Free University, Amsterdam, The Netherlands

H. T. A. Whiting
Department of Psychology, University of York, York, UK

H. van der Brug
Faculty of Social Sciences, The University of Amsterdam, The Netherlands

JOHN WILEY & SONS
Chichester · New York · Brisbane · Toronto · Singapore

Copyright © 1995 by John Wiley & Sons Ltd,
Baffins Lane, Chichester,
West Sussex PO19 1UD, England

Original title: *Sportpsychologie*
© 1984 Samson Uitgeverÿ, Alphen aan den Rijn, The Netherlands

Reprinted January 1996, December 1997

Other Wiley Editorial Offices

John Wiley & Sons, Inc., 605 Third Avenue,
New York, NY 10158-0012, USA

Jacaranda Wiley Ltd, Box 859, Brisbane,
Queensland 4001, Australia

John Wiley & Sons (Canada) Ltd, 22 Worcester Road,
Rexdale, Ontario M9W 1L1, Canada

John Wiley & Sons (SEA) Pte Ltd, 37 Jalan Pemimpin #05-04,
Block B, Union Industrial Building, Singapore 129809

Library of Congress Cataloging-in-Publication Data
Bakker, F.C.
 [Sportpsychologie. English]
 Sport psychology : concept and applications / F.C. Bakker, H.T.A.
Whiting, H. van der Brug.
  p. cm.
 Translation of: Sportpsychologie.
 Includes bibliographical references and index.
 1. Sports—Psychological aspects. I. Whiting, H.T.A. (Harold
Thomas Anthony), 1929– . II. Brug, H. van der. III. Title.
GV706.4.B3513   1990
796´01—dc20   90–36199
                                                     CIP

British Library Cataloguing in Publication Data
Bakker, F.C.
 Sport psychology : concepts and applications.
 1. Sports. Psychological aspects
 I. Title. II. Whiting, H.T.A. (Harold Thomas Antony)
 III. Brug, H. van der IV. Sportpsychologie. *English*
 796.01

 ISBN 0 471 93913 7

Typeset by Setrite Typesetters Ltd
Printed and bound in Great Britain by
Biddles Ltd, Guildford and King's Lynn

CONTENTS

Preface   ix

1 INTRODUCTION   1

   1.1 Departure points   1
   1.2 The role of the sport psychologist   3

2 MOTIVATION AND SPORT   8

   2.1 Introduction   8
   2.2 Motivation psychology   9
   2.3 Motives and motivation   10
   2.4 Motives for participation in sport   14
   2.5 Intrinsic motivation   21
   2.6 Exploring boundaries and taking risks   27
   2.7 Motivation and achievement   33
        2.7.1 Motivation and performance: an optimal level?   34
        2.7.2 Attribution   39
        2.7.3 Goal setting   41
        2.7.4 The influence of the public   43
   2.8 Summary and conclusions   46

3 PERSONALITY AND SPORT   53

   3.1 Introduction   53
   3.2 Sport and personality: two streams   54
   3.3 Personality   55
   3.4 Personality traits   57
        3.4.1 Criticism of personality traits   59
   3.5 Personality and sport: what is the relationship?   60
   3.6 Influence of sport participation on personality   63
   3.7 Differences between athletes and non-athletes   65
   3.8 Personality and motor learning   70
        3.8.1 Cognitive style and motor learning   71
        3.8.2 Anxiety and motor achievement   73
   3.9 Summary and conclusions   75

v

4 SPORT AND AGGRESSION 81

4.1 Introduction 81
4.2 Psychological theories about aggressive behaviour 82
   4.2.1 Aggression as inborn behaviour 82
   4.2.2 Physiological activation, emotion and aggression 83
   4.2.3 Aggression and learned behaviour 84
4.3 Disinhibiting influences 86
4.4 Reactive and instrumental aggression 87
4.5 Sociological theory-forming 87
4.6 Research into sport and aggression 89
   4.6.1 Aggressive behaviour of sport performers 89
      4.6.1.1 Aggressive behaviour and the nature of the sport 91
      4.6.1.2 Situational factors 93
      4.6.1.3 Socialisation processes 98
   4.6.2 Aggression of spectators 99
      4.6.2.1 The effect of watching sport competitions on the aggression of the spectator 99
      4.6.2.2 Situational factors that have an influence on the aggression of spectators 104
      4.6.2.3 Violent sub-cultures and attendance at sport competitions 111
4.7 Conclusions 121

5 MOTOR LEARNING 127

5.1 Introduction 127
5.2 General characteristics of the learning process 128
5.3 Classical and operant conditioning 131
5.4 Social learning theory 137
5.5 Information processing 140
5.6 Feedback 146
5.7 Mental training 148
   5.7.1 Symbolic learning 148
   5.7.2 Attention and activation 149
   5.7.3 Muscular excitation 149
5.8 Conclusion 150

6 DECISION-MAKING IN SPORT SITUATIONS 154

6.1 Introduction 154
6.2 Psychology and decision-making 158
   6.2.1 Signal detection theory 159

6.2.2 Behavioural decision theory 161
6.2.3 Decision-making in sport 165
6.3 Uncertain outcomes 165
6.3.1 The home-field advantage 166
6.4 Subjective probability 167
6.5 Ballistic actions 173
6.5.1 Individual differences 183
6.6 Perception−action coupling 189
6.7 Conclusion 192

7 SPORT PSYCHOLOGY AND PRACTICE 197

7.1 Introduction 197
7.2 Sport psychology and (top-level) performance 198
7.2.1 The problem of generalisation 201
7.2.2 The problem of suitable subjects 202
7.2.3 The problem of the small margins 202
7.2.4 The probabilistic nature of (sport) psychological 203
pronouncements
7.3 Sport, psychology and well-being 203
7.4 Sport, well-being and prejudice 206
7.5 Maintaining prejudices 211

Author index 215
Subject index 221

PREFACE

In contrast to existing textbooks on the subject of sport psychology, which are often of an encyclopaedic nature, the present text attempts to provide examples of empirically based answers to questions arising directly from the field of sport. The departure point, in this respect, lies in the posing of ecologically valid questions — that is to say, questions which have meaning within the context of sport — and thereby to make a start with the development of a meaningful body of knowledge in the field of sport psychology. The extent to which the field is, at the present time, dependent on knowledge 'borrowed' from the field of general psychology, and the consequent ecological limitations thereof, is a reflection of the present state of affairs in sport psychology.

Each chapter in this book (except Chapter 1) is set up in the following way: first, a number of typical questions raised by participants and coaches in the field of sport at all levels are signalled and superficially addressed within the context of the chapter heading. This is followed by a discussion of the psychological concepts pertinent to the answering of such questions (the 'pure' approach) and a selection of empirical findings stemming from the field of general and/or sport psychology (the 'applied' approach) are presented and discussed in the context of the questions posed. Each chapter concludes with an evaluation of the present state of affairs with respect to the topic area being discussed as well as speculation about future possibilities. The chapter on 'Sport and aggression' differs from the rest of the book in that it also introduces sociological perspectives and findings. The book was originally published in the Dutch language in 1984 and has been rewritten and updated for the present edition.

Chapter 5 — 'Motor learning' was written by a guest contributor, P. C. W. van Wieringen (in cooperation with F. C. Bakker).

F. C. Bakker
H. T. A. Whiting
H. van der Brug

ix

1 INTRODUCTION

1.1. Departure points

In his Foreword to Hendry's (1978) book *School, Sport and Leisure* Nisbet writes:

> *Sport, for example, promises to become an integral element of the culture of modern society, and insofar as it contributes to personal health and social interaction, it has a considerable potential. If it were to be ignored by our educational institutions, there is a risk that the potential might be lost in mere spectator interest and commercialism.*

Sport is not, indeed, an isolated phenomenon in our society; rather it is inseparably linked to many aspects of daily life. Decisions made outside the direct context of sport often have indirect consequences for the field of sport. The allocation of funds for sporting occasions by national governments and the boycott by different countries of particular sporting events on political grounds are but two examples. The reverse is also true: what goes on in sport has repercussions beyond the field of sport. A final place for any country in a World Championship football competition not only brings with it considerable disruption in the everyday life of that country but matches played at home in that context will probably result in considerable absences from work on the grounds of 'sudden illness'!

In studying the behaviour of people in sport situations (both players and spectators) account must be taken of these mutual influences. The chapter on 'Decision-making in sport' presents many illustrations in this respect. It also holds true for the chapter on 'Sport and aggression' from the spectator viewpoint; this chapter ends with the conclusion that violent behaviour at football matches and behaviour in other circumstances are structured by the same values and norms. The fact that attempts to reduce such violence have

1

little effect is not surprising, given the contention that the causes of such violence are closely connected to societal changes in general. Thus, counteractive measures which are restricted only to problems in sport *per se* are unlikely to have much effect or, where they do, the effect is likely to be short-lived.

With respect to the two faces of sport and sport training signalled by Nisbet — contribution to personal health or decline into passivity — there are a diversity of meanings and opinions. In the last chapter some of these will be discussed, and it will be made clear that expressions made about the positive and negative aspects of sport are seldom based on empirical evidence. Sport psychology as a research field is in its early stages of development. This, in spite of the existence of international and national organisations for sport psychology, and in spite of the fact that, already, in the *International Survey on the Psychology of Sport and Physical Activity* (Salmela, 1981) around 1000 people from 35 different countries are cited as people who claim to be sport psychologists! Perhaps not surprisingly, national societies of psychology have been slow to welcome this newly developing sub-field into their organisation, since many would-be sport psychologists do not have the kind of formal training in academic psychology that would make their membership of such societies acceptable. That there are changes to be expected in this respect is evidenced by the recent discussions taking place both in England and The Netherlands between representatives of sport psychology societies and the national psychological bodies (British Psychological Society and Netherlands Institute for Psychology, respectively).

To date, a large proportion of the literature pertaining to sport psychology is addressed to questions about personality and motivation. In fact, in many quarters, sport psychology is artificially constrained by considerations of only dynamic factors in performance. It is understandable that people should be aware that within these conceptual areas a lot of fascinating questions can be raised which, at the same time, have important implications for the field of sport — in Chapters 2 and 3 these areas receive considerable attention — but it is hoped, even within this relatively limited text, to show that these are not the only topics of interest, and also that they are not necessarily the most important.

The field of psychology, ranging as it does from the more biological to the more social, embraces a large number of sub-fields and recognises many different approaches and methodologies. From these sub-fields and approaches much information can be gleaned which has relevance for the field of sport. However, it would be difficult to conceive of these 'pockets' of information as providing an integrated body of knowledge which might merit the label 'sport psychology'. To this end, *systematisation* of sport-relevant questions and empirical findings must serve as the guiding principle. In this respect there has been little progress to date.

Wilberg (1973), in this respect, makes a distinction between *recipient* knowledge (knowledge borrowed from the parent discipline) and *generated* knowledge (which arises as a consequence of empirical work directly related to the field in question—in the present context, 'sport'). He warns about the danger of uncritically accepting recipient knowledge from the field of general psychology for answering questions concerned with sport—they can, in the extreme, be misleading. Nevertheless, in the past, this has often been done. Tyldesley & Whiting (1982) attribute this to the ambivalent position of the sport psychologist. On the one hand he is striving to obtain the recognition of sport psychology as a field of scientific endeavour with its own identity and, on the other hand, it is precisely this need for recognition which makes it easy for the sport psychologist to fall back on 'established' psychology, with its academically accepted methods. His position is not helped by the reluctance of 'established' psychology, until comparatively recently, to recognise sport psychology as a separate field of study.

In this book the contrast between recipient and generated knowledge, as it relates to the developing field of sport psychology, will be recognised for what it is, and repeatedly returned to in what follows, as will the problems which may arise following a too literal acceptance of concepts and methods from the parent discipline psychology.

1.2. The role of the sport psychologist

Given the present lack of clarity about the extent and function of sport psychology, it should not occasion too much surprise that there are problems about the precise role that a sport psychologist might be able to fill.

To begin with, it should be clear that, given the demands of present-day sport, the coach can no longer make do with only his specific knowledge about a particular sport coupled to a subjective feeling for the 'right' decision in countless different situations. While there would be considerable agreement that coaching is an art, in the sense that the successful coach must have a feeling for decisions that lead to results, this does not mean that such decisions might not be better made if account were to be taken of existing empirical evidence—quite the reverse (Whiting, 1975). In turn, such evidence should not be restricted to one field of scientific endeavour. When a sportsman or woman (or coach for that matter) fails to achieve, produces disappointing results or does not live up to his own or other people's expectations, diverse causes may be invoked: physiological, social, emotional, biomechanical or supervisory—either separately or in mutual cohesion. Knowledge from a number of different scientific fields, coupled to the coach's more sophisticated knowledge of the sport and the individual sportsman, is necessary in order to decide on an appropriate course of action. Empirical findings from diverse disciplines have to be considered and, where possible, integrated.

For the time being the coach/teacher would appear to be the only person suitably placed to fulfil that role. If, in fact, he is suitably equipped is another question which needs to receive considerable attention in some future science of coaching.

Cooperative working between coaches, medical practitioners and sport scientists (particularly exercise physiologists) is not unusual. The position of the sport psychologist, however, is unclear in spite of Bannister's (1980) contention that:

> *While physiological limitations by physical exercise are important, psychological factors are decisive for winning or losing: they determine how close an athlete is able to know how close he can approach his absolute limits.*

Likewise, the results of an investigation by Gowan (1979) do little to clarify the role of the sport psychologist. This author made an inventory of the opinions of coaches, and those responsible for the technical leading of the Canadian National Sport organisations, about the importance of different sport science disciplines. The results of this investigation are given in Table 1.1.

These results were confirmed in a similar research enquiry in Switzerland in 1980, shortly before the Olympic Games in Moscow. Sportsmen, trainers and sporting organisations were asked if they had need for advice of a psychological nature. In spite of the fact that 60% of the respondents had no direct experience of such advice, the majority of them were of the opinion that such advice was valuable and needed to be available.

Sport psychologists can provide such advice by presenting research reports, for example, at conferences attended by those active in the sporting world or publishing in journals accessible to coaches and other sport scientists. In

Table 1.1. Importance that Canadian coaches and technical staff attach to different sport science disciplines.

Sport science discipline	Importance	
	Score*	Rank order
Sport psychology	2.1	1st
Physiology	2.5	2nd
Biomechanics	2.7	3rd
Sport medicine	3.0	4th
Theories about motor learning	3.3	5th
Theories about growth and development	3.9	6th
Sport sociology	4.4	7th

Adapted from Gowan (1979).
* Scores are averaged and based on a seven-point scale in which 1 is the most important and 7 the least.

addition, the provision of courses on appropriate psychological topics for the sporting world could be more commonplace. In this respect there is much room for development in the relationship between theory and practice. Advice that is not directly coupled to sport is of little value, and usually resort has to be made to the application of knowledge borrowed from the field of general psychology without its relevance being made apparent.

It has also to be realised that *research does not tell one what to do*. While research — particularly sport-relevant research — provides *some* of the evidence on which decisions might be made, its piecemeal nature has to be realised. Subjective factors, value judgements and knowledge of sport-specific situations play just as important, if not a more important, role. The sport psychologist, if he is to function effectively, must be cognisant of this and must be able to estimate the value of such information alongside his own contribution. As in any good functioning system, feedback is necessary — in this case, feedback between the field and the laboratory.

In order to fulfil his advisory role effectively the sport psychologist must recognise his place and contribution within the constellation of coaches, trainers, sportsmen, medical and paramedical advisers, sport scientists and sport organisations. Figure 1.1 suggests a *possible* model in this respect; a model which undoubtedly will need to be modified as the contribution of the sport psychologist becomes clarified.

Direct channels of information exchange are suggested between coach and athlete and between the athlete and the medical/paramedical team (doctors, physiotherapists, etc.) in which the first channel reflects the *essential* relationship. Generally speaking, the sport psychologist will not have a *direct* communication channel to the athlete (unless as a clinical specialist he forms part of the medical team); his involvement with the athlete is more indirect,

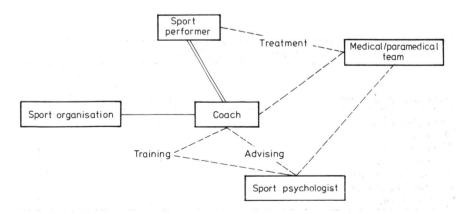

Figure 1.1. The place of the sport psychologist in the infrastructure of sport.

via the coach. A situation might also be conceived in which the coach, especially given the pressure and stresses of high-level competition, may well need personal advice from a sport psychologist.

In order for such a system to function effectively it is necessary that the sport psychologist maintain close contact with the practical field of sport as well as with the other branches of the sport sciences (Figure 1.2.) since his contribution is only one aspect of the scientific knowledge pertinent to sport. The recent national trend to set up sport science societies with sub-sections for the different scientific specialisations has advantages in this respect — cross-fertilisation being easier.

This book provides information from both general psychology and psychological information generated by attempts to provide answers to questions arising in the context of sport. By so doing it is hoped to demonstrate some of the contributions that psychology has made, and can make, to the field of sport. The topic areas addressed in this book represent only a small choice out of a potentially large field of knowledge. This field is dynamic: knowledge

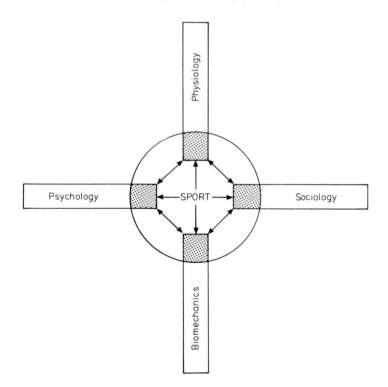

Figure 1.2. Structure of sport science — the hatched areas stand for sport psychology, sport physiology, sociology of sport and biomechanics.

must not only *inform* but also *stimulate* new ideas and further development. This book is written with these two criteria in mind.

References

Bannister, R. (1980). What's it all about? *Sports Coach*, **5**, 4–5.

Gowan, G.R. (1979). Bridging the gap between sport science and sport practice. In P. Klavora and J.V. Daniel (Eds), *Coach, Athlete and the Sport Psychologist*. Toronto: Publication Division, School of Physical and Health Education, University of Toronto.

Hendry, L.B. (1978). *School, Sport and Leisure*. London: Lepus.

Salmela, J. (1981). *International Survey on the Psychology of Sport and Physical Activity*. Champaign, IL: Human Kinetics.

Tyldesley, D.A., & Whiting, H.T.A. (1982). Sport psychology as a science. In E. Geron (Ed.), *Introduction to Sport Psychology*. Wingate, Israel: Institute for Physical Education and Sport.

Whiting, H.T.A. (1975). *Readings in Sport Psychology—2*. London: Kimpton.

Wilberg, R.B. (1973). Criteria for the definition of a field. IIIrd International Symposium on Sports Psychology, Madrid, Spain.

2 MOTIVATION AND SPORT

2.1. Introduction

The training schedule of a good marathon runner would be in the region of 200−300 km per week, i.e. 10−20 hours engaged in 'nothing but running'! Top-level gymnasts spend several hours a day at their sport, during which time they run the risk of painful, and sometimes serious, injuries. During the Tour de France, cyclists spend many hours each day 'in the saddle' often at the one extreme in temperatures above 30°C, and at the other in snow and hail storms. Anyone who has watched such competitors slaving away to reach the brow of a hill knows what is meant by persistence! Parachutists take the risk that there comes an occasion when their parachute does not open, and alpinists know, that in the Mont Blanc region alone, in some seasons over 50 mountaineers do not return. Seemingly such people are motivated not to give up, to exert themselves to extremes and to defy danger, i.e. particular things to do and others to leave undone in order to practise their sport. This assertion does not hold only for top-level sport. Mountaineers who climb only during their vacation often face the same risks as professional alpinists. Some 'joggers' apparently suffer as much as a professional cyclist in attempting 'not to give in', even though their colleagues are half an hour ahead.

The question that these examples evoke is 'why?'. Why would a mountaineer take such a risk, why would a 'jogger' be prepared to suffer, why would anyone run for 20 hours in a week?

To such questions the psychology of motivation tries to provide an answer. In this respect it is good to bear in mind that the examples provided are not the prerogative of the *sport* participant. They are equally applicable to practitioners of music, ballet or whatever hobby or professional activity.

The task of the psychology of motivation is, in this respect, two-fold. In

8

the first place to: 'discover what dimensions of individual differences are really needed to explain why people do what they do *when* they do it' (Atkinson, 1981, p. 119); and secondly, to answer the question: 'what is it about the sport or activity itself that helps to determine whether or not the person actually engages in it?' (Alderman, 1976, p. 205).

Questions such as the following, that relate to sport and motivation, fall within these two broadly formulated tasks: Why do some people participate in sport and others not? What motives lead to some people playing football while others cycle or parachute jump? In what way is it possible to influence a person's motivation in the direction of such activities and what factors, in this respect, are important? Under what circumstances is anyone 'optimally' motivated and how is this optimal level to be reached and maintained?

In the following paragraphs an indication will be given of the kind of answers that motivation psychology has provided or can provide to such questions.

2.2. Motivation psychology

Motivation psychology sees its task as that of providing answers to the question 'why' with respect to behaviour. Why does one person play tennis while another plays football, why does a 'jogger' run himself into the ground? Why go parachute jumping — or why, having once started, stop? Generally speaking, motivation psychology is concerned with the question of 'the origin, the direction and the persistence of behaviour' (Orlebeke, 1981, p. 13). In this respect the 'why-question' has three separate aspects: why do people invest energy in the carrying out of particular activities, why in those particular activities and not some others, and why do they persist in the chosen direction or give it up?

There are a number of different theories about motivation (instinct theories, theories in which the reduction of a drive is central or in which an optimal level of stimulation is assumed, expectation theories — to name but a few; see Atkinson, 1964; Deci, 1975; Murray, 1964 and Orlebeke, 1981 for overviews). Some theories are directed particularly to the question of where people get the energy for their activities from. Others are more suitable for explaining the direction which particular behaviours take, or answering questions that relate to persisting in a chosen activity or giving up. Theories differ above all in those aspects of behaviour to which they are directed (achievement, aggression, cooperation). Finally, there is a difference in the emphasis placed on the study of animal as against human behaviour, and thereby the extent to which development follows a more biological or a more cognitive orientation.

In looking for answers to the kinds of questions put forward in this Introduction, different theories will be evoked without being discussed in any great detail. The interested reader who requires more theoretical detail is directed to the many, readily available, psychological handbooks on motivation. Having said this, it should be noted that in what follows a particular emphasis has been placed on theories in which cognitive factors of motivation play a leading role.

2.3. Motives and motivation

While, in everyday language, motives and motivation are often used synonymously, it is useful to keep these two concepts separate from one another. Motives (reasons for doing) are relatively stable characteristics that induce a person to begin particular activities. Motives are dispositions, that is to say they become active under particular circumstances, or become actualised in behaviour — they are characteristics in which people may differ. As examples, achievement motive, affiliation motive (the need for friendship and emotionally tinted relationships), power motive and exploration motive — a catalogue that is easy to extend, as will be evident in what follows.

Motivation, in contrast, relates to the state of an organism held responsible for the carrying out of a particular activity at a particular point in time. This state of the organism is, as a rule, the consequence of a combination of internal (personal) and external (situational) factors. When motives are actualised there is talk of motivation. Motives, however, are only one of the factors that determine a person's motivation. Situational factors and biologically entrenched needs play an equally important role. The motivation of an athlete to achieve or to excel will, for example, be dependent not only on his achievement motive (his wish to excel) but also on the reputation of his opponents and the public interest of the competition, to name but two of the potential situational factors. Different motives can, moreover, be active at the same time — in which case they may also be antagonistic — and, together, determine the strength of motivation at a particular moment.

'Need' is closely tied to the concept 'motive' or the more biologically oriented concept 'drive'. With respect to biological drives this is particularly easy to illustrate: a biological deficiency (for example lack of oxygen) results in a need (for oxygen). This need is the drive that motivates the organism to behave in a manner which reduces that drive, i.e. the satisfaction of the need. The acquisition of food (or oxygen) is the goal of the organism, and behaviour that leads to this goal is reinforcing. The need activates the organism, the nature of the need gives direction to the behaviour (trying to surface from under water in order to breathe again). Satisfaction of the need leads to a cessation of the behaviour.

The majority of motivated behaviour cannot be traced back to the satisfaction of biological needs, i.e. to biological drives (for example making friends, playing music, participating in sport, etc.). However, the terminology used for biological drives could also be applied to motives. For example we speak of 'the need to excel' (achievement motive) or 'a lack of affection' (affiliation motive). Closely related to the concept 'motive' are the goals that a person sets himself (or strives towards) and the expectations that he has about the actions necessary to achieve these goals. The achievement motive is what urges a person to be the best in his team, a goal that he can achieve by training more often than his team-mates. By the formulation of goals and the actions that will lead to their fulfilment important learning processes are involved.

The athlete who decides to undertake extra training will consider this to be a useful investment of time if, indeed, in the course of time he becomes the best in the team. Also, the reaching of the goal set will be experienced as valuable, with the possible consequence that the wish to excel by means of a similar experience will be strengthened. Certainly, when repeated positive experiences of a similar kind occur, the achievement motive will be strengthened — and, inversely, this motive will be weakened if the goal is not reached (Hermans, 1971). From the latter can be deduced that realistic goal-setting is important to the development of motives.

In Heckhausen's (1974) description of the concept 'motive', the intimate relationships between motive, goals and value of the actions in relation to these goals as well as the importance of learning experiences are expressed: 'Motives comprise relatively abstract goals and action expectations, which have been developed in continuous interaction with the environment' (p. 147).

Deci (1975), in particular, emphasises the importance of learning experiences to the development of human motives. In this respect he directs his attention not so much to motivation with a clear biological (hunger, thirst, sex) or emotional (fear, joy) background — in spite of the fact that learning experiences are also involved here — but rather to intrinsic motivation. Intrinsically motivated behaviour manifests itself in the desire to feel competent. From this basic need (or motive) for competence and self-determination, more specific motives develop.

As the child interacts with his environment, the basic undifferentiated need for competence and self-determination begins to differentiate into specific motives. Therefore, adults may be high-need achievers, or self-actualizers, or intellectuals. These needs (for achievement, for actualization, for cognizance, etc.) are all specific intrinsic motives which develop out of the basic intrinsic need as a result of the person's interaction with his environment. (Deci, 1975, pp. 65, 66).

The development of different motives is thus dependent on the extent to which the environment provides the child (and later the adult) with the opportunity to express his need to feel competent in particular behaviour. When behaviours that are coupled to a particular need are encouraged and when, as a consequence, a positive feeling is invoked in the child then a motive will develop. For example, when independent behaviour is encouraged and the child, through the behaviour, feels 'competent', an independence motive develops out of the more basic competence motive. The same holds for the need for novelty, for knowledge, for skill mastery, for power, or for achievement.

The more social motives, such as the need for approval, for acceptance and for affection arise out of environmental reactions to the behaviour of the child. These motives, however, are only likely to originate if the child, in his striving for competency, receives only little support from his immediate environment. To illustrate this last point: the child who is confronted with a novel situation can try to handle it himself but can also seek the protection of parents or other adults in order to reduce his uncertainty. If the latter behaviour is encouraged, the child sees this kind of behaviour as valuable with, as possible consequence, the development of a need for support instead of the development of an independence motive.

The question as to the motives that drive a person to participate in sport can be reversed — which motives can, in a sport participation context, be developed. In the next paragraph both of these questions will be returned to. First, the way in which motives are active (become actualised) will be pursued further. To this end, use is made of Deci's (1975) cognitive motivation model that is schematically reproduced in Figure 2.1.

Central to the model is the second box: awareness of potential satisfaction. Someone is aware that he can achieve a particular state of affairs that will be experienced by him as more pleasant, more satisfactory than the situation in which he now finds himself. In this respect reference can be made to:

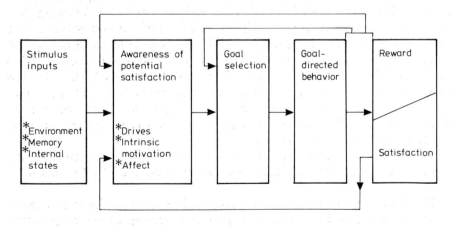

Figure 2.1. Deci's cognitive model of motivated behaviour. From Deci, (1975); reprinted with permission of Plenum Press and author.

1. The satisfaction of a biological need (hunger, thirst).
2. The satisfaction of the intrinsic need for feelings of competence (or of one of the specific motives that have developed out of this basic motive).
3. The experiencing of more positive or less negative emotional feelings.

Out of this 'awareness of' — Deci speaks about 'cognitive representation of a desired future state' (p. 96) — the person derives the energy for his motivated behaviour. A feeling of hunger starts him thinking about what he should eat; the conviction that he will die if he comes in last can result in a pupil making an apparently senseless, final sprint.

The awareness that potential satisfaction is possible arises from environmental stimuli (seeing a table set for a party, for example), from memory (the satisfaction of more clearly setting one's own record) or from an internal state of the organism (blood sugar level). The awareness, actuated by internal and external stimuli, directs the person in the selection of this goal; he will get something to eat, he wishes to become the best in his team or to feel less down-hearted. As a consequence he chooses to behave in a manner that he assumes will, indeed, bring him closer to his goal; he is going to eat something, to do extra training or go more often to see a film.

Eventually, the chosen behaviour results in, more or less, the expected results, i.e. the satisfaction of the felt need.

Several points arising from the Deci model need to be emphasised. In the first place, in making decisions about the goal that must be strived for at a particular moment, people weigh up also the expected consequences of any actions they may make. These decisions relate to the setting of priorities when diverse motives and drives play a role at the same time (or lead to consciousness of potential satisfaction), but where the striving to satisfy one need conflicts with that of the other. A night out and, the following day, achieving a top performance are likely to be a difficult combination. The decisions that people take also relate to the choosing of goals. A person can excel in sport, in music, in ballet or in different school subjects. This suggestion gives rise to a new point — the role of feedback. It is by this means that some people learn to develop particular motives and others not. By such means a person learns that some actions are more suitable for reaching his goals than others and that, in order to feel more competent, he can better play chess than football.

A last point from Deci's model on which attention must be focused, is the fact that, in coming to their decisions, people make use of information:

1. From the environment, from memory and out of their internal state of affairs that together result in a person becoming aware of potential satisfaction.
2. About desirable and undesirable effects of particular actions (that, for

example, aggressive behaviour can have a certain instrumental value, but can also bring with it negative effects — see Chapter 4).
3. About the probability that particular behaviour will lead to the desired outcome.
4. About the value of particular actions for the person carrying them out.

The above implies that others can, by providing information, exert influence on a person's motivation. Information about the usefulness of particular training activities, about the strength of the opponent or his weak spots and about the consequences of a particular performance for an athlete form, for example, important sources for bringing about motivational changes in an athlete.

2.4. Motives for participation in sport

Why does someone participate in a particular sport, why participate in sport at all, or in other words: what motives lie behind a person's decision to participate in (a particular) sport? In the course of the history of psychology a number of attempts have been made to develop a classification system under which all human motives can be brought. Classic, in this respect, is Murray's (1938, out of Hilgard, Atkinson & Atkinson, 1971) list of 12 motives which owe their origin to biological needs and 28 motives that arise out of 'psychological needs'. To the latter belong, amongst others:

1. Construction: the need to organise and build.
2. Achievement: the need to overcome obstacles, to strive to do something difficult as well and as quickly as possible.
3. Exhibition: the need for self-dramatisation: to excite, amuse, stir, shock, thrill others.
4. Defensiveness: the need to justify one's actions.
5. Dominance: the need to influence or control others.
6. Autonomy: the need to strive for independence.
7. Aggression: the need to assault or injure others.
8. Affiliation: the need to form friendships and associations.
9. Nurturance: the need to nourish, aid, or protect others.
10. Play: the need to relax, amuse oneself, seek diversion and entertainment.
11. Cognisance: the need to explore, ask questions, satisfy curiosity.
12. Exposition: the need to point and demonstrate, to give information, explain, interpret, lecture.

The existence of different classification systems of human motives (in addition to that of Murray can be mentioned, amongst others, Birch & Veroff, 1966; Cattell & Child, 1975; Deci, 1975; Heckhausen, 1974;

McClelland, 1985) makes the giving of conclusive answers to the question 'which motives lie at the basis of sport participation?', very difficult. Results of empirical work are linked to the classification system used such that mutual comparisons are not always possible. Moreover, there are important differences in the procedures used. In some cases the most important motive underlying sport participation is asked for, in others a number of motives can be given. Further, use is made of widely divergent methods in order to elicit information from people, e.g,. lists of motives, interest questionnaires, interviews and projective tests (such as the Thematic Apperception Test in which subjects, on the basis of presented photographs, have to compose a short story: subsequently, the contents are analysed for indications of particular themes, for example achievement, fear of failure, friendship). Finally, different scaling techniques would appear to be used.

Nevertheless, there has been sufficient research carried out into the motives of sport performers to present a number of general conclusions about the reasons underlying their participation. In Table 2.1 an overview is presented of the most important motives named in the different studies. From the table it is apparent that very diverse groups have been researched, ranging from recreational to top-level sport performers.

From this table, in the first place, it is obvious that very different motives can underlie the same behaviour—the practice of sport. Secondly, it can be concluded that a number of motives are closely linked to the activity in question, i.e. they are relatively specific (pleasure in movement and the intrinsic pleasure of swimming are two examples). Thus, they lose something of their explanatory value (see, for example, the conclusion of Brackhane & Fischhold, 1981 that long-distance runners have a need for movement). However, the fact that joy or pleasure often appears as the most important motive does have some meaning. Apparently participation in sport has important intrinsic value. In addition to the relatively specific motives, the motives which appear in the different studies reported are, in part, attributable to the basic need to feel competent (see Deci's theory, p. 11). The affiliation motive and the wish to achieve and excel are reported in almost all studies. With respect to the achievement motive it can, on 'common-sense grounds', be assumed that sport situations are, indeed, an area of activity in which this motive can be expressed and developed. Finally, it would seem that a health motive—the need to feel fit and healthy—as well as the need for compensation for study and work load—play a role.

The question as to why people participate in sport can provisionally be answered as follows:

1. The activities involved have intrinsic value (joy, pleasure) and, consequently, are worth striving for.
2. Such activities, it is claimed, have positive effects on health.

Table 2.1. Motives and reasons for participation in sport.

Study	Subjects	N	Sex	Motives
Alderman & Wood (1976)	Young hockey players	425	Male	Affiliation (need for friendship), need to excel, need for excitement, need for success, autonomy
Artus (1971)	14–21-year-old recreational and competitive athletes	1625	Male and female	Compensation, intrinsic pleasure, achievement, affiliation, health
Bielefeld (1979)	Students	418	Male and female	Achievement, self-determination, health, catharsis, affiliation
Bloss (1971)	Students	160	Male and female	Joy, pleasure, physical fitness, compensation, health, affiliation
Brackhane & Fischhold (1981)	Long-distance runners	21	Male	Need to move, 'need to feel one's own body', achievement, affiliation, compensation, feeling relaxed afterwards
Van Dellen & Crum (1975)	Participants in recreation sport	158	Male and female	Intrinsic pleasure, health, physical fitness, compensation
Gabler (1971)	(Top-level) swimmers (12–26 years)	154	Male and female	Intrinsic pleasure of swimming, competition, need for social contact, need to demonstrate skills, health
Hahmann (1971)	Students	986	Male and female	Health, intrinsic pleasure, achievement, compensation
Manders (1980)	Recreational and competitive athletes (15–50 years)	2000	Male and female	Entertainment/relaxation, health, sociability, achievement
Robertson (1981)	Children (12 years)	2261	Male and female	Intrinsic rewards (pleasure, excitement, 'feeling fine'), achievement
Sabath (1971)	Students	218	Female	Intrinsic pleasure, health, physical fitness

3. Opportunities are provided for people to gain the feeling of competence.

An additional insight into the motives for sport participation can be provided by a comparison between athletes and non-athletes. If athletes find some things more important than non-athletes, attach value to other goals or distinguish themselves by the development of particular motives, it is possible, indirectly, to discern what are the motives underlying sport practice.

Fodero (1980) provides an overview of studies into differences in motives between groups of people that differ with respect to the level at which they practise sport and the intensity of that practice. Some studies conclude with respect to the achievement motive that differences do exist, in the sense that with an increasingly higher level of sport practice, athletes have a stronger achievement motive (Vanek & Hosek, 1970; Ogilvie, Tutko & Young, 1965). In other studies such a difference would not appear to be shown (for example, Gorsuch, 1968; Pyne, 1956). From Fodero's own research it would seem that within a gymnastics club operating at national level, no difference exists between high-level and lower-level gymnasts with respect to achievement motive, the need for self-respect or the need to perfect what the gymnast is capable of doing. The scores of the gymnasts on the achievement motive and the need for self-respect were, however, in comparison to the national norms, relatively high.

Dunleavy & Rees (1979) demonstrated that the achievement motive was closely related to a greater interest in competitive sport. People with a strong achievement motive showed more interest in competitive sport than those with a weak achievement motive — who tended to be more interested in recreation sport. If, however, the concern is participation in sport activities *per se* there would not appear to be any differences between competitive and recreative sport performers in strength of achievement motive. Gabler (1972) came to this conclusion following a comparison between top-level swimmers and a control group. There were no statistically significant differences between the two groups in personality characteristics, under which heading achievement motive was also included (see also Chapter 3 on personality).

In a carefully organised longitudinal study by Gabler (1976) it seemed that top-level sport performers who remained in training had a higher achievement motive than top-level swimmers who dropped out during the 4-year research period. In general, it would seem that the differences between athletes and non-athletes in motives of a more general kind are relatively small. It might well be supposed, however, that the achievement motive in sport situations plays an important role but, with the exception of this motive there are few indications that the field of 'sport' makes demands on particular, very general motives, on which other areas of activity do not call. Also, in the comparison between competitive and recreational sport performers, it was interesting to note that there were more similarities than differences in reasons for sport participation. In the study by Manders (1980), the results of which are reproduced in Figure 2.2, a similar conclusion is drawn.

It is important to note that the results reported so far are based on the

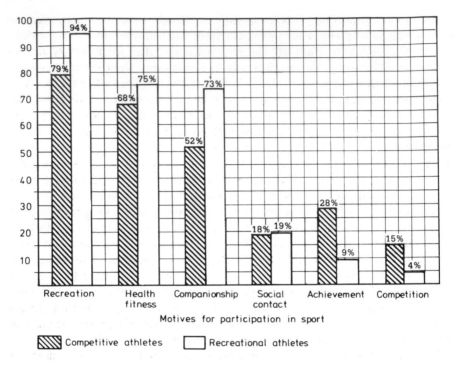

Motives for participation in sport

Competitive athletes   Recreational athletes

Figure 2.2. Motives to take part in sport by participants in competitive and recreative sport. From Manders (1980).

verbal reports of athletes, about their reasons for participation. Butt (1976) comes to somewhat different conclusions than those reported above. She provides three categories which she considers to constitute the source of the motivation of (top-level) sport participants. In Butt's conception, the basis of the motivation to participate in (top-level) sport is aggression, a neurotic conflict or the striving for competency. An athlete whose motivation is related to aggression would be characterised as active, strongly motivated and especially directed towards trying to master his opponent(s). As an example of an athlete whose motivation can be traced back to aggression Butt names the boxer Sonny Liston. When the source of the motivation is a neurotic conflict, motives, according to Butt, such as 'exhibitionism' and 'narcissism' play an important role. The chess master Bobby Fisher would be typified in this way. The need to be competent is the third—and by Butt the most positively valued—motive that lies at the basis of the motivation of athletes.

In addition to these individual sources of the motivation of athletes, Butt names two motives of a more social kind, competition and cooperation. The motive to cooperate with others is easy to link to the competency motive, the motive to compete with aggression and neurotic conflict.

Butt makes use mainly of 'case-histories' for the confirmation of the existence of the named motivation sources. Moreover, such explanations are mainly concerned with the energetic aspect of motivated behaviour. The athlete will derive the energy for his activities from the need to find an outlet for his aggression, on the need to reduce the tension of internal conflicts or on the need to feel himself competent. It is true that Butt's description can be criticised—not least for the absence of empirical evidence to support her propositions—nevertheless, her work provides a warning: the picture generally presented of the motives of sport performers may be less rosy than would appear from their own statements.

As indicated earlier, relatively specific motives play an important role in explaining why people participate in sport. In this connection it is worthwhile to recall Heckhausen's description of motives (see page 11). Motives comprise relatively abstract goals and action expectations. Athletes have apparently experienced learning situations in which participation in sport has become an important goal, and they have positive expectations about the consequences of actions in this field of activity. An important question is then 'what learning experiences have athletes gone through in comparison to non-athletes?', or 'which learning processes are important?'.

From Deci's cognitive motivation model (see Figure 2.1), a number of factors which have meaning in this connection can be deduced:

1. It can be seen that the feedback which occurs between the setting of goals and their realisation has an effect on the development of motives. Failure to reach a goal has implications for the appraisal of the means used to reach that goal (e.g. the chosen training form was unsuitable). Alternatively, the person might decide that the goal selected was inappropriate. Applied to sport situations, the failure to reach goals leads either to a change in those goals or a change in action expectations within that sport activity. In both cases it might be expected that a person, on grounds of such experiences, would turn away from this field of activity. Illustrative in this respect is the research of Gabler (1976). This author showed that top-level swimmers who stopped swimming at national level during the four-year period of the research had a higher level of aspiration than swimmers who continued with their training. The higher aspiration level led to not, or only partly, reaching the goals set and a turning away from the activity.

   Earlier research by the same author (Gabler, 1972) also allowed practical indications in this connection. Gabler was able to show that the goals that swimmers set themselves in the long run—as is normal in (top-level) sport—were partly determined by social factors. Amongst others, the influence of the trainer, the group in which training took place and the atmosphere within the association—more or less directed to achievement—were the factors signalled. In the light of the 1976 results, and the theoretical expectations about the goals set, it can be said that influencing goal-setting, in a more realistic way, is an important variable in the development of sport-directed motives.

2. As an extension of this point, there is a need to achieve success in the relatively short term. This holds equally well for top-level sport (where attaining, for example, a place in the finals of the Olympic Games must never be the only goal) and for sport at a lower level. The announcement that, by the end of one's school career, one will be able to strike a baseball in nine out of 10 attempts is not really motivating if, in the first two-years, one is unable to make a single strike—notwithstanding the question of whether or not this goal, in itself, is realistic. Regular positive experiences (e.g. reaching goals) is a necessary learning condition for the development of sport motives.

3. General principles with respect to the provision of information (or feedback) during the process of learning are also applicable to the domain of motivation psychology. Two aspects are particularly worthy of mention (Alderman, 1978, p. 143):
   (a) such information should be provided immediately following the behaviour (e.g. if good training performances give the possibility to promote a person from reserve to player, it is better that this statement is made directly after the training than just before the competition);
   (b) information about behaviour and results should be both specific and clear.

4. The question of why people take part in sport gives rise to a complementary question: 'What are the reasons underlying the fact that some people do not participate in sport?' It would seem that an answer to this question can provide indications as to the nature of the learning processes that influence a person's choosing to participate in sport. Both Bielefeld (1979) and Bloss (1971) have researched the contra motives for not participating. Using cluster and factor analysis Bielefeld, on the basis of 71 statements against the practice of sport, ended up with four factors:
   (a) a negative stereotypy of sport ('because it is foolish to do so', 'because you do not learn anything from it');
   (b) frustrating experiences ('because by doing so you become ridiculed');
   (c) conflicting interests ('because I have other interests');
   (d) desire for a restful life ('because I do not find it pleasant to exercise').
   Bloss asked 49 school-children the reasons why they no longer participated in sport. By far the most frequently named reason was 'insufficient time'. In addition to this reason, the children gave: tiredness, no interest, didn't feel like it, risk of injury and lack of accommodation. It is true that in

this research it was not so much about motives in the real sense of the word, but such studies provide a good insight into background reasons for (not) choosing sport as a field of activity.

2.5. Intrinsic motivation

In the previous section 'intrinsic pleasure' was given as one of the motives underlying the reason for sport participation. People often undertake activities without there being any indication of a reward being coupled to their behaviour. The activity itself is the reward; it is also the goal in itself and not a means to a particular goal. This is called 'intrinsic motivation'. Intrinsically motivated behaviour is behaviour in which the value lies in the behaviour itself. In this section intrinsic motivation and its counterpart, motivation arising from external reward, will be discussed. Particular attention will be paid to the consequence of extrinsic rewards for behaviour that, in the first instance, is intrinsically motivated.

As stated, an important characteristic of intrinsically motivated behaviour is that people participate in an activity without receiving any apparent external reward. Defining intrinsic motivation in this way, however, gives rise to objections, the most important of which is that such a definition: 'merely describes what intrinsically motivated behavior looks like, but (it) fails to explain why the behavior occurred' (Halliwell, 1978a, p. 85). It is therefore more accurate to speak of an activity which, in the eyes of the individual, has certain worthwhile consequences. Characteristic of intrinsically motivated behaviour is—in general terms—that it gives rise to feelings of competence and self-determination (Deci, 1975; see also page 11): 'Intrinsically motivated behaviors are behaviors which a person engages in to feel competent and self-determining' (p. 61).

Intrinsically motivated behaviour has the important characteristic that even after the goal has been reached, the need for feelings of competence remains. In contrast to extrinsically motivated behaviour, achieving the goal and thereby gaining the reward does not result in satiation. The need for self-actualisation, to have control of one's environment and to feel 'valued' remain also—and perhaps only—when successful actions give rise to similar feelings. Because the motivation does not decrease following the reaching of the goal, intrinsic motivation is a 'positive' form of being motivated, of which, for example in education the importance has always been realised. Interest in mathematics because, as a subject, it presents a challenge, does not disappear following an examination. Interest, exclusively for the reason that it is necessary to pass in order to be able to continue with a course mostly disappears following the completion of the examination.

The same can be said about the continuance of training, the following of gymnastic lessons or participation in sport. When a person is intrinsically motivated towards these activities, when they give rise to feelings of competence, interest remains. If the person is active, because such activity will result in extrinsic reward, avoidance of punishment by staying away from training sessions, receipt of a monetary reward, then interest in the activity will almost certainly disappear with the reward.

This leads to the second important characteristic of intrinsic motivation, that the person himself controls his own behaviour. In contrast to behaviour that is motivated by extrinsic reward, the behaviour is independent of what goes on outside the person and over which he has no control.

The influence of external reinforcement on intrinsic motivation is related to the nature of control (by oneself or some external agency). De Charms (1968) formulated the hypothesis that increasing external reinforcement will lead to a person perceiving his behaviour as being under the control of the reinforcement and this, in turn, results in a decrease in intrinsic motivation. Deci (1975) provides an overview of different studies which, in general, lend support to the hypothesis of De Charms.

Halliwell (1978a), using a quote from Casady (1974), illustrates, in a nice example, how the process runs its course:

> *An old man lived alone on a street where boys played noisily every afternoon. One day the din became too much, and he called the boys into his house. He told them he liked to listen to them play, but his hearing was as failing and he could no longer hear their games. He asked them to come around each day and play noisily in front of his house. If they did, he would give them each a quarter. The youngsters raced back the following day, and made a tremendous racket in front of the house. The old man paid them, and asked them to return the next day. Again they made noise, and again the old man paid them for it. But this time he gave each boy only 20 cents, explaining that he was running out of money. On the following day, they got only 15 cents each. Furthermore, the old man told them, he would have to reduce the fee to five cents on the 4th day. The boys became angry, and told the man they would not be back. It was not worth the effort, they said, to make noise for only five cents a day.*

An explanation of the disappearance of intrinsic motivation can lie in the following: when two possible causes of a behaviour are available (namely internal, i.e. intrinsic motivation and external, i.e. reward) and each, in itself, is sufficient to produce the behaviour, the person gives priority to the one over the other. This so-called 'discounting principle' has its roots in attribution theory (Heider, 1958; Kelley, 1967). Because more often than not, the external cause is more readily verifiable and more salient than the internal cause, the person will be inclined, in situations in which internal and external causes are both available at the same time, to discount the importance of internal factors to the extent that external factors are sufficient to cause a behaviour. He attributes the behaviour exclusively to the reward.

In a discussion of the above principle Halliwell (1978b) points out that making use of the 'discounting principle' by a person supposes a 'rather sophisticated logical causal analysis' (p. 404). In a research study, carried out by him — it would appear that very young children do not operate on such a principle but use, instead, an additive schema. That is to say that young children (from the Kindergarten) find an intrinsically pleasant task even more pleasant when it is duly rewarded. The 'discounting principle' is, however, apparent in older children (from approximately age 7). They consider a task that is intrinsically attractive and moreover is rewarded, less attractive than a task in which the extra reward is not given. This result supports the explanation given above, of the influence of extrinsic reward on intrinsic motivation.

A research study by Orlick & Mosher (1978) showed the undermining effect of extrinsic reward on intrinsic motivation, utilising a motor task. In this research children were required to carry out a balance task on a (so-called) stabilometer. Before beginning it was checked that only those children took part who found the task, in itself, pleasant to do. On two successive days the children individually performed on the balance task for 10 minutes. Four groups of children participated:

1. Control group 1: no reinforcement given.
2. Control group 2: the reward consisted of a compliment provided by the experimenter ('you really did a good job').
3. Experimental group 1: every child had the possibility to gain an award following a good performance; every child received such an award;
4. Experimental group 2: every child, without having prior knowledge of the fact, received an award because 'you did such a good job you are getting this special award'.

In pre- and post-tests was assessed how long the children, of their own volition, were engaged in the balance task. In addition to this task they could choose from three other motor tasks. The time spent on the balance task by each of the four groups is reported in Table 2.2. There were no significant differences between the groups on the pre-test. On the post-test control group one (no reward) spent significantly more time on the balance task than experimental group two (unexpected reward). It seemed, also, that when control and experimental groups were combined, children who received an award spent less time on the balance task in the post-test than children out of either control group.

There are two sides to the problem of extrinsic reinforcement and the influence thereof on intrinsic motivation. In the first place the control aspect illustrated by the example provided by Casady (see page 22). Behaviour can be carried out on account of a prospective reward, in which the person attributes the reason for his actions to the reward *per se* (which can also

Figure 2.3. Young children find an intrinsically pleasant task even more pleasant when it is duly rewarded. (ANP Foto.)

Table 2.2. Mean time in minutes and seconds that subjects chose to play with the target activity during pre- and post-10 minute free play periods, by treatments.

Experimental condition	N	Pre-test	Post-test
Control group 1: no award and no social reinforcement	12	2.35	4.15
Control group 2: social reinforcement only	11	2.48	3.25
Experimental group 1: conditionally expected award	14	2.59	2.57
Experimental group 2: unexpected award	12	2.36	1.06

From Orlick & Mosher (1978); reprinted with permission of the authors.

occur in retrospect — as in the research of Orlick and Mosher). In the absence of the reward the reasons for the actions also disappear.

In the second place reinforcement can also have a second function. A mark of 8 (out of 10) for a mathematics test does not only mean a pass, it also indicates that a good level has been reached, giving rise to feelings of competence. Deci (1975, 1978), in particular, has drawn attention to this dual role of extrinsic reinforcement. Deci predicts that a decrease in intrinsic motivation will be apparent only when the control aspect of the reinforcement is in the forefront. If the informative function predominates then the intrinsic motivation for the task will increase.

A relevant aspect for sport is that competition can be an extrinsically motivating factor. Deci, Betley, Kahle, Abrams & Porac (1981) give the following reason why this should be so:

> *The reward for intrinsically motivated behavior is the feeling of competence and self-determination that is associated with the behavior. The reward for extrinsically motivated behavior is something that is separate from and follows the behavior. With competitive activities, the reward is typically 'winning' (that is, beating the other person or the other team), so the reward is actually extrinsic to the activity itself* (p. 79).

In one of their research studies, 40 female and 40 male students tried to solve interesting puzzles. Their efforts were reported in the presence of someone who already knew the solutions. Half of the subjects were instructed to compete with those who already knew the solution (although, of course, the subjects were not aware of this). The other half were instructed to solve the puzzles as quickly as possible. Five puzzles were provided and, in every case, the subject 'won' four times. Subjects were then left alone for a period of eight minutes. The number of seconds that subjects spontaneously spent on two other puzzles available in the experimental room served as the

Table 2.3. Means for intrinsic motivation, free-choice scores, for male and female subjects in the competition and no-competition conditions.

	Competition	No-competition
Males	105.2	143.1
Females	55.9	170.8

From Deci, Betley, Kahle, Abrams & Porac (1981).

dependent variable (the measure of intrinsic motivation). Table 2.3 reports the findings.

An analysis of covariance—in which scores for intrinsic interest in this type of activity served as covariant—showed a significant ($p<0.05$) effect of the experimental condition. Carrying out the task in competition led to a significant decrease in intrinsic motivation. Nevertheless, it cannot be concluded from this study that the carrying out of activities in a competitive setting will always have a negative influence on intrinsic motivation. After all, the result of a competition also provides information about the achievement of the participant. Weinberg & Ragan (1979) and Weinberg & Jackson (1979) manipulated the outcomes of competitions. From these experiments it appeared that the successful or unsuccessful completion of a competition had a large influence on intrinsic motivation of participants. Being told that a win had been achieved led, on different measures, to higher scores on intrinsic motivation than being told about a losing result. Weinberg and Ragan also found, by comparing the results of carrying out the task under, or not under, competitive conditions, that the intrinsic motivation under the former circumstances was greater. This result is contrary to the research findings of Deci *et al* (1981). It must be realised, in this respect, that the meaning that a subject attributes to winning (or losing) can be influenced by a host of circumstances—his judgement of his opponent's abilities; that he has the idea that he is in with an equal chance, etc.

Such factors were not controlled in the experiments discussed and herein, perhaps, lies the explanation of the conflicting findings.

In conclusion, it can be said that there are clear indications of a disadvantageous effect of extrinsic reinforcement on a person's intrinsic motivation and that competition can serve as an extrinsically motivating factor. However, in this connection a warning must be issued against too simple generalisations:

1. In the first place, intrinsic and extrinsic motivation are often interwoven. A person may play football because he finds it enjoyable and because in that way he may earn money. So long that he is aware that his interest in football is an important driving force, the disadvantageous effects of reward will have little chance to manifest themselves.
2. Secondly, it has been shown that reward can have both a controlling and

an informative function and its effect upon intrinsic motivation depends upon which of these functions is in the foreground, i.e. the variables that are important are those that together, in mutual interaction, finally determine the specific effect of the reward. To name but a few of these variables: (a) the extent to which the reward is contingent on the way in which the task is carried out; (b) if it is known, beforehand, that a reward will be gained; (c) the nature of the reward (material, social recognition, verbal, etc.).

3. Finally, it must be signalled that the research discussed relates only to the immediate effects of reward on intrinsic motivation. There has been hardly any research carried out on the long-term consequences.

2.6. Exploring boundaries and taking risks

One of the most intriguing questions in the area of sport and motivation relates to the reasons for participation in sports involving unmistakable risk. From mountaineering or alpinism — as well as motor racing, parachute jumping and skiing — a host of typical examples can be derived. In the Alps a number of 'North Walls' with which the average mountaineer, using pick, pietons and safety ropes has his hands full have been descended on skis. Apart from the extreme difficulty of such an undertaking, there is no way back for the skier if, after 50 metres, the snow gives rise to hard ice. A fatal fall is the result of his audacity. Finding explanations for people's motivation to participate in parachute jumping, hang gliding and mountaineering is a challenge for motivation psychology. To illustrate the point, data on fatal accidents in these sports in the U.S.A., presented by Brannigan & McDougall (1983) are given in Table 2.4. The estimation of the number of victims is conservative and the question is why would anyone do such things? In addition to the taking of risks, many people are just as prepared during their sport participation to suffer pain, and to go to the limits of their potential.

A possible explanation of the fact that participants in some (sport) situations can bear far more pain than normal, is to be gleaned from psychological research into pain experience. In this respect, concepts such as anticipation and attention play a key role. Nisbett & Schachter (1966) describe how subjects can feel pain without the nature and intensity of the stimulus really being capable of giving rise to such pain. By giving misleading instructions prior to the experiment, false expectations about the (light and benign) stimulus were evoked. In reverse this would mean that the anticipation of a painful stimulus as not too severe, can lead to a reduced experience of pain. Further, pain tolerance could be increased by distracting the attention of the subject from the painful stimulus (Kanfer & Goldfoot, 1966). It can be proposed that particular activities can so completely capture a person's attention that painful stimuli are no longer consciously experienced as painful.

Table 2.4. Number of people killed while climbing, parachuting and hang-gliding in the U.S.A.

	Number of people killed	Year	Estimated number of people participating
Mountaineering	19	1975	*ca.* 60 000
	54	1976	
Parachuting	54	1976	*ca.* 25 000
	49	1977	
Hang-gliding	2	1971	
	40	1974	
	38	1976	
	18	1977	
	26	1978	*ca.* 40 000 (in 1978)

A boxer is so concentrated on the match that he has no attentional capacity left to allow him to think about the pain following a blow or punch by his opponent. A good example, in this respect, is provided by Muhammad Ali in his autobiography. In a competitive fight against Jeff Merritt he received, in the second round, a fractured jaw. Nevertheless, he reported completing the fight without feeling much pain. This came after the finish when he became troubled by severe attacks of pain (Muhammad Ali, 1975). Nevertheless, what has been written above would seem to be an insufficient explanation of the phenomena targeted in the introduction to this chapter. After all, even if pain was not (perhaps) felt at the moment, afterwards one would be thoroughly aware of having been injured (compare Muhammad Ali). Moreover, many situations are known in which the athlete is, at the moment, certainly conscious of the painful experiences. Statements such as 'all to pieces', 'must give up', and 'all-in' are illustrations of this. Finally, painful experiences, whether experienced at the time or afterwards, are in any case anticipated. In most cases one is aware of what one is doing and of potential outcomes.

In an attempt to understand people's motivation for extremely strenuous sports (i.e. marathon, triathlon), attention might be directed to the phenomenon of addiction to these types of exercises. Apparently, some people have become addicted to these activities, and their addiction provides an answer to the question why they take part.

Addiction is characterised by dependency on the activity and by withdrawal symptoms if one stops. Dependency manifests itself in an excessive dominance of the activity in one's life, at the cost of other important areas, as for example, the family, social contacts or work. Withdrawal symptoms are, amongst others, feelings of nervousness, guilt and anxiety, and physiological reactions (e.g. headaches, physical discomfort).

Specifically in relation to running, the phenomenon of addiction has gained interest. Summers, Machin & Sargent (1983) questioned more than 450 participants in a marathon. Fifty-two per cent of them described themselves as somewhat addicted to running, and 30% to be strongly addicted. However, the validity of these percentages might be questioned, since the respondents probably did not use the same definition of addiction as stated above.

Sachs (1981) and Summers & Hinton (1986) distinguish between commitment and addiction to running. According to Sachs, commitment to running is based on a logical analysis of the benefits of running—such as attaining social contacts, health benefits or monetary rewards—whereas addiction is characterised by dependency and withdrawal symptoms. Only recently has a questionnaire designed to measure and distinguish between addiction and commitment to running become available, so that it has not previously been possible to provide a reliable estimation of the number of runners that might be typified as addicted to running.

It is not surprising therefore that only speculative explanations for the phenomenon of running addiction are available. Of these, one of the most popular deals with so-called beta-endorphins, and the available evidence in this respect will be briefly discussed.

In 1971 Goldstein discovered receptors for narcotics and their antagonists (Goldstein, 1978), a finding that gave rise to the hypothesis that the body was able to produce these substances itself. Soon after Goldstein's discovery, several endogenous opioide peptides—proteins, produced by the body itself and exhibiting morphine-like effects—were found. Apart from beta-endorphins, which are best known, several enkephalins and dynorphins were discovered.

Beta-endorphins are found in the central nervous system, where they function as neurotransmitters and neuromodulators (influencing stimulus transmission) and in the blood stream, where their function is that of a hormone. Beta-endorphins (can) lead to anxiety-reduction, have an anaesthetic effect and give rise to euphoria. They also may lead to hypothermy and a decrease in ventilation rate (Grossman & Sutton, 1985; Hardley, 1984).

Relevant and interesting in relation to the phenomenon of running addiction is the finding of an increase in beta-endorphin concentration in the blood during and after physical exercise (i.e. Colt, Wardlaw & Frantz, 1981; Elliot, Goldberg, Watts & Orwoll, 1984; Howlett, Tomlin, Ngahfoong, Rees, Bullen, Skrinar & McArthur, 1984). However the increase does not seem to be related to the amount of exercise. Moreover, results of a number of studies differ with respect to several important variables; for example, the reported resting values and the amount of increase after exercise. These results suggest, however, some relationship between exercise, the production of the morphine-like substance beta-endorphin and the need to be (again) physically active.

More light on this possible connection can be provided by studies in which the effect of training on the concentration of beta-endorphin is pursued. However, to date only a few such studies have been carried out. While they do not permit any firm conclusions to be drawn they certainly give rise to interesting hypotheses. Lobstein & Ismail (1983), for example, confirmed in a sample of 10 untrained men that following a period of training of 16 weeks duration the resting level of beta-endorphins in the plasma was significantly lower than before the training. One possible explanation of this finding was provided by Goldstein in 1978. He proposed the presence of a negative feedback loop; as a consequence of the frequent higher production of beta-endorphin during exercise, the body reacts by producing less of this chemical. In order to satisfy this deficiency in beta-endorphin and to once again bring it to an appropriate level, the person becomes stimulated to train regularly. In this way a certain measure of addiction can arise.

Another explanation put forward by Goldstein for the phenomenon that some people appear to be addicted to bodily exercise is that, from the outset, their bodies have produced insufficient beta-endorphin. Thus they suffer from a chronic deficiency: a deficiency that can be temporarily remedied by means of physical activity.

Before any definite conclusion is possible about the relationship between exercise, beta-endorphin and addiction, much more research is needed and several problems have to be resolved. One of the most serious of these concerns the relation between beta-endorphin concentration in the blood (which is measured) and the production of endorphins in the central nervous system. There is no evidence that the concentration of beta-endorphins in the blood gives a reliable indication of its concentration in the cerebrospinal fluid. However, this latter concentration is essential for addiction effects, if any.

An attempt to explain the motivation for risky sports has recently been undertaken by Piët (1987). She interviewed several mountaineers and racing drivers and asked them to fill in personality questionnaires. The findings of her research indicate clearly the important role of the need for competence as a motive. Mountaineers mentioned as reasons for their climbing, amongst others, managing the challenge of a very difficult and risky task, successfully performing tasks which are too difficult for most people, the experience of feelings of self-confidence, and knowing one's own boundaries and expanding on them. The challenge of coping with the stress of climbing seems to be a separate, but important, reason for participation. Frequently mentioned as a drive by mountaineers (and racing drivers) were the feelings of competence experienced when they managed to control their stress reactions beyond the point where these reactions would normally give rise to fear and anxiety.

This type of competence is quite specific to 'risk' sports.

An effort to place both the 'willingness to suffer pain' and the 'taking of risks' in one motivational—theoretical framework was undertaken by Solomon (1980). While the theory cannot call upon extensive empirical support, it is interesting enough to receive attention here. In Solomon's 'opponent-process theory of acquired motivation' the concept 'affective contrast' stands central. This involves the following: when a situation (or stimulus) has given rise to a positive feeling (affect), this feeling becomes negative following the removal of the stimulus and, vice-versa, a negative affect changes in the course of time to a positive affect. Solomon provides an illustration of the phenomenon by citing, amongst others, a study by Epstein (1967) of the emotional reactions of military parachutists:

'During their first free-fall, the parachute opens, military parachutists may experience terror: They may yell, pupils dilated, eyes bulging, bodies curled forward and stiff, heart racing and breathing irregular. After they land safely, they may walk around with a stunned and stony-faced expression for a few minutes, and then they usually smile, chatter and gesticulate, being very socially active and appearing to be elated (p. 693).

Also, the 'hangover' following a euphoric feeling and the relief after an unpleasant event are examples of affective contrast. When stimuli are repeatedly presented, habituation tends to occur. However, in this respect there is a marked difference between primary and secondary affective reaction. Habituation to the stimulus results in a reduction in the intensity of the primary reaction (State A), while the secondary reaction (State B), in contrast, increases. Figures 2.4 and 2.5 reproduce the reactions to a new stimulus and to a stimulus repeatedly presented.

The affective process described leads to the formation of new drives or motives, the origin of which lies in the secondary affective reaction. This is equally true when the secondary reaction is positive (with, as first reaction, therefore, a negative feeling) as when it is negative. Table 2.5 gives an example of someone who is motivated to using narcotics. Table 2.6 to parachute-jumping.

Directed to the examples provided in the introduction to this chapter Solomon's theory suggests that with respect to pain, opting out and danger, a certain habituation comes about while the after-effects (feelings of relief, satisfaction, feeling good), in contrast, become much more pronounced. This secondary affect functions as motive. Danger, pain and opting-out are sought after because of the positive, euphoristic state of mind that follows.

For the phenomenon of affective-contrast, considerable empirical support is available. This is also the case for the differences between 'State A' and 'State B' that arise with habituation. These differences are crucial to the relationship between affective-contrast and development of motives. As

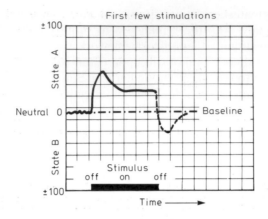

Figure 2.4. The standard pattern of affective reactions produced by a relatively novel stimulus. From Solomon (1980); Copyright (1980) by the American Psychological Association; reprinted by permission of the publisher and author.

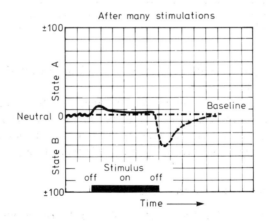

Figure 2.5. The standard pattern of affective reactions produced by a familiar, frequently, repeated stimulus. From Solomon (1980); Copyright (1980) by the American Psychological Association; reprinted by permission of the publisher and author.

stated earlier, there is not yet much empirical evidence for the motivational working of the system. There are, however, indications in that direction. The examples provided by Solomon, of which some have been described here, function as such. Furthermore, it seems, from the earlier reported research of Brackhane & Fischhold (1981, see page 16) that the relaxed feeling after an exhausting competition (marathon running) or following

Table 2.5. Changes in affect before, during and after each stimulation (self-dosing with opiates) for the first few experiences and after many experiences.

Period	First few	After many
Before	Resting state	Craving
During	Rush, euphoria	Contentment
After	Craving	Abstinence-agony
	Resting state	Craving

From Solomon (1980); copyright (1980) by the American Psychological Association; reprinted by permission of the publisher and author.

Table 2.6. Changes in affect before, during and after each stimulation (free-fall in military parachuting) for the first few experiences and after many experiences.

Period	First few	After many
Before	Anxiety	Eagerness
During	Terror	Thrill
After	Relief	Exhilaration
	Resting state	Resting state

From Solomon (1980); copyright (1980) by the American Psychological Association; reprinted by permission of the publisher and author.

intensive training by the runners, was very much appreciated and put forward as one of their motives.

For the time being the opinion is advanced that the theory of Solomon provides an important addition to more conservative approaches, in which, for activities such as mountain climbing, only motives such as the need for competence are suggested (for example, Lefebvre, 1980).

2.7. Motivation and achievement

It goes without saying that the question of the relation between motivational level and achievement—particularly in the practice of physical education and sport—is very important. This question becomes particularly important in the context of its application in the ascending part of the motivation curve. After all, it is inherent in the description of the concept of motivation that, in a situation where there is little motivation, low achievement levels will result. The central issue is whether or not there is a particular optimal level of motivation, in the sense that exceeding that level will lead to a deterioration in performance. An alternative possibility is that increasing motivation will produce increasing gains in performance. Both possibilities are sketched in Figure 2.6.

Closely related to the question of optimality are related problems such as

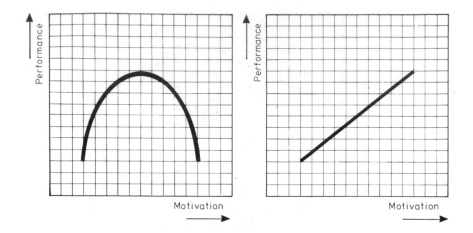

Figure 2.6. The relationship between performance and level of motivation; (a) for an optimal level of motivation, (b) for a positive relationship between level of motivation and performance (in this example, linear).

(1) what determines the level of one's motivation, (2) what factors have an influence on the relationship between motivation and achievement, and (3) in what ways is it possible to influence a person's motivation.

2.7.1 MOTIVATION AND PERFORMANCE: AN OPTIMAL LEVEL?

The hypothesis of an optimal level of motivation can be traced back to the experiments of Yerkes & Dodson (1908, see Hilgard, Atkinson & Atkinson, 1971). On the basis of their research those authors concluded that for each level of task difficulty an optimal level of motivation could be identified which would lead to the best performance. For an easy task this motivation level is high and, as the task increases in difficulty, the optimal level of motivation decreases. That is to say, for a difficult task the optimal level is reached earlier than for an easy task. This formulation is known as the 'Yerkes–Dodson law' as illustrated in Figure 2.7.

Ferguson (1976) discusses an experiment of Broadhurst (1957) that provides convincing support for the Yerkes–Dodson Law. Animal subjects (rats) were held under water for periods of 0, 2, 4, or 8 seconds prior to being able to obtain air via an under-water Y-shaped maze. The animals had to learn which of the two passageways (the light or the dark) would lead to their escape. The animal subjects were divided into three groups based on the extent to which the passageways they had to negotiate differed from one another (little contrast, i.e. difficult; moderate or much contrast, i.e. easier). The number of correct attempts out of a total of 100 provided a score for the

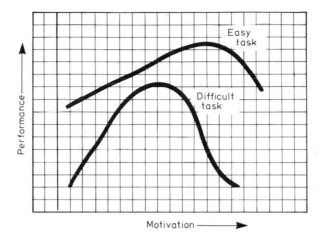

Figure 2.7. The relationship between motivation and performance by a difficult and an easy task (following Yerkes and Dodson, 1908).

learning achievement (see Table 2.7). The results of this study are reproduced three-dimensionally in Figure 2.8.

The advantage of these experiments is that the level of motivation can be accurately assessed. The longer the rat stays under water, the greater its need for oxygen, and thus the stronger its motivation. For people, however, motivation is, in general, more difficult to asssess unequivocally, and this makes the demonstration of relations difficult. The choice of the strength of a motive as a measure of a person's motivation is, as was shown previously, not really suitable. Motivation level is determined by a number of factors, of which motive is only one.

In research studies the difficulty of the operationalisation of motivation level is often resolved by introducing the concept of activation (also known

Table 2.7. Average number of correct attempts out of a total of 100.

Motivation level (air deprivation)	Difficulty of Discrimination			
	Easy	Moderate	Difficult	All
0 s	84.8	81.3	71.1	79.1
2 s	86.4	84.7	79.5	83.5
4 s	87.7	83.0	71.6	80.8
8 s	86.8	83.2	66.1	78.7
All	86.4	83.1	72.1	80.5

Adapted from Broadhurst (1957).

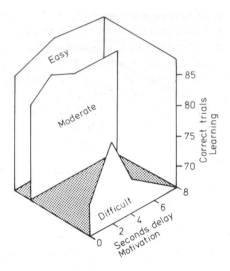

Figure 2.8. The relationship between learning achievement (number of correct attempts) and level of motivation (oxygen deprivation) for three levels of task difficulty (distinguishability of passages). Adapted from Broadhurst, (1957).

as arousal, excitedness, and energy mobilisation). The idea underlying this procedure is that increasing motivation leads to higher activation levels and activation (or arousal) refers to the degree of energy release of the organism (e.g. Landers, 1978, 1980). By activation is to be understood a one-dimensional intensity continuum, with deep sleep at one end and high excitement at the other (Malmo, 1959).

The concept of activation or arousal has also been used to refer to emotional states of the organism, specifically anxiety. The inverted-U hypothesis has been popular for describing the relationship between anxiety (arousal, activation) and motor performance since Martens (1971) reviewed the literature in this area (Klavora, 1978; Landers, 1978, 1980; Martens, 1974, 1977).

Activation is indexed by changes in diverse physiological variables: heart rate, blood pressure, pupil dilation, galvanic-skin resistance, EEG activity and hormonal secretion. Changes in activation are to be traced back to different brain centres. Structures that play an important role in this respect are the amygdala, the basal ganglia, the reticular formation and the hippocampus (Pribram & McGuinness, 1975). A large number of factors can influence the level of activation. Amongst those named are: diverse psychopharmacotics (stimulating as well as sedating), environmental factors such as noise and heat, signals that give rise to an orientation or defence reaction and lack of sleep (Sanders, 1980).

The explanation of a lower performance with reduced activation is obvious: the organism is not alert, not in a state to process information and is therefore insufficiently prepared to act. The reduction in performance by a too high activation level can be a consequence of too great a demand on central, information processors. The large number of stimuli associated with a high activation level makes high demands on the available processing capacity of the central mechanisms (Welford, 1968) or requires so much attention that little remains over for the task itself (Kahneman, 1973). The latter can be recognised in everyday language — for example when people speak about over-concentration.

In Easterbrook's (1959) 'cue utilisation theory' the idea of attentional changes is worked out as follows:

Increases in the level of activation lead to a narrowing of attention. Thus, a low level of activation means that many signals from the environment will be observed (the theory does not seem to be appropriate for that part of the intensity continuum characterised by deep sleep) — both task-relevant and task-irrelevant. Gradually, more and more signals will fail to be detected as activation increases; in the first instance, task-irrelevant cues, whereby attention is better directed to the task resulting in an improvement in the carrying out of the task, but later, task-relevant cues will also be 'missed' resulting in a decrease in performance.

It must be assumed that the explanatory principles discussed above are too simple. Activation is not uni-dimensional, a number of different components of activation are to be distinguished. These do not show the same reactive patterns and are under the influence of different brain centres. Moreover, the activation concept, used in this way, is related to the 'energetic' component of motivation and not to 'persistence' and 'direction'. It is, apparently, just these aspects of motivation that play an important role in task performance.

Related difficulties are apparent when activation or arousal is used to operationalise anxiety. Anxiety as an emotional state is associated with heightened activation or arousal of the autonomic nervous system, but it is only the combination with particular affective and cognitive variables that make a particular state experienced as anxiety (see also Chapter 3).

Because of these and other arguments, Neiss (1988) recently heavily criticised the inverted-U hypothesis. In his opinion it is true but trivial: 'it reveals only that the motivated outperform the apathetic and the terrified' (p. 355). Neiss argues that the empirical evidence supporting the relationship is weak. Conceptually his main criticism is that arousal or activation cannot distinguish between debilitating states (e.g. anxiety) and states that are optimal for performance (e.g. the state of being 'psyched-up'), 'because it is an excessively broad physiological construct, artificially severed from its psychological context' (p. 345). Consequently, Neiss proposed to abandon the concept and to investigate discrete psychobiological states, which include affect and cognition as well as physiology.

Kerr's (1985, 1987) position is less extreme. In his contention the inverted-U hypothesis between arousal/activation and performance has been an over-simplification. Referring to Apter's (1982) reversal theory, he exemplifies the complex nature of arousal/activation: the experience of arousal depends on how the person interprets his own motivational state. If, for example, a person is oriented towards some essential goal, he will experience arousal as unpleasant and it will give rise to feelings of anxiety. In that state low arousal is experienced as pleasant and felt as relaxation. However, if the person is oriented towards some aspects of his continuing behaviour, high arousal is experienced as excitement and low arousal as boredom. The effects of high and low arousal on performance will also depend on the interpretation of one's own motivational state. Sometimes high arousal will give rise to debilitating effects; at other times the same level of arousal will facilitate performance.

Recently, Jones & Hardy (1989), in an elaborated discussion of the relationship between stress and performance in sport, came to the same conclusion as Kerr: 'the inverted-U hypothesis is too vague and simplistic' (p. 41). In addition to the criticisms mentioned above—i.e. arousal or activation is not a uni-dimensional construct and cannot be artificially severed from its psychological context—Jones & Hardy criticise the symmetry of the performance curve. The symmetrical nature of the inverted-U curve implies that when an individual is 'over-stressed', all he has to do is lower the stress (or arousal) until peak performance is regained. The authors point to the fact that this description is extremely unlikely and propose a 'catastrophe curve'. This indicates:

> that under low levels of stress and physiological arousal performance should improve as stress increases up to a certain critical threshold. At this point the performer begins to perceive an imbalance between the demands of the situation and his capability to match them. Anxiety occurs and performance suddenly and dramatically falls, causing a discontinuity in the graph (p. 46).

Jones & Hardy discuss several models of stress and performance which are multi-dimensional in nature and which seem more suitable for under-standing the complex relationship between stress and sports performance. In addition, they point to several implications of these models for the types of intervention aimed at—for example, anxiety reduction.

In conclusion, it can be said that there are indications of a reduction in performance under high levels of activation. However, the establishment of the reasons for this decrement, and the conditions under which debilitating effects are apparent, must await further research and theory-forming. It might sometimes be necessary to reduce an excessively high level of activation. Often, however, it is an improvement in motivation that needs to be brought about. The factors that play a role, in this respect, will be discussed in what follows.

2.7.2. ATTRIBUTION

To whom or to what a person attributes the results of his actions is one of the factors that might have an effect on the strength of his motivation. This process of attributing causes to the outcome of a particular action is known as the attribution process.*

It is obvious that the experiences a person has had in particular situations are important in determining the strength of his motivation in similar kinds of situation. To give but one example: not being chosen for a representative team does not directly serve as a stimulus to work very hard during the next training session, whereas being chosen might well serve as a stimulus to train particularly hard during the next training session. The meaning to which the experience of being or not being chosen gives rise is, to a large degree, determined by the explanation provided by the person involved.

The way in which a person explains the outcome of his actions (in this case, being or not being chosen for a representative team), can vary along two important dimensions. The first relates to where the responsibility is placed: internal (by the person himself) or external (by others, by the circumstances). The second dimension refers to the stability of the causal factor — stable or unstable. Own capabilities or degree of difficulty are stable factors, commitment or chance are unstable factors (Weiner, Frieze, Kuhla, Reed, Rest & Rosenbaum, 1971). In the schema in Table 2.8 the four factors to which success or failure can be attributed are brought together, with some examples being provided in each cell.

The way in which the attribution process progresses has consequences for the expectations that someone has about the outcomes of his own actions in future situations and, hence, for his motivation. Heckhausen (1971) provides a good example:

Thus, it makes a great difference if a sportsman/woman attributes a failure to lack of talent, to a temporary relapse or to a poor condition. In each of these

---

* It should be noted that attribution theory is 'concerned with how people perceive, interpret and process information associated with their own, and others' behaviour' (Biddle, 1984, p. 145). The explanation of the outcomes of achievement oriented behaviour, dealt with in this section, is but one aspect of attribution theory. Elaborated discussion of attribution theory and its applicability in sport is to be found in, for example, Biddle (1984) and Rejeski & Brawley (1983).

Table 2.8. Factors to which the outcome of an action can be attributed.

	Stable attributions	Unstable attributions
Internal attributions	Abilities	Fatigue, motivation
External attributions	Task difficulty, coach	Bad luck, weather

cases a different influence on motivation is to be expected. The first case should lead to a decrease in motivation, because what can one do if the talent is not there? In the second case, no change in motivation is to be expected: a temporary relapse is hard luck, pure chance, and will quickly pass. In the last case, motivation will increase: a poor condition can, after all, only be counteracted by extra efforts (p. 37).

In the attribution of causes the stability dimension in particular is important for the expectation that a person has about the result of his future actions. When the outcome of an action is seen as a consequence of stable factors, the person is inclined to expect the same outcome in the future. If attributed to unstable factors, there is no reason to expect the same result.

The consequences that a particular attribution pattern has for someone's motivation is strongly dependent on whether success or failure has to be explained. It seems that people, in general, are more inclined to attribute failures to external factors and success more to their own capabilities (i.e. internal factors) (Bergen, Alberts & Peters, 1980; Frieze & Weiner, 1971; Lefebvre, 1979). It must, however, be noted that the attribution process that actually is in operation is dependent on a great number of variables. The meaning that the task has for the person carrying it out, for example, would appear to play a role. Bierhoff-Alfermann (1979) was able to show that in important swimming competitions a different pattern of causes was attributed to success and failure than in friendly competitions. Furthermore, the skill level of the participants played a role. Highly skilled participants are inclined to attribute success more to their own capabilities than less gifted people (Schwenkmezger, Voigt & Müller, 1979).

Finally, with respect to the attribution process, individual differences are of importance. In the first place the personality trait 'locus of control' can be mentioned.

Rotter (1966) developed a scale for the measurement of this factor. This internal−external (I-E) scale is concerned to measure the extent to which a person thinks he has particular events under his own control (I), or attributes these to forces controlled from outside himself (E).

In the second place, achievement motivation and fear of failure must be mentioned as personality characteristics that have an influence on the attribution process. Thus, people with a strong achievement motive are more inclined to attribute success to internal factors, while persons with a weak achievement motive are more inclined to attribute this to external factors (Lefebvre, 1979).

The number of factors that play a role in the attribution process makes it difficult to speak about an optimal attribution pattern for the motivation. What can be said is that the cause of a decreasing motivation can lie in an unfavourably developing attribution process. This is illustrated by the example of Heckhausen, presented earlier. This means that changes in attribution may possibly give rise to an improvement in motivation. In the light of the relationship between attribution process and personality characteristics such as self-confidence and fear of failure it would seem to the present writers that corrections to a particular attribution pattern are more difficult to bring about than is often suggested (Heckhausen, 1971, p. 37).

2.7.3. GOAL SETTING

The importance, for the development of motives, of setting oneself realistic goals has already been alluded to (see Section 2.3). The choice of goal, in addition to the attribution process, is an important factor for strength of motivation. One person might try to run his 10 kilometres within 40 minutes, another might try to cover the same distance without having to stop on the way. The top-level athlete, in the framework of his training schedule, has set a time of 29 minutes as his goal for his 10 kilometres.

For the relationship between motivation and performance it would seem that setting oneself goals is of great value. Locke, Shaw, Saari & Latham (1981) provide an overview of 110 studies in which the effect of this process on performance was researched. In 90% of the studies it appeared that the setting of specific goals, and goals which presented a real challenge, led to better performances than easier goals, goals that were imprecisely specified ('do your best') or when no goal at all was set. The reason for this positive effect lies in the fact that goals give direction to the attention, they 'mobilise' the person, they increase his powers of persistence and they make the development of a strategy easier (Locke et al, p. 125). The use of 'schedules' in speed skating, whereby the coach provides information about how much above or below his schedule the speed skater is performing, provides a practical example of the way in which goals play a role: the four explanatory principles named also appear to be applicable to this example. Starting with a particular schedule in mind means that the skater is ready to produce a particular performance. In the beginning, skating far above the schedule is a signal to change the strategy, while being behind schedule towards the end of a competition often leads to a last, extreme effort. The skater keeps his attention completely on his performance because he is permanently engaged with his schedule.

The motivational effect of goals in a sport-related task was shown, amongst others, by Nelson (1978). Subjects were tested on an arm-strength perseverance task. Groups of subjects who were made aware of norms for the task delivered significantly better performances than the control group, who were only stimulated to do their best.

From the above it can be deduced that the attainment of accurately specified goals in which, in addition, a certain challenge is presented (by coach, trainer) is probably useful as a procedure for improving motivation. The same can be said about teaching oneself to set concrete and realistic goals. After all, the concern is always with goals that the person accepts as goals for himself. Goals provided by outside agencies would appear to have scarcely any function to fulfil in the motivation process (Locke *et al*, 1981; Locke & Latham, 1985).

An important aspect must also be pointed out — namely, that the goals are realistic. A skating schedule that is unachievable makes no sense at all; on the contrary, it is more likely to be 'demotivational'. Setting oneself realistic goals is closely connected to level of aspiration — that is to say, the level of achievement that may be reached. A realistic level of aspiration means that neither too difficult nor too easy goals will be strived for.

The influencing of a person's level of aspiration can, for example, be achieved by providing information about what for him or her would be an acceptable result (according to the research of Nelson just mentioned, in which people received information about the norms associated with the task). The suggestion that one is in an advantageous (or disadvantageous) situation with respect to an opponent — for example, by suggesting that one has access to better or, respectively, worse equipment — would equally seem to have an influence on level of aspiration (Dalton & Maier, 1977). Those who had the idea that they had been manoeuvred into a disadvantageous situation had a lower level of aspiration and performed at a lower level than those who considered themselves to be in an advantageous position. It must expressly be stated that this concerned the *suggestion* of having better or worse equipment available than the opponent; in point of fact there were no differences. Nevertheless, the suggestion produced differences in level of aspiration and in performance.

Level of aspiration is also related to a person's attribution pattern, as the following example makes apparent:

> *If, for example, success is perceived as the consequence of personal factors, a person will build up the expectation that he will, on other occasions, also have success and/or that he will increase his level of aspiration (the level of difficulty someone thinks himself capable of)* (Orlebeke, 1981, pp. 47/48).

That is to say that a person's level of aspiration may also be affected by influencing his attribution pattern.

2.7.4. THE INFLUENCE OF THE PUBLIC

As a last factor in the relationship between motivation and performance the 'public' deserves attention. In this respect it has to do with questions such as: what are the consequences of the presence of spectators, of their encouragement or their apparent condemnation?

To begin with, it must be stated that research studies directed towards the answering of these questions give rise to problems in respect of their 'ecological validity'. The size of the audience in a laboratory situation — usually, at the most 10 people and often far fewer — sets limitations on the generalisability of the findings to sport situations. There is, in such cases, after all, talk of at least tens of spectators, while sometimes 10000 people are watching. It is hardly conceivable that such numbers would not result in a separate effect. In view of the fact that the research to be reviewed here relates exclusively to laboratory studies, the meaning of these for the sport situation is limited.

In research into the influence of the public on the performances of subjects, spectators can be classified into different classes (Streng, 1980):

1. Passive (or neutral) spectators who show no evidence of approval or disapproval.
2. Active spectators, who take a positive stance with respect to the performances of the subject.
3. Active spectators, who take a negative or critical stance.
4. Spectators 'imagined' by the subject.
5. So-called co-actors (team-mates).

In laboratory studies it is often found that subjects achieve better performances in the presence of others than do subjects who perform alone. To explain this phenomenon, Zajonc (1965) formulated the social facilitation hypothesis. This states that the presence of an audience has a facilitatory effect on activation or arousal (see also Section 2.7.1). The increased level of activation is responsible for the fact that dominant responses are carried out with greater intensity. This means that in the early stages of learning a task, when faulty responses dominate, the presence of spectators is unfavourable. Later, when correct responses dominate, the presence of an audience has a favourable effect upon performance. In an overview article, Geen & Gange (1977) conclude that Zajonc's hypothesis can call upon a reasonable amount of support. Also, research carried out by Martens (1969) — using a motor task — provides support for Zajonc's hypothesis, although Martens's results could only be replicated, in part, by Landers, Bauer & Feltz (1978).

Figure 2.9. Spectators: facilitating performance or distracting attention?

Kozan (1973) did not find any significant difference in performance between subjects who learned a task (balancing on a stabilometer) alone, in the presence of encouraging or critical spectators. For the absence of a difference between subjects who learned alone and subjects who learned in the presence of others, Kozan put forward the possibility that subjects in the 'alone' condition had imagined 'spectators' for themselves. This he deduced from the interest that the subjects showed, on completion, for the performances of others on the task. Apparently, other subjects functioned as a reference framework. While the explanation of Kozan is of an *ad hoc* kind, it is meaningful in that it implies that a performance can, in retrospect, be looked at or appraised and that this can lead to an increase in the level of activation. After all, sporting achievements are often followed in precisely this way—via the press or the increasingly popular computer rank lists for diverse sports—that is to say, outside the framework of the actual availability of spectators.

In addition to the arousal or activation-increasing effect that arises as the result of the presence of spectators, Landers (1980) points to a second important consequence of an audience—namely, a distracting (from the task) effect (see also Sanders, 1981). On the basis of this contention Landers considers it necessary for a shift in related research to take place from the motor (i.e. output) to the perceptual (i.e. input) side. The consequence of the availability of an audience on the carrying-out of the task will not be primarily dependent on the dominant response of the subject, but much more on the amount of attention that is required to carry out the task. The increase in the level of activation as a consequence of the presence of spectators has an influence on performance in the way described in Easterbrook's 'cue utilisation theory' (see page 37). That is to say, that only by tasks demanding relatively little attention will the availability of an audience lead to better performances. Naturally, this will hold more often for tasks that are already under control than for tasks in which the person is still in a learning phase (see also Chapter 5). It is characteristic of top-level sport performers that they are masters of the skills necessary for their sport to such a degree that these require little attention. Attempts to distract tabletennis players — by means of noise, music, prodding with a stick, to unbalance by pushing or pulling or by requiring a secondary task to be carried out (during play, sums to work out) — did not seem to be in any way successful (Blitz, 1980). This author remarked with reference to these findings:

No one had expected such a course of events. Seemingly, sports such as tabletennis are concerned with perceptual-motor activities, that are so automatised that their carrying out makes little demand on the information-processing capacity (compare piano playing, writing and such like) (p. 83).

In spite of the limitations imposed by the laboratory in experiments discussed so far, it is not difficult to appreciate either of the effects on an athlete (increase in activation, distraction) that arise as a consequence of the presence of spectators.

An enthusiastic public, giving spontaneous applause after every successful jump or pirouette during the skating of the 'kür', can give rise to an excited feeling in the skater. It is equally possible to imagine that the skater pays so much attention to the reactions of the public that the spectators indeed have a distracting effect. In the practical situation it is apparent that, in some sports, attentional or concentration disturbances are easier to bring about than in others. The behaviour of the public at a boxing match is completely different from their behaviour at a tennis match. The ritual whispering of commentators at billiards events radiates respect for the (assumed) labile concentration of the billiard player. In view of the fact that, in this particular sport, movements can often not be carried out in an automatic way, this habit of the commentators may be of more than ritual significance.

For the sake of completeness a last aspect of the influence of spectators on the athlete should be indicated. It might well be supposed that the reactions of the public would have a certain informative value. If the speed skater is outside the schedule which would lead to him becoming world champion the stadium is generally very quiet. The speed skater deduces from this that all is not going as he had wished, but how far this information adds to that provided by the trainer/coach, or to what the speed skater himself experiences, is questionable. On the other hand it might be expected that information stemming from the public is, in general, non-specific and lacking in precision and thus is likely to contribute little (see also page 20).

2.8. Summary and conclusions

In the first part of this chapter the central focus was the motives for sport participation, or, to put it in another way, which individual differences provide an explanation for the fact that some people participate in sport and others do not? Coupled to this is the question: 'What makes a sport activity so attractive to someone that he lets it determine his lifestyle, while another can scarcely conjure up any enthusiasm?'

It would seem that, in addition to a health motive, motives that can be attributed to the basic motive competency (i.e. affiliation and achievement motives) have just as much a role to play as motives that lie close to the activity itself (intrinsic pleasure, enjoyment of movement). Seemingly, some people have developed goal images and action anticipations with respect to the field of activity 'sport', in which sport represents an important positive value. The question as to which learning experiences are, in that connection, of importance would seem pre-eminently a question to which sport psychology should direct its research. In this connection, just as much attention should be paid to the learning experiences of persons active in sport as those of people who do not practise sport.

Two aspects of the question why people have taken part in sport have, separately, received attention. In the first place was the role of intrinsic motivation and the effect thereon of extrinsic rewards, whereby the interest centred on whether competition or rivalry can function as an extrinsically motivating factor. While extrinsic rewards in different situations have a negative effect on a person's intrinsic motivation, the problem with research carried out in that area is that it is limited to short-term effects. In the light of the question of why people do or do not participate in sport, it would seem worthwhile to direct research more to the effects of extrinsic rewards in the long term, *in casu* to the development of a person's motives. The second aspect related to the motives to explore boundaries and to take risks. In view of the particularly intriguing nature of the question, Solomon's (1980) theory merits further elaboration and testing in sport situations.

The second part of this chapter examined the relationship between motivation and achievement. The inverted-U hypothesis rejoices in a certain popularity; nevertheless, it would seem that in some situations the problem is particularly to increase motivation. Several factors that play a role in this respect were explored. The attribution process (to what does a person attribute his successes or failures), setting oneself clear, realistic goals and the presence of the public, are factors which clearly have an influence on the relationship between motivation and achievement.

References

Alderman, R.B. (1976). Incentive motivation in sport: an interpretive speculation of research opportunities. In A.C. Fisher (Ed.), *Psychology of Sport*. Palo Alto, CA: Mayfield.

Alderman, R.B. (1978). Strategies for motivating young athletes. In W.F. Straub (Ed.), *Sport Psychology. An Analysis of Athlete Behavior*. Ithaca, NY: Mouvement Publications.

Alderman, R.B., & Wood, N.L. (1976). An analysis of incentive motivation in young Canadian athletes. *Canadian Journal of Applied Sports Sciences*, **2**, 169–176.

Apter, M.J. (1982). *The Experience of Motivation: The Theory of Psychological Reversals*. London: Academic Press.

Artus, H.G. (1971). Untersuchungen zur Motivation bei Jugendlichen im Breitensport (Investigations into the motivation of young recreational sport performers). In P.W. Henze (Ed.), *Motivation im Sport (Motivation in Sport)*. Schorndorf: Karl Hofmann.

Atkinson, J.W. (1964). *An Introduction to Motivation*. London: Van Nostrand.

Atkinson, J.W. (1981). Studying personality in the context of an advanced motivational psychology. *American Psychologist*, **36**, 117–128.

Bergen, T.C.M., Alberts, R.V.J., & Peters, V.A.M. (1980). Transferproblemen bij motivatietrainingen voor docenten (Transfer problems in the motivation training of teachers). In S.A.M. Veenman and J.J.M. Kok (Eds), *Opleiding van Onderwijsgevenden (Education of Teachers)*. Den Haag: Staatsuitgeverij.

Biddle, S.J.H. (1984). Attribution theory in sport and recreation: origins, developments and future directions. *Physical Education Review*, **7**, 145–159.

Bielefeld, J. (1979). Gründe für und wider das Sporttreiben (Reasons for (not) participating in sport). In G. Bäumler, E. Hahn and R. Nitsch (Eds), *Aktuelle Probleme der Sportpsychologie (Current Questions in Sport Psychology)*. Schorndorf: Karl Hofmann.

Bierhoff-Alfermann, D. (1979). Ursachenerklärung für Erfolg und Misserfolg bei einem Schwimmwettkampf: defensive Attribution und die Bedeutsamkeit des Wettkampfes (Explanation for success and failure in a swimming competition). In G. Bäumler, E. Hahn and J.R. Nitsch (Eds), *Aktuelle Probleme der Sportpsychologie (Current Questions in Sport Psychology)*. Schorndorf: Karl Hofmann.

Birch, D., & Veroff, J. (1966). *Motivation: a Study of Action*. Belmont, CA: Brooks/Cole.

Blitz, P. (1980). Sport en psychologie (Sport and psychology). In H. Bergman and H. van der Ploeg (Eds), *Sport en Wetenschap (Sport and Science)*. Haarlem: De Vrieseborch.

Bloss, H. (1971). Motive und Einstellungen von Berufsschülern zur sportlichen Betätigung (Student's motivation for physical education). In P.W. Henze (Ed.), *Motivation im Sport (Motivation in Sport)*. Schorndorf: Karl Hofmann.

Brackhane, R., & Fischhold, R. (1981). Freizeitsport als Leistungssport (Recreational and competitive sport). *Sportwissenschaft*, **11**, 309–317.

Brannigan, A., & McDougall, A.A. (1983). Peril and pleasure in the maintenance of a high risk sport: a study of hang-gliding. *Journal of Sport Behavior*, **6**, 37—51.

Broadhurst, P.L. (1957). Emotionality and the Yerkes—Dodson law. *Journal of Experimental Psychology*, **54**, 345—352.

Butt, D.S. (1976). *Psychology of Sport*. New York: Van Nostrand Reinhold.

Casady, M. (1974). The tricky business of giving rewards. *Psychology Today*, **8**, 52.

Cattell, R.B., & Child, D. (1975). *Motivation and Dynamic Structure*. London: Holt, Rinehart & Winston.

Colt, E.W.D., Wardlaw, S.L., & Frantz, A.G. (1981). The effect of running on plasma beta-endorphin. *Life Sciences*, **28**, 1637—1640.

Dalton, J.E., & Maier, R.A. (1977). A self-fulfilling prophecy in a competitive psychomotor task. *Journal of Research in Personality*, **11**, 487—495.

De Charms, R. (1968). *Personal Causation*. New York: Academic Press.

Deci, E.L. (1975). *Intrinsic Motivation*. New York: Plenum Press.

Deci, E.L. (1978). Intrinsic motivation: theory and application. In D.M. Landers and R.W. Christina (Eds), *Psychology of Motor Behavior and Sport*. Champaign, IL: Human Kinetics.

Deci, E.L., Betley, G., Kahle, J., Abrams, L., & Porac, J. (1981). When trying to win: competition and intrinsic motivation. *Personality and Social Psychology Bulletin*, **7**, 79—83.

Dellen, T.J. van, & Crum, B.J. (1975). *De Sportinstuif in Amsterdam (The Informal 'Sports Party' in Amsterdam)*. Internal publication, Free University, Faculty of Human Movement Sciences, Amsterdam.

Dunleavy, A.O., & Rees, C.R. (1979). The effect of achievement motivation and sports exposure upon sports involvement of American college males. *International Journal of Sport Psychology*, **10**, 92—100.

Easterbrook, J.A. (1959). The effect of emotion on cue utilization and the organization of behavior. *Psychological Review*, **66**, 183—201.

Elliot, D.L., Goldberg, L., Watts, W.J., & Orwoll, E. (1984). Resistance exercise and plasma beta-endorphin/beta-lipotrophin immunoreactivity. *Life Sciences*, **34**, 515—518.

Epstein, S. (1967). Toward a unified theory of anxiety. In B.A. Maher (Ed.), *Progress in Experimental Personality Research*, Vol. 4. New York: Academic Press.

Ferguson, E.D. (1976). *Motivation, an Experimental Approach*. New York: Holt, Rinehart & Winston.

Fisher, A.C. (1976). *Psychology of Sport*, Palo Alto: Mayfield.

Fodero, J.M. (1980). An analysis of achievement motivation and motivational tendencies among men and women collegiate gymnasts. *International Journal of Sport Psychology*, **11**, 100—112.

Frieze, I., & Weiner, B. (1971). Cue utilization and attributional judgments for success and failure. *Journal of Personality*, **39**, 591—606.

Gabler, H. (1971). Zur Entwicklung der Leistungsmotivation von jugendlichen Hochleistungssportlern (Development of achievement motivation in young top-level sport performers). In P.W. Henze (Ed.), *Motivation in Sport (Motivation in Sport)*. Schorndorf: Karl Hofmann.

Gabler, H. (1972). *Leistungsmotivation im Hochleistungssport (Achievement Motivation in Top-level Sport)*. Schorndorf: Verlag Karl Hofmann.

Gabler, H. (1976). Entwicklung von Persönlichkeitsmerkmalen bei Hochleistungssportlern (Development of personality traits in top-level sport performers). *Sportwissenschaft*, **6**, 247—276.

Geen, R.G., & Gange, J.J. (1977). Drive theory of social facilitation: a decade of theory and research. *Psychological Bulletin*, **84**, 1267–1288.

Goldstein, A. (1978). Endorphins: physiology and clinical implications. *Annals of the New York Academy of Sciences*, **311**, 49–58.

Gorsuch, H.R. (1968). The competitive athlete and the achievement motive as measured by a projective test. Dissertation, Pennsylvania State University.

Grossman, A., & Sutton, J.R. (1985). Endorphins. What are they? How are they measured? What is their role in exercise? *Medicine and Science in Sports and Exercise*, **17**, 74–81.

Hahmann, H. (1971). Die Auswirkung von Dauer und Intensität sportlicher Aktivität in Kindheid und Jugend auf die Motivation im Sport bei Studierenden (The effects of sporting activities in childhood on student's motivation for sport). In P.W. Henze (Ed.), *Motivation im Sport (Motivation in Sport)*. Schorndorf: Karl Hofmann.

Halliwell, W.R. (1978a). Intrinsic motivation in sport. In W.F. Straub (Ed.), *Sport Psychology, an Analysis of Athlete Behavior*. Ithaca, NY: Mouvement Publications.

Halliwell, W.R. (1978b). The effect of cognitive development on children's perceptions of intrinsically and extrinsically motivated behavior. In D.M. Landers and R.W. Christina (Eds), *Psychology of Motor Behavior and Sport—1977*. Champaign, IL: Human Kinetics.

Hardley, M.E. (1984). *Endocrinology*. Englewood Cliffs, NJ: Prentice Hall.

Heckhausen, H. (1963). *Hoffnung und Furcht in der Leistungsmotivation (Hope and Anxiety in Achievement Motivation)*. Meisenheim/Glan: Hain.

Heckhausen, H. (1971). Leistungsmotivation und Sport (Achievement motivation and sport). In P.W. Henze (Ed.), *Motivation im Sport (Motivation in Sport)*. Schorndorf: Karl Hofmann.

Heckhausen, H. (1974). Motive und ihre Erstehung (The origins of motives). In F.E. Weinert (Ed.), *Funk-Kolleg 'Paedagogische Psychologie'*, Band 1 *(Broadcast lectures on pedagogical psychology)*. Frankfurt a.M.: Fischer.

Heider, R. (1958). *The Psychology of Interpersonal Relations*. New York: Wiley.

Hermans, H.J.M. (1967). *Motivatie en Prestatie (Motivation and Achievement)*. Amsterdam: Swets & Zeitlinger.

Hermans, H.J.M. (1971). *Prestatiemotief en Faalangst in Gezin en Onderwijs (Achievement Motivation and Debilitating Anxiety in Family and at School)*. Amsterdam: Swets & Zeitlinger.

Hilgard, E.R., Atkinson, R.C., & Atkinson, R.L. (1971). *Introduction to Psychology*, 5th edn. New York: Harcourt Brace Jovanovich.

Howlett, T.A., Tomlin, S., Ngahfoong, L., Rees, L.H., Bullen, B.A., Skrinar, G.S., & McArthur, J.W. (1984). Releases of beta-endorphin and met-enkephalin during exercise in normal women: response to training. *British Medical Journal*, **288**, 1950–1952.

Jones, J.G., & Hardy, L. (1989). Stress and cognitive functioning in sport. *Journal of Sport Sciences*, **7**, 41–63.

Kahneman, D. (1973). *Attention and Effort*. Englewood Cliffs, NJ: Prentice-Hall.

Kanfer, F.H., & Goldfoot, D.A. (1966). Self-control and tolerance of noxious stimulation. *Psychological Reports*, **18**, 79–85.

Kelley, H.H. (1967). Attribution theory in social psychology. In D. Levine (Ed.), *Nebraska Symposium on Motivation*, Vol. 15. Lincoln, NA: University of Nebraska Press.

Kerr, J.H. (1985). The experience of arousal: a new basis for studying arousal effects in sport. *Journal of Sport Sciences*, **3**, 169–179.

Kerr, J.H. (1987). Structural phenomenology: arousal and performance. *Journal of Human Movement Studies*, **13**, 211–229.

Klavora, P. (1978). An attempt to derive inverted-U curves based on the relationship between anxiety and athletic performance. In D.M. Landers and R.W. Christina (Eds), *Psychology of Motor Behavior and Sport—1977*. Champaign, IL: Human Kinetics.

Kozan, B. (1973). The effects of a supportive and non-supportive audience upon learning a gross motor skill. *International Journal of Sport Psychology*, **4**, 27–38.

Landers, D.M. (1978). Motivation and performance: the role of arousal and attentional factors. In W. Straub (Ed.), *Sport Psychology, an Analysis of Athletic Behavior*. Ithaca, NY: Mouvement Publications.

Landers, D.M. (1980). The arousal–performance relationship revisited. *Research Quarterly for Exercise and Sport*, **51**, 77–90.

Landers, D.M., Bauer, R.S., & Feltz, D.L. (1978). Social facilitation during the initial stage of motor learning: a re-examination of Martens' audience study. *Journal of Motor Behavior*, **10**, 325–337.

Lefebvre, L.M. (1979). Achievement motivation and causal attribution in male and female athletes. *International Journal of Sport Psychology*, **10**, 31–41.

Lefebvre, L.M. (1980). Somato-psychological experiences during rock-climbing. *International Journal of Sport Psychology*, **11**, 153–164.

Lobstein, D.D., & Ismail, A.H. (1983). Regular exercise training may decrease resting blood beta-endorphin in middle-aged men. *Medicine and Science in Sports and Exercise*, **15**, 150–151.

Locke, E.A., & Latham, G.P. (1985). The application of goal setting in sport. *Journal of Sport Psychology*, **7**, 205–222.

Locke, E.A., Shaw, K.N., Saari, L.M., & Latham, G.P. (1981). Goal setting and task performance: 1969–1980. *Psychological Bulletin*, **90**, 125–152.

Malmo, R.B. (1959). Activation: a neuropsychological dimension. *Psychological Review*, **66**, 367–386.

Manders, T.G.W.M. (1980). Vormen van sportbeoefening (Types of sport). In H. Bergman and H. van der Ploeg (Eds.), *Sport en Wetenschap (Sport and Science)*. Haarlem: De Vrieseborch.

Martens, R. (1969). Effect of audience on learning and performance of a complex motor skill. *Journal of Personality and Social Psychology*, **12**, 252–260.

Martens, R. (1971). Anxiety and motor behavior: a review. *Journal of Motor Behavior*, **3**, 151–179.

Martens, R. (1974). Arousal and motor performance. In J.H. Wilmore (Ed.), *Exercise and Sport Sciences Reviews*, Vol. 2. London: Academic Press.

Martens, R. (1977). *Sport Competition Anxiety Test*. Champaign, IL: Human Kinetics.

McClelland, D.C. (1985). *Human Motivation*. New York: Scott, Foresman.

Muhammad Ali (1975). *The Greatest: My Own Story* (with R. Durham). New York: Ballantine Books.

Murray, E.J. (1964). *Motivation and Emotion*. Englewood Cliffs, NJ: Prentice-Hall.

Murray, H.A. (1938). *Explorations in Personality*. New York: Oxford University Press.

Neiss, R. (1988). Reconceptualizing arousal: psychobiological states in motor performance. *Psychological Bulletin*, **103**, 345–366.

Nelson, J.K. (1978). Motivating effects of the use of norms and goals with endurance testing. *Research Quarterly*, **49**, 317–321.

Nisbett, R.E., & Schachter, S. (1966). Cognitive manipulation of pain. *Journal of Experimental Social Psychology*, **2**, 227–236.

Ogilvie, B.C., Tutko, T.A., & Young, I. (1965). The psychological profile of Olympic champions: a brief look at Olympic medalists. *Swimming Technique*, 1, 97−99.

Orlebeke, J.F. (1981). Motivatie (Motivation). In J.F. Orlebeke, P.J.D. Drenth and C. Sanders (Eds), *Compendium van de Psychologie (Compendium of Psychology)*. Muiderberg: Coutinho.

Orlick, T.D., & Mosher, R. (1978). Extrinsic awards and participant motivation in a sport related task. *International Journal of Sport Psychology*, 9, 27−39.

Piët, S. (1987). *Het Loon van de Angst (The Benefits of Anxiety)*. Baarn: Ambo.

Pribram, K.H., & McGuinness, D. (1975). Arousal, activation and effort in the control of attention. *Psychological Review*, 82, 116−149.

Pyne, F.F. (1956). The relationship of measures of self-concept, motivation, and ability level to success in competitive athletics. *Dissertation Abstracts*, 57−887.

Rejeski, W.J., & Brawley, L.R. (1983). Attribution theory in sport: current status and new perspectives. *Journal of Sport Psychology*, 5, 77−99.

Robertson, I. (1981). Children's perceived satisfactions and stresses in sport. Paper presented at ACHPER 13th National Biennial Conference.

Rotter, J.B. (1966). Generalized expectancies for internal versus external control of reinforcement. *Psychological Monographs*, 80 (whole no. 609).

Sabath, I.M. (1971). Einstellung und Verhalten von Studentinnen zu den Leibesübungen und Folgerungen für den Hochschulsport (Attitudes to and behaviour in physical education of female students: consequences for top-level sport). In P.W. Henze (Ed.), *Motivation im Sport (Motivation in Sport)*. Schorndorf: Karl Hofmann.

Sachs, M.L. (1981). Running addiction. In M. Sacks and M.L. Sachs (Eds), *Psychology of Running*. Champaign, IL.: Human Kinetics.

Sanders, A.F. (1980). *Stress activatie en verrichtingen (Stress activation and performance)*. Inaugural lecture, Catholic University, Tilburg.

Sanders, G.S. (1981). Driven by distraction: An integrative review of social facilitation theory and research. *Journal of Experimental and Social Psychology*, 17, 227−251.

Schwenkmezger, P., Voigt, H.F., & Müller, W. (1979). Leistungsmotivation, Ursachenattribuierung und Spielerleistung im Sportspiel Volleybal (Achievement motivation, causal attribution and achievement in volleyball). In G. Bäumler, E. Hahn and J.R. Nitsch (Eds), *Aktuelle Probleme der Sportpsychologie (Current Questions in Sport Psychology)*. Schorndorf: Karl Hofmann.

Solomon, R.L. (1980). The opponent−process theory of acquired motivation: the costs of pleasure and the benefits of pain. *American Psychologist*, 35, 691−712.

Streng, J. (1980). *Sportpsychologie (Sport Psychology)*. Internal publication, Faculty of Human Movement Sciences, Free University, Amsterdam.

Summers, J.J., Machin, V.J., & Sargent, G.I. (1983). Psychosocial factors related to marathon running. *Journal of Sport Psychology*, 5, 315−331.

Summers, J.J., & Hinton, E.R. (1986). Development of scales to measure participation in running. In L.E. Unestahl (Ed.), *Contemporary Sport Psychology*. Orebro: VEJE.

Thomas, A. (1978). *Einführung in die Sportpsychologie (Introduction to Sport Psychology)*. Göttingen: Verlag fur Psychologie Dr C.J. Hogrefe.

Vanek, M., & Hosek, V. (1970). Need for achievement in sport activity. *International Journal of Sport Psychology*, 1, 83−92.

Weinberg, R.S., & Jackson, A. (1979). Competition and extrinsic rewards: effect on intrinsic motivation and attribution. *Research Quarterly*, 50, 494−502.

Weinberg, R.S., & Ragan, J. (1978). Motor performance under three levels of trait anxiety and stress. *Journal of Motor Behavior*, **10**, 169–176.

Weinberg, R.S., & Ragan, J. (1979). Effects of competition, success/failure, and sex on intrinsic motivation. *Research Quarterly*, **50**, 503–510.

Weiner, B., Frieze, I., Kuhla, A., Reed, L., Rest, S., & Rosenbaum, R.M. (1971). *Perceiving the Causes of Success and Failure*. New York: General Learning Press.

Welford, A.T. (1986). *Fundamentals of Skill*. London: Methuen.

Yerkes, R.M., & Dodson, J.D. (1908). The relation of strength of stimulus to rapidity of habit-formation. *Journal of Comparative Neurology and Psychology*, **18**, 459–482.

Zajonc, R.B. (1965). Social facilitation. *Science*, **149**, 269–274.

3 PERSONALITY AND SPORT

3.1. Introduction

The subject of personality and sport almost invariably gives rise to two questions:

1. Does a person's personality change as a consequence of participation in sport and, if so, how?
2. Is the possession of particular personality characteristics necessary, or at least a predisposing factor, for the practice of a particular sport at a particular level?

In many 'common-sense' conceptions of sport both questions would be implicitly answered in the affirmative. A confirmatory answer to the first question, for example, lies at the basis of the often-quoted statement that sport is character-forming. Participation in sport, it is proposed, will have a favourable influence on the development of such characteristics as perseverance, sportsmanship, courage, the ability to accept defeat, stamina and other characteristics that have to do with social functioning. A confirmatory answer to the first question is, in the same way, the basis for notions in which a 'deformatory' effect is attributed to sport. Replacing the positive characteristics named above are negative ones like aggressiveness, egoism, intolerance, jealousy or other less favourable traits that might be a consequence of sport participation.

Sometimes a differentiation is made according to the level at which sport is practised. The 'deformatory hypothesis', for example, is especially related to the consequence of practising top-level sport. Character-forming, in contrast, is mostly attributed to the practising of sport at a somewhat lower level. Also, for different sports, the character-forming ethic can be further specified: judo is useful in the learning of self-control, boxing in offsetting intolerance, and springing from a climbing frame in promoting courage.

The second question—whether particular personality characteristics are *necessary* in order to practise sport at a particular level—also gives rise to many answers based on intuition and common sense. Perseverance, for example is, for most sports, a required attribute, and for each separate sport one or more attributes can be thought of which, while not a requirement for that particular sport, do provide a useful starting point. For parachute jumping it is low anxiety; for car racing, courage; and for billiards or chess, the power of concentration, to name but a few examples.

In this chapter we shall try to show to what extent these ideas about the relationship between personality and sport can be supported by research findings. In doing so it will become apparent that, in spite of the fact that no other topic in the field of sport psychology has received quite so much attention as the relationship between sport and personality, the findings are not particularly impressive. After we have discussed the reasons for the 'disappointing' empirical evidence supporting a close relationship between personality and sport, we will give some thought to developments that do provide a perspective from which statements about the relationship between sport and personality might meaningfully be made.

3.2. Sport and personality: two streams

The questions posed in the introduction to this chapter have given rise to two streams in the sport psychology world. Morgan (1978, 1980) speaks, in this connection, about the *sceptical* and the *credulous* viewpoints in his discussion about the importance of personality traits for sporting behaviour. The sceptics (for example Martens, 1975; Rushall, 1975) maintain that personality traits have scarcely any importance for the explanation or prediction of differences between athletes and non-athletes, between athletes who practise their sport at different levels or between athletes who participate in different sports. The critics of the so-called 'trait' psychology (see, for example, Mischel, 1968), attribute little weight to the usefulness of personality traits for the prediction of behaviour. They claim that the extent of the variation in criterion behaviour, which could be explained with the help of personality traits, is so low (in the order of 10% to a maximum of 20%) that, to all intents and purposes, it is of no practical use.

The sceptical standpoint can be illustrated by means of a Czechoslovakian book on sport psychology (Vanek, Hosek, Rychtecky & Slepicka, 1980) published some years ago. The authors decided not to devote any space in this book to a chapter on 'the personality of the sportsman'. They provide the following reasons for their decision:*

---

* We express our thanks to Misa Nerad of the Karels University of Prague who drew our attention to this publication and translated the relevant passages.

1. When the 'personality of the athlete' is spoken about, it implies a static description of personality as a reasonably stable collection of characteristics that express themselves in all situations. They label this the 'structural static approach to personality of the sportsman'. They are of the opinion that this approach, in which personality is described by means of psycho-diagnostic methods (for example, standard personality questionnaires), is completely unsuitable.
2. Research in this field provides no evidence of differences between athletes and non-athletes.
3. In the same way, it is not possible to show any significant relationship between the personality traits of sportsmen established by means of psychometric methods and the achievement they produce.
4. The so-called 'general personality of the sportsman' is an abstraction that does not exist in reality. What do exist are sportsmen, active in particular sports, each with his own personality. In attempting to come to generalisations, the variability would appear to be so great that it would be senseless to speak about a particular personality for (a particular) sport.

So much for the arguments of Vanek *et al* (1980). In Sections 3.6 and 3.7 it will become apparent that not all these arguments are correct.

In contrast to the sceptics, other authors take a much more optimistic standpoint. Personality traits are a suitable means of selecting athletes and establishing how different sport teams should be composed (see for example, Kane, 1970, 1978). Tutko & Richards (1971) describe a number of personality traits which are related to good athletic performance. Morgan (1980), while certainly not representative of an unbridled optimism, provides an overview of more than 30 studies in which significant differences between athletes and non-athletes, in terms of personality traits, have been reported—although the differences reported are not great.

Which of the two standpoints presented is the correct one cannot yet be determined—we shall return to this issue later in the chapter—although Morgan (1980) is probably right when he states: 'it appears reasonable to conclude that sport psychologists who have adopted the sceptical or the credulous position are equally wrong' (p. 72).

3.3. Personality

Before discussing research that has been carried out on the relationship between personality and sport it is worthwhile clarifying further the concepts of personality, personality characteristics and personality trait.

Within psychology there is no more uniform definition of the concept personality than there is talk of a single psychology of personality. Where overall agreement is reached it is with respect to the uniqueness of a person. Personality psychology tries to describe and explain this uniqueness. This means that it has to do with the description and explanation of individual differences (Epstein, 1979, 1980; Guilford, 1959; Wiggins, 1979). People differ from one another in a large number of respects: anatomically and physiologically, in feelings and attitudes, in activities, in the effect that they have on others, in social background and so forth.

In personality psychology, individual differences in the *behaviour* of people stand central: why is one person cheerful and the other depressed, one quickly anxious and the other afraid of nothing, or why do some people choose to go on holiday with a group, while others prefer to go alone? These arbitrary questions point to a second aspect of the personality concept that is at least as important as that of individual differences; namely, that personality implies a degree of stability. A person becomes characterised on the basis of his personality, and in his behaviour there must be something that is recognisable, something that is peculiar to him and which therefore manifests itself with a certain regularity. To bring these two aspects together it can be said that in personality psychology the concern is with the study of those characteristics in which the inter-individual differences are very pronounced and the intra-individual differences relatively small.

As already indicated, the approaches to the study of these characteristics differ considerably in the different theories. These different approaches to personality psychology will not be discussed in what follows (see in this connection, for example, Maddi, 1976; Mischel, 1986).

A very useful definition of the personality concept in which the two aspects referred to above are combined, is provided by Guilford (1959): 'an individual's personality is his unique pattern of personality characteristics' (p. 5). Actually, Guilford talks about a 'unique pattern of traits'. In the psychological literature this concept of 'trait' has, however, a rather narrower meaning (namely, a behavioural disposition) than that implied by Guilford. A preference is expressed, therefore, for referring to personality characteristics and to reserve the concept 'personality trait' for behavioural dispositions. In this definition the uniqueness of personality is emphasised, while the second aspect is expressed in the description of personality characteristic as: 'any distinguishable, relatively enduring, way in which one individual differs from others' (p. 6).

Guilford distinguishes between different classes (or modalities) of personality characteristics, that represent different sides of personality. These are reproduced in Figure 3.1. Physiological and morphological characteristics relate, respectively, to bodily functions (frequency of heart beat, body temperature, etc.) and aspects of bodily make-up (length, weight, facial features, etc.). Aptitudes pertain to abilities to perform. The number of these characteristics is, in principle, very large, since all the motor, intellectual and social skills can be grouped in this class. Needs, interests and attitudes are brought together under the umbrella term 'motivational traits' and

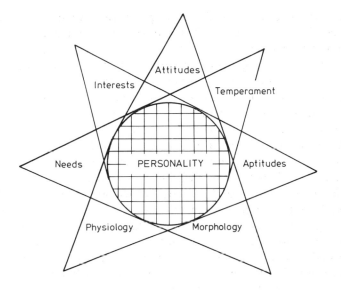

Figure 3.1. Modalities of personality characteristics that represent different aspects of personality. Adapted from Guilford (1959).

pertain to things we strive to do or to obtain. Finally, temperamental characteristics include all behavioural traits left over when the other classes have been accounted for. Confidence, cheerfulness, impulsiveness and nervousness are examples of this class.

A very important part of personality psychology is concerned with the behavioural traits or 'personality traits' while, at the same time, action with respect to the controversy sketched above takes place in this area. In the following section we will, therefore, pay separate attention to personality traits.

3.4. Personality traits

A personality trait is a relatively stable disposition towards particular behavioural patterns (Epstein, 1977). A large number of personality traits are in evidence both in everyday language usage and in the psychological literature. As an illustration: Allport & Odbert (1936, referred to by Cattell, 1965), using dictionaries, compiled a list of more than 3000 words that referenced personality traits. The large number indicates that there are very many terms that can be used to describe aspects of a person's personality.

With respect to the establishment of names for personality traits, Guilford (1959, p. 52) comments that the first step lies in the observation of behaviour. We observe differences in the things that people do and the way in which they do them. One player brought to the ground during a soccer match immediately reacts in an angry way, while another, under the same circumstances, shows hardly any annoyance. In the first instance such an observation leads to characterising the behaviour as an angry, friendly or half-hearted reaction. Almost in the next breath, the person who demonstrated the behaviour becomes characterised as angry, friendly and so forth. It is precisely the differences in reaction between people that lead to the suspicion that the reaction to being brought down is not entirely dependent upon the environment, but is related to the person who experienced it: we expect that one will more quickly become angry than the other. If, during a game, the same thing happens a number of times, then our expectation is confirmed and to the first person will be attributed a greater inclination (tendency, disposition) to react angrily than to the second. Terms such as quick-tempered, touchy and aggressive would be deemed applicable.

From what has been said, it is especially important to note that personality traits are not observable but are inferred from the behaviour shown by people. Particularly consistent, behavioural patterns give rise to the formulation of personality characteristics — a child that cries for nothing is touchy and over-sensitive; someone who often and quickly reacts aggressively is quick-tempered; a person who seldom or never shows anxiety is self-assured.

Guilford speaks of 'trait indicators' in the case of behaviours that give rise to the postulation of a trait. Diverse 'sorts' of personality traits exist. In this connection two important aspects can be signalled. The first relates to the relation between the personality trait and the indicators of that trait. For the prediction of the behaviour of a person, the way in which the indicators of a particular trait mutually interact is significant, and this relation probably differs (for some traits) from individual to individual. Guilford illustrates this point as follows:

> For example, one individual's sociability is more often or more clearly shown by his liking of friends and acquaintances, whereas another individual's sociability is more often shown by his love of social affairs. If we were to obtain seven scores, one for each of the seven indicators of sociability mentioned above,* we should find that not all individuals are shown to be equally sociable in all respects. Two persons with the same total score (where the total is a sum of the seven indicator scores) would not often have identical part scores (p. 77).

The second aspect in which personality traits may differ is the extent to which the trait is 'general' — that is to say expresses itself in almost everything that a person does — or is more specific, i.e. limited to a particular class of

---

* The seven indicators of sociability, mentioned by Guilford are: (1) liking friends and acquaintances, (2) being gregarious, (3) liking social affairs, (4) leading on social occasions, (5) having social poise, (6) liking to be in the limelight, and (7) not being shy or bashful.

situations. Is the aggressive reaction of those 'brought to the ground' in soccer restricted to the soccer field (thus rather specific) or is there an underlying habit of reacting in a hot-tempered way?

These two aspects mentioned above are not separate from one another. A relatively specific personality trait permits a far less changing pattern of trait indicators than a very general personality trait. In the latter case the number of indicators is greater than by the specific trait; consequently the chance of a divergently constructed 'total score' is also greater.

3.4.1. CRICITISM OF PERSONALITY TRAITS

Since the 1960s considerable criticism has been directed towards the usefulness of personality traits as descriptions or explanations of individual differences in behaviour (e.g. Mischel, 1968, 1979; for overviews of these criticisms see Feij, 1978; Hogan, De Soto & Solano, 1977). Representatives of the sceptical viewpoint (see page 54) in dismissing personality traits as useful concepts in sport psychology invoke, amongst other reasons, this criticism. The arguments of such critics will be briefly discussed.

The two most important aspects of the criticism relate to:

1. The explanatory status of the concept personality trait—a trait being wrongly used as an explanation of behaviour.
2. The limited consistency of behaviour and, related to this, the moderate to poor predictability of behaviour on the basis of personality traits.

In short, it has to do with the following: personality traits emerge specifically as a response to the need of people for a certain constancy in their social intercourse with others. They therefore attribute to their fellow-men particular, stable characteristics that make it possible to predict how they will react. It is, for example, much simpler to hold the stereotype that someone is a pleasant, social type than that today he will be social and tomorrow not. Having stereotyped someone as 'social' we do our utmost to maintain this opinion—at least, that is the reasoning. Personality traits are, in these terms, more constructions of those who perceive the behaviour of others than that they are, in reality, available in that behaviour (Mischel, 1979).

The method by which personality traits are measured has also come in for a considerable amount of criticism, notwithstanding the fact that the reliability of many such measures has gradually reached an acceptable level. People fill in two versions of the same questionnaire in approximately the same way, even if a period of some weeks or months intervenes. This indicates, at the same time, that people attribute a certain constancy in behaviour not only to others, but also to themselves.

In view of the fact that in carefully designed research (Block, 1977;

Epstein, 1979, 1980) it would seem that a substantial consistency in behaviour can be shown, the criticism brought forward here would appear to be too strong (though this does not deny that the point that Mischel signalled is of importance and can often play a meaningful role).

It is important to remember that personality traits diverge with respect to their measure of generality. As stated, some traits are very specific to particular situations (fear of heights), while others span a broad scale of situations. A greater inconsistency is to be expected in the latter case, and not only on the grounds of different patterns of trait indicators. Interactions between situational variables and general characteristics of the person will occur more easily than they will with relatively specific traits such as fear of heights. Thus, predictions based upon specific traits are, in general, likely to be more accurate than predictions based upon more general personality traits. This contention gave rise, in sport psychology in particular, to a certain demand for the use of personality traits that are specific to sport situations (amongst others, Fisher, Horsfall & Morris, 1977; Martens, 1977; Rushall, 1975). In spite of the somewhat better predictions that are possible on the basis of these — often very specific — personality traits, there clings to this approach an important negative aspect — namely, that all kinds of '*ad hoc*' traits will be postulated that contribute little to the explanation of behaviour. In this connection recall the list of Allport & Odbert, in which more than 3000 personality characteristics were listed. A further extension of this list would not seem to be the most valuable contribution that the psychologist in the area of personality study could deliver.

The discussion about the usefulness of personality traits has resulted in situational aspects receiving more attention in personality research (see, for example, Magnusson & Endler, 1977, for an overview of this approach). Indeed, also in the classical trait theory, space was made for situational factors. Dispositions always require particular circumstances in which they become actualised in behaviour and, in this sense, there is always talk of interaction. Furthermore, it hardly needs to be demonstrated that both situational and personal variables are determinants of behaviour. The concern of personality psychology is with the relative contribution of the personal variables in the explanation of behaviour. The description of individual differences with the help of personality traits is, in this respect, a first step.

3.5. Personality and sport: what is the relationship?

Research into the relationship between personality and sport is principally directed towards answering two categories of question. The prototypes of these questions were presented in the introduction to this chapter. In the first category, questions relate to the influence of (participation in) sport on personality: is there a change in a person's personality traits as a consequence of his or her participation in sport? Questions of the second category have to do with attempts to predict individual differences in sport participation and sporting achievement and, eventually, to explain these in terms of personality or personality traits. Hypotheses attached to such research might be of the following kind: a person who scores high on aggression is inclined to choose combat sports in his free time; extraverts will be more likely to opt for team sports, introverts for more individually based sports; amongst top-level swimmers are to be found people with a strong achievement motivation, and so forth.

The distinction is important from many points of view. In the first place, it can be deduced that, even when descriptive research shows differences, for example between athletes and non-athletes, almost nothing can be concluded.

Sack (1975) indicates, by means of a flow diagram, the statements which one may make with respect to one or both questions (Figure 3.2). From this schema it seems that in the comparison of athletes who practise sport at different levels (e.g. recreative versus competitive, athletes who participate at regional as against national levels), account must be taken, with respect to eventual differences in personality, of two principally different possibilities. In the first place there is the question of selection: people with particular personality traits become particularly attracted to intensive participation in competitive sport (the same is, naturally, possible with respect to particular sports, individual or team sports). In the second place it is possible that, as a consequence of participation in sport at a particular level, changes in the personality of the athlete become apparent. In addition, it is conceivable that there is a regression towards the population mean, or that the practice of sport leads, precisely, to a deviation from this mean.

There is a second reason why the distinction is important. Research that is directed towards demonstrating change (e.g. when it has to do with the influence of participation in sport on personality) requires a different kind of research design than that which investigates whether particular personality traits predispose people towards the practice of sport or constitute a favourable condition for the achievement of top performance. The first type of question demands longitudinal research, in which a group of athletes must be investigated over a period of successive years. For obvious reasons such research is the exception rather than the rule.

If the research question has to do with the influence of personality traits on sport participation or sport achievement, longitudinal research is not a strict requirement, although this assumes that controls are built into the experimental design so as to make it possible to determine if an eventual influence of sport on personality has taken place.

A last reason why the distinction between the two types of questions is of importance is related to the following. In research directed towards demonstrating a change in personality traits as a consequence of participation in

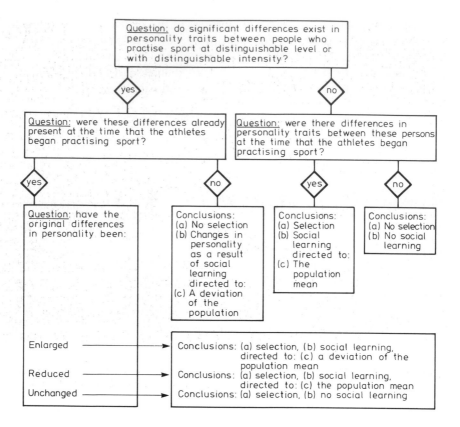

Figure 3.2. Schematic reproduction of the hypothetical relationships between sport participation and personality. Adapted from Sack (1975); adapted with permission of the publisher.

sport, account must be taken of the nature and duration of the influencing processes that, in themselves, are necessary to bring about such a change. It holds for the majority of personality traits—which are, by definition, characterised by a reasonable amount of stability—that the influencing must be very intensive in order for it to be possible to show change. The comparison of groups of athletes who, for example, practise sport at regional or at national level, is thus a procedure from which, on theoretical grounds, little result can be expected. However, not only theoretically, but also empirically, it would seem that there is little evidence of personality change as a consequence of participation in sport, even when the research relates to top-level athletes. In the following section this issue will be pursued further.

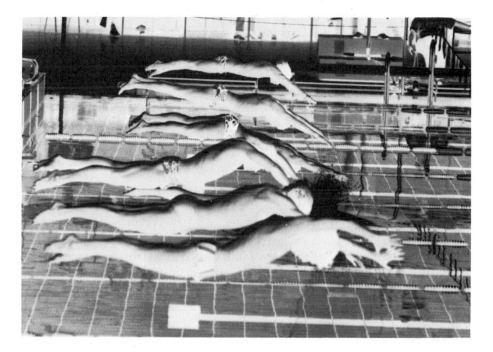

Figure 3.3. The demands made by training for top-level swimmers do not apparently lead to radical changes in general personality characteristics. (Benelux Press.)

3.6. Influence of sport participation on personality

One of the few investigations which allows direct statements to be made about this question is the research of Gabler (1976), already cited in Chapter 2. Gabler researched 154 male and female top-level swimmers. After a period of five years, 102 of these subjects were again investigated. Both during the first investigation in 1969/1970 and during the second the '16 Personality Factor' (16 PF) — amongst others — was completed. The swimmers completed six of the 16 scales of this Personality Questionnaire (developed by Cattell & Eber, 1964) which, in turn, gave rise to scores for emotional stability, dominance, light-heartedness, venturousness, apprehension and tenseness. In addition to these so-called primary factors, scores could also be calculated for the second-order factors 'neuroticism' and 'extraversion—introversion'. Following on the first test completion it was apparent that the scores of the top-level swimmers deviated little from the norm. On the basis of a similar investigation five years later it could be concluded, moreover, that hardly any change had taken place in the personality traits measured.

Gabler summarises his results as follows:

> The demands made by training for top-level swimming do not apparently lead to radical changes in general personality characteristics. This holds particularly for male swimmers. With respect to male and female swimmers, the following generalisations can be made: they are no more emotionally balanced or unbalanced than average; they are not unduly indulgent, pessimistic, withdrawn, uncertain of themselves or tense; neither can they be characterised as particularly dominant, optimistic, 'pushing', self-assured or tense. This holds equally well before they actually begun their training. There are no indications that point to neurotic tendencies.

McCloy-Layman (1974), Sack (1975), Stevenson (1975) and, more recently, Folkins & Sime (1981) and Eysenck, Nias & Cox (1982), in overviews of research in this field, come to the same conclusion as Gabler—namely, that personality changes as a consequence of participation in (top-level) sport or physical activities ('physical fitness training') have not been demonstrated. Folkins & Sime state, for example, 'It appears that there is no evidence to support a claim that global changes on personality tests follow from fitness training' (p. 380). Eysenck, Nias & Cox summarise their findings as follows:

> The effects of sporting activities on personality are not really known, although there are many theories in this connection. It is often suggested that sporting activities may have a beneficial effect on personality, particularly in reducing depression and anxiety, but the evidence does not support such a view (p. 48).

An exception holds with respect to the 'self-concept' (i.e. a person's attitude towards himself and his self-esteem—e.g. bodily characteristics, own potential, etc.). A number of investigations lead to the conclusion that the 'self-concept' changes positively following participation in condition-training (see Folkins & Sime, 1981, p. 381). It is not clear, however, if this change is a consequence of the *idea* that the bodily condition and health has improved or that the actual physical improvement is the cause. That fitness *per se* is not the decisive factor may be concluded from a study by Bakker (1988), who demonstrated that self-concept and other self-attitudes of young ballet dancers was considerably and significantly less positive than that of control subjects.

These results are in conflict with the widespread and intuitive idea that participation in sport and physical education will have favourable effects on a person's personality characteristics. A possible explanation for this discrepancy between intuition and research findings can be sought in the methodological shortcomings of the research into personality changes, such as the paucity of longitudinal research and the general deficiencies in experimental research designs. However, it is unlikely that this is the only reason for the influence of sport on personality not being demonstrated. In this connection some doubt about the validity of intuition is equally appropriate, and one must also bear in mind the fact that people are exposed to a great many influences. Of these, sport is but one. All these factors, in combination with the relative stability of personality traits, would seem to indicate that high expectations of changes in personality as a result of participation in sport are not appropriate (see also Chapter 7).

3.7. Differences between athletes and non-athletes

Much of the work on 'sport and personality' relates to the comparison of athletes and non-athletes, groups of athletes who practise sport at different levels or participants in different types of sport. If the conclusion drawn in the previous paragraph is correct and sport, indeed, has little or no influence on a person's personality, this means that the establishment of personality differences between groups of athletes provides support for the 'selection hypothesis' (Figure 3.2).

Sack (1975) provides a very broad and scholarly overview of research in this area. He distinguishes three categories: people who do not participate in sport at all, those who participate in sport at recreational level and those who participate in sport at competitive and top level.

Based on 151 studies in which around 15000 people were involved, Sack concluded that there is a small deviation from the mean for only a few personality traits, and then only for people who are considerably more or considerably less involved in sport than the average. The author summarises his findings in Figure 3.4.

Although there is some lack of clarity about the way in which the divisions on the x-axis (deviations from the mean with respect to participation in sport) were arrived at, it can be seen from the figure that athletes who deviate markedly from the mean with respect to their activities (i.e. competitive and top-level sport performers) only score higher than average on extraversion. With respect to the personality traits of dominance, aggressiveness and achievement orientation there are indications of higher scores in this group. The results in this respect are not, however, uniform. People who, on the whole, are not active in any sport score somewhat higher on neuroticism, anxiety and introversion than the population mean.

The differences between (top-level) athletes and non-athletes seem to be, over the whole range, relatively small; a conclusion that can also be drawn from the overviews of McCloy-Layman (1974) and Stevenson (1975). What must be noted, however, is that the division of Sack into three categories (see above) is rather gross, and no distinction is made between individual and team sport performers.

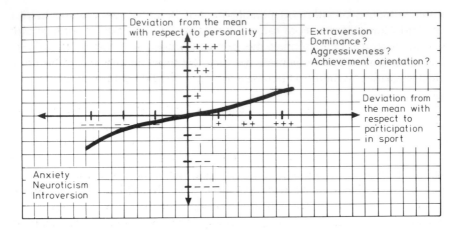

Figure 3.4. Deviations in personality by more or less participation in sport. Adapted from Sack (1975); adapted with permission of the publisher.

Eysenck *et al* (1982) come, in what to date is the most exhaustive overview of research into sport and personality, to somewhat different conclusions than the above. That is to say, they attribute greater significance to the differences reported between athletes and non-athletes than the authors named above are inclined to do. An important reason for this difference in interpretation of research findings lies in the fact that Eysenck *et al* view the research findings against the background of Eysenck's personality theory (see, amongst others, Eysenck, 1967, 1973, 1981). The extremely divergent personality traits measured in the diverse studies—a consequence of the large number of personality tests from which researchers can make their choice—are brought into line with one or other of the three personality dimensions that Eysenck distinguishes. By so doing, it is possible that results to which others attach no significance, because of the relatively small range in differences shown, can still be of importance against the background of a theoretical framework.

The three personality dimensions distinguished by Eysenck are: extraversion—introversion (E), neuroticism—stability (N) and psychoticism—strength of the super-ego (P). These dimensions, identified by means of factor-analytic techniques, form what are termed 'second-order' factors, that is to say that each of the named dimensions has its origin in a number of correlated personality traits.

Extraverts can be characterised, in a social sense, as active, optimistic, impulsive and making social contacts easily. Introverts, in contrast, are typified as reserved, careful and thoughtful, and as having difficulty in forming social contacts. People with a high N-score can by characterised as moody, depressed, restless and stubborn. Those with a low N-score can be described as even-tempered, calm and unworried. The person with a high P-score, lastly, is egocentric, cold, non-conformist, aggressive, impulsive, hostile, suspicious and antisocial, while at the other end of this continuum traits such as an inclination to cooperate, empathy and carefulness are to be found.

These different dimensions of personality have a strong hereditary component, the origins of which lie in biological differences, namely the central nervous and the hormonal systems. The 'cortical arousal' of the more introverted person is, for example, high, and that of the more extraverted person low, a difference originating in the brainstem reticular formation. The neuroticism—stability dimension (N) relates to the activity of the limbic system and the P-dimension has associations with the hormonal system.

Eysenck's personality theory, especially the extraversion—introversion dimension, gives rise to a number of predictions that might lead to the expectation of there being differences on this continuum between athletes and non-athletes. The predictions arise out of the differences in cortical arousal between more or less extraverted/introverted persons. The low

Figure 3.5. The extravert can also be described as someone with a strong need for excitement ('sensation-seeking'). (Benelux Press.)

arousal of the more extraverted person results in a greater need for stimulation, an inclination to seek exciting situations, i.e. an intolerance of boredom, a better ability to bear pain, but also means that he is quicker to react aggressively, puts fewer constraints on himself and is more inclined to infringe (game) rules. In the terms of Zuckerman (1979), the extravert can also be described as someone with a strong need for excitement ('sensation-seeking'), who is inclined to seek bodily sensations, activity and adventure and one who reacts impulsively, in a non-conformist way and displays little anxiety. On the basis of this 'typing' relatively more extraverted people would be expected to be found amongst athletes. Against this background, Sack's finding that (top-level) athletes score higher than non-(competitive)-athletes with respect to extraversion, is brought into relief.

The findings of Fiegenbaum (1981) (cited in Eysenck et al, 1982) are along the same lines. Fiegenbaum compared 53 long-distance runners (athletes who completed the marathon in less than $3\frac{1}{2}$ hours) with 62 'joggers' (who had either taken longer than $3\frac{1}{2}$ hours for the marathon or who had never participated in this event) and 52 control subjects. As can be seen from Table 3.1, the long-distance runners have a higher extraversion score than joggers who, in turn, have higher scores than the control group. For emotional lability (N), the picture is reversed—the control group scoring the highest.

The results of the research of Martin & Myrick (1976) into the influence of personality on the choice of leisure-time activities also fit the predictions of Eysenck's theory. These authors compared the personality characteristics of parachutists, deep-sea divers and skiers with those of a control group comprising students. Participants in the activities named appeared to differ from the control group on the characteristics 'behaviour' (on which they scored higher) and 'anxiety' (on which they scored lower). A high score on behaviour is indicative of rather crude and ill-mannered behaviour in social situations while a low score reflects social behaviour more in keeping with convention—behaviours that can be named as typical of the more extraverted or more introverted person, respectively.

A high score on 'anxiety' is an indication of tenseness and irritability, a low score indicates a relatively stable, emotional condition (thus, this characteristic shows a relationship to the N-dimensions of Eysenck's theory).

Table 3.1. Scores on extraversion and emotional lability of runners, joggers and controls.

	Extraversion	Emotional lability
Runners	3.65 ± 2.06	1.40 ± 1.41
Joggers	3.09 ± 2.09	1.86 ± 1.60
Controls	2.46 ± 2.19	2.22 ± 2.25

Adapted from Fiegenbaum (1981).

Participants in the three forms of leisure-time activities differed little on these two characteristics.

In summary, it would seem that extraversion, in the same way as the need for excitement (sensation-seeking), is a personality variable on which (top-level) athletes can be distinguished from non-(competitive)-athletes. Despite these results it is still not easy to decide on possibilities for practical applications — for example, in the sense of making a selection on the basis of these characteristics. Extraversion also predisposes one to behaviour which is not compatible with the practice of sport — such as smoking and an irregular life pattern.

With respect to both of the other personality dimensions — psychoticism — strength of the super-ego and, neuroticism — stability — the available research findings suggest that athletes, and particularly top-level athletes, have a lower N-score than non-athletes (compare, in this respect, the research findings of Fiegenbaum, and of Martin and Myrick) while, at the same time, they score higher on the P-dimension. Research results that relate to this dimension are, however, to say the least ambiguous, and the differences found have often been small (Eysenck et al, 1982).

The fact that differences in personality between (top-level) athletes and non-athletes seem to be much more limited than those based on common-sense ideas necessitates some comment in ending this section.

In the first place, it is important to note that the groups compared were often heterogeneously composed so that differences are less obvious. Extraverts will particularly excel when it becomes necessary to produce fast performances under a certain time pressure; introverts perform better in the absence of time pressure. Dependent on the style of play, top-level billiard players will be likely to comprise both extraverted and introverted players, and the comparison of a group of top-level billiard players with those of average talent will miss this kind of nuance. Given the fact that much of the research into sport and personality is rather atheoretical, such nuances will often be missing and result in an underestimation of the differences.

If this is a reason for underestimating the differences, it must be remembered that in research of this kind *groups* are nearly always compared. Common-sense notions, in contrast, will more often be based on single cases, top-level athletes who very clearly deviate from the norm and will therefore tend towards an overestimation of the differences.

Furthermore, characteristics that are important for the practice of top-level sport are, naturally, also of use in other fields. In order to excel in work, art or any other area for that matter, persistence, self-assurance, and achievement orientation are just as necessary as are these characteristics for reaching the top in a particular sport. None to large deviations from the population norm in personality by top-level sports performers are then less strange than appear, in the first instance, to be the case.

Figure 3.6. Depending on the style of play, top billiard players will be likely to comprise both extraverted and introverted players. (ANP Foto.)

Finally, it is important to note that sporting achievements are determined by a large number of variables. Natural ability, motivation, social milieu, stimulation from the immediate environment, school experience and such-like, play a role. Personality variables then form but one of the possible influences, and from this point of view, to expect an all-too-great influence of personality on sport (participation), is not realistic (see also Chapter 7).

3.8. Personality and motor learning

In addition to the research discussed in the previous section, in which comparisons between diverse categories of sport performers were made, there is another type of research in the field of personality and sport that merits attention. This is research based on theory-formation around particular personality characteristics, on the basis of which predictions are made about narrowly prescribed behaviours or particular behavioural aspects. Thus, the concern is no longer with global explorations such as typified much of the research discussed above but, for example, differences in motor learning achievements between people with extreme cognitive styles, reactions to stress situations by people with differing anxiety dispositions or relations between extraversion and introversion *apropros* particular learning strategies.

By referring to Eysenck's work we have shown that findings are more fruitful when research is based on a particular theoretical position rather than a 'shot-in-the-dark' approach. The type of research addressed in this section will be clearly characterised by such a theoretical approach and a number of examples of this kind of research will be discussed in what follows.

3.8.1. COGNITIVE STYLE AND MOTOR LEARNING

As a first example of such research, the relationship between cognitive style or cognitive style aspects and motor learning can be cited. The origin of the cognitive style concept and research into cognitive styles can, for an important part, be traced back to the research of Witkin dating from 1942 into individual differences in spatial orientation. The personality dimension brought out in Witkin's research was, in the first instance, designated field dependence — field independence. Later Witkin talked about the 'analytical versus global field approach' and, later still, about psychological differentiation (Witkin, Moore, Goodenough & Cox, 1977). Field-dependent people become, in their perception, strongly influenced by the surrounding field, they perceive more globally than analytically in contrast to field-independent people. These cognitive style dimensions also manifest themselves in problem-solving in which a critical element must be taken out of its context — as would be required, for example, in many mathematical exercises — in tasks in which a person is involved with symbolic representations and in thinking. Finally, cognitive style is mirrored in social behaviour and interests. Field-dependent people have more difficulties in solving such (mathematical) problems than field-independent people, they are more sensitive to social 'cues' and are interested in what other people do and say. Field-independent people have a more impersonal orientation, are more distant from others and more individualistic (Witkin *et al*, 1977).*

There are now a large number of cognitive style tests in use, all of which claim to measure some aspect of cognitive style but which only correlate to a small degree (Arbuthnot, 1972). It is probably better, then, to talk about aspects of cognitive style in which field-(in)dependence is but one — other examples being reflexivity—impulsivity (Kagan & Kogan, 1970) and structuring-tendency (Span, 1973).

---

* It must be remarked in passing that a number of authors have reservations with respect to the generalisations propagated by Witkin (for a critical appraisal of Witkin's theory, see, for example, Span, 1973).

Theories about aspects of cognitive style form a fruitful base for the generation of hypotheses about links between style aspects and motor learning. MacGillivary (1979), for example, showed a relationship between field-dependence/field-independence and learning to catch a ball under three viewing time conditions. Forty-five field-dependent and 45 field-independent subjects were subdivided into three groups of 2×15 subjects each. These subgroups were randomly assigned to each of the viewing time treatments of 150, 250 and 350 milliseconds. The ball-catching task involved a ball-projection machine which delivered a tennis ball at a speed of 40 feet per second over a constant semi-parabolic trajectory. The ball travelled a distance of 20 feet from the machine to the subject. The subject attempted to catch the ball under one of the designated viewing time conditions using his preferred hand. For the total group it appeared that the field-independent subjects produced better learning achievements than the field-dependent. In the two conditions in which the light was on for, respectively, 150 and 250 ms the field-independent group scored significantly better than the field-dependent. In the condition in which the light was on for the longest period of time, no significant differences between the groups were found. This result was in accordance with the hypothesis that field-independent people can more quickly and easily identify the position of an object in space than field-dependent people, these differences only becoming apparent when the situation makes a demand on this capacity (i.e. those conditions in which the light was on for only a short period of time). When perception of objects is at stake and swift decisions must be taken — as in sport — field-(in)dependency can be a relevant variable.

In this research there was a clear link between cognitive style and perception in the carrying out of a motor task. Research of Pijning & Murris (1978) was directed to a lesser extent to the relationship between cognitive style and perception. The authors showed that in the learning of high-jump (Scotch spring) a relationship exists between structuring tendency and the learning strategy followed by the pupils. Pupils with a strong structuring tendency (in Witkin's terms: field-independent) showed, in the learning of high-jumping, a more fault-analytical approach: pupils with only very limited structuring tendency (i.e. field-dependent) were characterised by a 'momentary' approach. In a fault-analytic approach a person directs more attention to the active analysis of the movement pattern carried out; in a 'momentary' approach attention is more directed to the final result of the movement (I have succeeded (or failed) in the attempt) (see also Chapter 5, p. 150).

Bakker (1981) also found a connection between structuring tendency and relevant aspects of the motor learning process. In boys of around 12 years of age those with a strong structuring tendency produced better achievements in mini-trampoline jumping than those with a weak structuring tendency. Moreover, good 'structurers' had available a better visual image of the spring that they had to do ('norm-image') than poor 'structurers'. It was proposed that the 'norm-image' served as a mediating factor in the relationship between structuring tendency and 'spring' achievement. This proposition was partly based on the significant relationship between the norm-image and achievement. In other words: good 'structurers', because of their more complete image of the spring to be carried out, achieve better performances than poor 'structurers'.

3.8.2. ANXIETY AND MOTOR ACHIEVEMENT

The research into anxiety and motor achievement can be cited as a second example of research based on theory-formation around particular personality traits which tests hypotheses about relatively specific aspects of behaviour.

It is usual, with respect to anxiety, to distinguish between:

1. Anxiety as an emotional state, i.e. the emotional reaction of someone to a situation that he experiences as threatening — 'state anxiety'.
2. Anxiety as a personality trait, a disposition to react to situations in an anxious way — 'trait anxiety' (Spielberger, 1972).

In addition to this a second distinction is also usual; namely that between anxiety and fear. Fear is then coupled to an objective (real) danger, anxiety to an imagined or unreal danger. The reality of the source giving rise to the threat is partly dependent on the meaning that the person attributes to it; hence, that some authors consider the difference as redundant or at least only to a limited degree relevant.

In diverse studies the influence of anxiety on motor achievement and motor learning has been shown. Whiting (1970) demonstrated the role of anxiety (or fear) and learning to swim based on Eysenck's personality theory. Whiting's research was concerned with 'persistent' non-swimmers. It was proposed that one of the reasons for such a group of people not learning to swim would lie in their strong fear of water (or drowning). The personality trait anxiety relates both to the neuroticism—stability dimension (a person with a high neuroticism score has a stronger emotional reaction to aversive stimuli — such as pain) as to the extraversion—introversion continuum (a more introverted person is easy to condition). It can be deduced that fear of water is more likely to arise in people who are emotionally labile (high N-score) and/or are introverted than those who have low scores on (one of) the two dimensions. The hypothesised personality differences between swimmers and persistent non-swimmers were indeed shown. The group of non-swimmers appeared to have both significantly higher N-scores and to be significantly more introverted.

In an investigation by Weinberg & Hunt (1976) subjects had to learn to throw a ball to a particular target. Anxious subjects (state anxiety) performed worse than non-anxious subjects. What was interesting in this experiment was that, in addition to the achievement measure, the electrical activity of the muscles (EMGs) involved in the throw were registered. From this it was apparent that trait-anxious people threw in a different way than non-anxious (amongst other things there was more co-contraction of agonist and antagonist muscles and, in general, contractions lasted longer). Certainly in a rather explosive action, such as throwing, the muscle activity of the trait-anxious subjects is less efficient. As a possible — albeit speculative — explanation for the differences found, Weinberg and Hunt suggest that trait-anxious people, as a consequence of their uncertainty, have a greater need for permanent cortical steering and control of their movement.

Adam & van Wieringen (1983) investigated the effect of anxiety on the throwing accuracy of physical education students. To this end they formed three groups of subjects with respectively low, average and high scores on an anxiety questionnaire. There was no difference between the groups with respect to overhand throwing accuracy to a target with a tennis ball. If, however, this target had to be hit at the moment that a moving flag passed precisely in front of the bull's-eye, the least state-anxious subjects timed this better than subjects in the other two groups. The authors indicate in this respect that knowing when a movement should be initiated — an aspect of timing — is the most difficult and last to be learned aspect of complex motor skills (Tyldesley & Whiting, 1975). They suggest that for the subjects in their study, timing of the throw in relation to a change in the environment was more difficult than carrying out the throws well and was, therefore, more sensitive to anxiety. Further analysis of their data indicated that the deteriorating effects on performance were due to the cognitive, and not the somatic, aspects of state anxiety (Adam & van Wieringen, 1988).

An important effect of anxiety on the performance of a task has to do with changes in attentional and information-processing processes. Gaul (1977), for example, found that anxious people attend to different information than do the non-anxious, in carrying out a task. In this connection the following is also of interest: Thomas, Simons & Brackhane (1977) found that in answer to the question 'to what must people particularly attend in competition diving', the divers who participated in the experiment particularly named those aspects that were more difficult or related to anxiety-inducing factors (hitting the diving board, belly-flopping, etc.). Answers to such a question can be seen as an indication of the kind of image that a person has about his movement. The important point here is that if, indeed, aspects that go together with anxiety-inducing factors are included in a movement image (norm image), this will lead, in people with different anxiety dispositions, to differences in movement images. Bakker (1981) was able to demonstrate such a relationship in mini-trampoline jumping. Pupils with a high fear of failure had a different idea about the height and duration of the jump with extended body than pupils with a reduced fear of failure.

Finally, a completely different approach to the study of the relationship between anxiety and sport will be indicated. In this case the concern is with the influence of the learning process (or of increasing experience in a movement situation) on the level of state anxiety. Fenz & Epstein (1967) investigated changes in heart rate, respiration rate and skin conductance in beginners and experienced parachutists from the moment that they arrived on the airfield until the moment they jumped. These physiological measures were all considered to be indications of state anxiety.

It appeared that with the beginner parachutists the physiological reactions became stronger as the moment of jumping approached. With the experienced parachutists there was also evidence of an increase, but only until the moment that the plane from which they were to jump took off. From that time on they were able to maintain their physiological reactions at the same level (or sometimes to show a decrease). Thus, it is not the case that experienced parachutists experience no anxiety or tension before a jump, but simply that they have learned to control their anxiety or physiological reactions to a reasonable degree. As a consequence, the chances of an excessive level of activation that might interfere with the performance of the task is reduced. Figure 3.7 presents the findings of Fenz and Epstein on heart rate.

3.9. Summary and conclusions

In research into the relationship between personality and sport, two questions have received a great deal of attention. The first asks whether a person's personality changes as a consequence of his participation in sport and, if so, how? The second concerns itself with whether a particular personality type provides a favourable condition for the successful practice of sport, or a particular type of sport. These are also the questions most frequently put forward from the field of sport. On the basis of the evidence currently available, the first question must be answered in the negative. Participation in (top-level) sport has not, in general, been shown to lead to changes in particular personality traits. The same applies to the influence of physical fitness training on personality, whereby an exception has to be made with respect to the 'self-concept' for which some positive change has been confirmed.

The second question has been particularly addressed in comparisons between athletes and non-athletes, or between participants in different areas of sport. While the differences found are less extensive than is often implied, it would seem that with respect to extraversion and the need for excitement athletes clearly differ from non-athletes. (Top-level) athletes score, on these

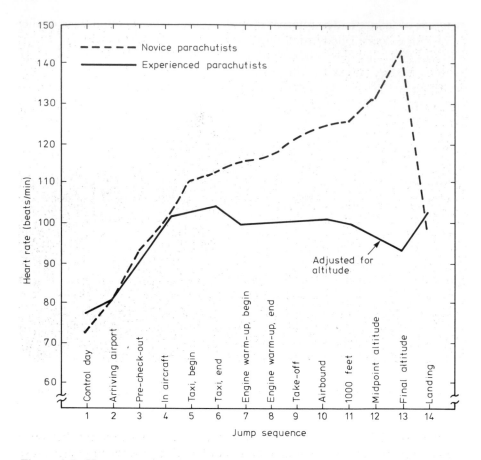

Figure 3.7. Heart rate, experienced and novice parachutists as a function of events leading up to and following jump. From Fenz & Epstein (1967).

characteristics, higher than non-(competitive)-athletes.

Much of the research related to these questions has the drawback that it is relatively atheoretical. The choice of a tight-knit theoretical framework leads to a markedly improved interpretation of results, as was apparent in the discussion of Eysenck's personality theory. The same holds true for the research described in the previous section, where predictions about particular behavioural aspects were tested, using as departure point the theory surrounding a particular personality trait. In this respect there was in the discussion a certain emphasis on the relationships between personality traits and the learning of motor skills. Motor learning processes undoubtedly carry different weight in the different areas of sport. In some areas the learning of the movement is central to achievement in that sport, e.g. ice-dancing,

Figure 3.8. Experienced parachutists have learned to control their anxiety. (ANP Foto.)

competitive diving and gymnastics. In other sports it would seem that once the basic skills have been learned the motor learning process no longer plays a crucial role (sprinting, cycling). For very many sports the significance of the learning process lies somewhere between these two extremes; the technique in soccer, volleyball, speed skating and tennis can always be improved. However, there is far more to be learned in sport than motor skills alone: tactical rules, cooperative play, anticipation of the opposing player(s), keeping emotions under control, etc. For these learning processes it is also useful to know what relationships exist with particular personality traits.

It would seem apparent that, along these lines in particular, research into the relationship between personality and sport is worth continuing. In so far as research into the 'classic' questions with respect to sport and personality is concerned, it is essential that the starting point also lies in theory-formation around the personality concept or in theories about particular personality traits.

In conclusion, and with respect to the 'sceptical−credulous controversy' in sport psychology, it would seem that both standpoints are incorrect. The credulous view that it is only a question of time (and good research) until, for example, athletes or sport teams can be selected or put together, respectively, on the basis of personality characteristics of those involved, has little status. The idea that personality traits have little relevance to the practice of sport is, in its turn, equally misplaced.

References

Adam, J.J.M.E., & Wieringen, P.C.W. van (1983). Relationships between anxiety and performance on two aspects of a throwing task. *International Journal of Sport Psychology*, **14**, 174–185.

Adam, J.J.M.E., & Wieringen, P.C.W. van (1988). Worry and emotionality: Its influence on the performance of a throwing task. *International Journal of Sport Psychology*, **19**, 211–225.

Allport, G.W., & Odbert, H.S. (1936). Trait-names: a psycho-lexical study. *Psychological Monographs*, **47** (whole no. 211).

Arbuthnot, J. (1972). Cautionary note on measurement of field independence. *Perceptual and Motor Skills*, **35**, 479–488.

Bakker, F.C. (1981). Persoonlijkheid en motorisch leren bij kinderen. (Personality and motor learning in children). Doctoral dissertation, Free University, Amsterdam.

Bakker, F.C. (1988). Personality differences between young dancers and non-dancers. *Personality and Individual Differences*, **9**, 121–131.

Block, J. (1977). Advancing the psychology of personality: paradigmatic shift or improving the quality of research. In D. Magnusson and N.S. Endler (Eds), *Personality at the Crossroads*. Hillsdale, NJ: Erlbaum.

Cattell, R.B. (1965). *The Scientific Analysis of Personality*. Harmondsworth: Penguin Books.

Cattel, R.B., & Eber, H.W. (1964). *Handbook for the 16 Personality Questionnaire*. Illinois, IL: Institute for Personality and Ability Testing.

Epstein, S. (1977). Traits are alive and well. In D. Magnusson and N.S. Endler (Eds), *Personality at the Crossroads*. Hillsdale NJ: Erlbaum.

Epstein, S. (1979). The stability of behavior: I. On predicting most of the people much of the time. *Journal of Personality and Social Psychology*, **37**, 1097–1126.

Epstein, S. (1980). The stability of behavior: II. Implications for psychological research. *American Psychologist*, **35**, 790–806.

Eysenck, H.J. (1967). *The Biological Basis of Personality*. Springfield, IL: C.C. Thomas.

Eysenck, H.J. (1973). Personality, learning and 'anxiety'. In H.J. Eysenck (Ed.), *Handbook of Abnormal Psychology*. Belfast: University Press.

Eysenck, H.J. (1981). *A Model for Personality*. New York: Springer.

Eysenck, H.J., Nias, D.K.B., & Cox, D.N. (1982). Sport and personality. *Advances in Behavior Research and Therapy*, **4**, 1–56.

Fenz, W.D., & Epstein, S. (1967). Gradients of psychological arousal in parachutists as a function of an approaching jump. *Psychosomatic Medicine*, **29**, 33–51.

Feij, J.A. (1978). Temperament. Onderzoek naar de betekenis van extraversie, emotionaliteit, impulsiviteit en spanningsbehoefte (Temperament. Investigation into the meaning of extraversion, emotionality, impulsiveness and sensation seeking). Doctoral dissertation, Free University, Amsterdam.

Fiegenbaum, T. (1981). Persönlichkeitsmerkmale von Langstreckenläufern (Personality traits of long distance runners). Paper presented at the Symposium on Sport Psychology, München.

Fisher, A.C., Horsfall, J.S., & Morris, H.H. (1977). Sport personality assessment: methodological re-examination. *International Journal of Sport Psychology*, **8**, 92–102.

Folkins, C.H., & Sime, W.E. (1981). Physical fitness training and mental health. *American Psychologist*, **36**, 373–389.

Gabler, H. (1976). Entwicklung von Persönlichkeitsmerkmalen bei Hochleistungssportlern (Development of personality traits in top-level sport performers). *Sportwissenschaft*, **6**, 247–276.

Gaul, M. (1977). The influence of anxiety level on evaluation of dimensional importance in risky tasks. *Polish Psychological Bulletin*, **8**, 171–176.

Guilford, J.P. (1959). *Personality*. New York: McGraw-Hill.

Hogan, R., DeSoto, C.B., & Solano, C. (1977). Traits, tests, and personality research. *American Psychologist*, **32**, 255–264.

Kagan, J., & Kogan, N. (1970). Individual variation in cognitive processes. In P.H. Mussen (Ed.), *Carmichael's Manual of Child Psychology*, Vol. 1. New York: Wiley.

Kane, J.E. (1970). Personality and physical abilities. In G.S. Kenyon (Ed.), *Contemporary Psychology of Sport*. Chicago, IL: Athletic Institute.

Kane, J.E. (1978). Personality research: the current controversy and implications for sports studies. In W.F. Straub (Ed.), *Sportpsychology: an analysis of athlete behavior*. Ithaca, NY: Mouvement Publications.

MacGillivary, W.W. (1979). Perceptual style and ball skill acquisition. *Research Quarterly*, **50**, 222–229.

Maddi, S.R. (1976). *Personality Theories: a Comparative Analysis*, 3rd. edn. Homewood, IL: Dorsey Press.

Magnusson, D., & Endler, N.S. (Eds) (1977). *Personality at the Crossroads: Current Issues in Interactional Psychology*. Hillsdale, NJ: Erlbaum.

Martens, R. (1975). The paradigmatic crisis in American sport personology. *Sportwissenschaft*, **5**, 9–24.

Martens, R. (1977). *Sport Competition Anxiety Test*. Champaign, IL: Human Kinetics.

Martin, W.S., & Myrick, F.L. (1976). Personality and leisure time activities. *Research Quarterly*, **47**, 246–253.

McCloy-Layman, E. (1974). Psychological effects of physical activity. In J.H. Wilmore (Ed.), *Exercise and Sport Sciences Reviews*, Vol. 2. London: Academic Press.

Mischel, W. (1968). *Personality and Assessment*. London: Wiley.

Mischel, W. (1979). On the interface of cognition and personality. Beyond the person–situation debate. *American Psychologist*, **34**, 740–754.

Mischel, W. (1986). *Introduction to Personality*, 4th edn. New York: CBS.

Morgan, W.P. (1978). Sport personology: the credulous–skeptical argument in perspective. In W.F. Straub (Ed.), *Sport Psychology: an Analysis of Athlete Behavior*. Ithaca, NY: Mouvement Publications.

Morgan, W.P. (1980). The trait psychology controversy. *Research Quarterly for Exercise and Sport*, **51**, 50–76.

Pijning, H.F., & Murris, R.F. (1978). Leren hoogspringen (Learning the high jump). *De Lichamelijke Opvoeding*, **66**, 568–573, 620–625.

Rushall, B.S. (1975). Alternative dependent variables for the study of behavior in sport. In D.M. Landers (Ed.), *Psychology of Sport and Motor Behavior*, Vol. II. College Park, PA: Pennsylvania State University.

Sack, H.G. (1975). *Sportliche Betätigung und Persönlichkeit (Sport Participation and Personality)*. Ahrensburg: Czwalina.

Span, P. (1973). De structureringstendentie als cognitieve-stijlaspect (Structuring tendency as an aspect of cognitive style). Doctoral dissertation, University of Utrecht.

Spielberger, C.D. (1972). Anxiety as an emotional state. In C.D. Spielberger (Ed.), *Anxiety: Current Trends in Theory and Research*, Vol. 1. London: Academic Press.

Stevenson, C.L. (1975). Socialization effects of participation in sport: a critical review of the research. *Research Quarterly*, **46**, 287−301.

Thomas, A. (1978). *Einführung in die Sportpsychologie (Introduction to Sport Psychology)*. Göttingen: Verlag für Psychologie Dr C.J. Hogrefe.

Thomas, A., Simons, D., & Brackhane, R. (1977). *Handlungspsychologische Analyse Sportlicher Uebungsprozesse (Action Psychology. Analysis of Training Processes in Sport)*. Schorndorf: Karl Hofmann.

Tutko, T.A., & Richards, J.W. (1971). *Psychology of Coaching*. Boston, MA: Allyn & Bacon.

Tyldesley, D.A., & Whiting, H.T.A. (1975). Operational timing. *Journal of Human Movement Studies*, **1**, 172−177.

Vanek, M., Hosek, V., Rychtecky, A., & Slepicka, P. (1980). *Psychologie Sportu (Psychology of Sport)*. Praha: Statni Pedagogicke Nakladatelstvi.

Weinberg, R.S., & Hunt, V.V. (1976). The interrelationships between anxiety, motor performance and electromyography. *Journal of Motor Behavior*, **8**, 219−224.

Whiting, H.T.A. (1970). *The Persistent Non-swimmer*. London: Bell & Sons.

Wiggins, J.S. (1979). A psychological taxonomy of trait-descriptive terms: the interpersonal domain. *Journal of Personality and Social Psychology*, **37**, 395−412.

Witkin, H.A., Moore, C.A., Goodenough, D.R., & Cox, P.W. (1977). Field-dependent and field-independent cognitive styles and their educational implications. *Review of Educational Research*, **47**, 1−64.

Zuckerman, M. (1979). *Sensation Seeking: Beyond the Optimal Level of Arousal*. Hillsdale, NJ: Erlbaum.

4 SPORT AND AGGRESSION

4.1. Introduction

Sport is a frequently used subject for reflections about aggressive behaviour. Barry M. Mangillo, during the 'Sixth Postgraduate Conference on Medical Aspects of Sport' held in Kingston, Rhode Island in 1968, put it this way:

> *Sports promote mental health and peace of mind...they can relieve natural hostilities, aggressiveness and competitiveness. They reduce delinquency, crime and violence* (cited in Singer, 1975).

In contrast to this standpoint, others emphasise the disastrous consequences of sport — reference often being made to the thousands of victims resulting from the international soccer match in 1969 between Honduras and El Salvador. At the end of this match the notorious soccer war, described in almost all articles about sport and aggression, broke out.

The discussion about the relationship between sport and aggression would seem to have become dominated by these opposing viewpoints. If evidence for the first standpoint should prove to be positive, sport would have demonstrated its great significance to society but, if positive evidence in support of the second standpoint were to be obtained, such consequences of sporting practice would need to be taken seriously. In this chapter an attempt will be made to examine empirically based opinions about the relationship between sport and aggression. Before this can be done a theoretical overview is necessary.

It is almost impossible to arrive at a decisive definition of aggression. The concept can be viewed as a personality trait, a learned habit or as a biological process. Intention or, on the contrary, consequences can be emphasised. Aggression can be expressed in socially acceptable or unacceptable forms.

81

The value of our definition also has limitations, but for sport research it is, perhaps, useful to have. We will define aggression, then, as *the intention to hurt or injure someone*. Aggression can be expressed in verbal or non-verbal ways and in socially acceptable or unacceptable forms.

4.2. Psychological theories about aggressive behaviour

In this section three psychological approaches to aggressive behaviour will be discussed. In the first place are the biologically oriented ideas of Freud and Lorenz, in which the notion of an inborn tendency towards aggressive behaviour is of special importance. Such aggression must be channelled in an acceptable way. Sport can, in this respect, play an important role. In the second place are theories postulating that an emotional reaction arises as a consequence of unwelcome stimuli (e.g. frustration) and that this, in turn, leads to aggressive behaviour. Finally, there are the social learning theories in which the learning of aggression through 'observation' and 'reinforcement' is emphasised.

4.2.1. AGGRESSION AS INBORN BEHAVIOUR

Most of the animal species cannot, according to Lorenz (1963), survive without aggression on account of its selective value for the species. Lorenz considers aggression as a normal and fundamental instinct with clear functions that lead to survival possibilities for the species. These functions are: delineation of living spaces or territories, selection via rivalry between representatives of the male sex and, in the social context, the forming of a status-hierarchy that provides discipline and leadership.

The idea of Lorenz boils down to the fact that aggression is healthy, necessary and inborn, and that its ritualisation or channelling serves to neutralise hostile tendencies and to direct them towards innocuous goals. It strengthens the idea that sporting competitions are necessary to allow aggressive tendencies to be expressed in a socially acceptable way. Comparable ideas are encountered in those of a psychoanalytical persuasion such as Freud (1946) and, in sociology, in representatives of structural-functionalism such as Parsons (1951).

All these theories are based on a corresponding motivational concept — namely, that people have a source of aggressive impulses, an aggressive drive that returns with a certain regularity.

The ways proposed by Lorenz for controlling instinctive energy — namely, ritualisation and channelling — deviate very little from the different possibilities put forward by psychoanalysts for catharsis and sublimation of aggression.

Neo-psychoanalysts no longer consider aggression as an autonomous drive but, instead, emphasise unfavourable life experiences, especially during youth, as the cause of aggression. This idea was extended by Vinnai (1970) to a social−critical theory of sport-happenings. The substance of his theory is that the viewing of sport competitions, allowing the dissipation of aggression built up as a consequence of the frustrations arising from unfavourable work conditions, helps to maintain the late-capitalist system. Ideas developed in the field of sociology are closely in agreement with this standpoint. Parsons, for example, maintained that social systems have 'safety-valves' to dissipate excessive and unwanted tensions. Dissatisfaction and hostility become channelled in such a way that the relationships that gave rise to the tensions remain. Similar propositions are also put forward by mass-psychologists such as Lang & Lang (1961) and Klapp (1972). They consider sport as a means of 'letting-off steam', a socially sanctioned circumstance during which behaviour, that under other circumstances would be considered as deviant, is tolerated.

The above-named theories show common agreement that during participation in, or looking at, sport people occasionally become angry and, in an acceptable way, aggressive; but that on the conclusion of the competition the aggressive drive diminishes. As a consequence, people will be less inclined in other circumstances to behave aggressively.

4.2.2. PHYSIOLOGICAL ACTIVATION, EMOTION AND AGGRESSION

In 1939, Dollard, Miller, Doob, Mowrer & Sears formulated the thesis that aggression is the consequence of frustration, and that frustration always leads to a form of aggressive behaviour. Frustration is considered by them to be the circumstance that blocks goal-directed behaviour. Criticism, supported by research findings, has been raised against this rather pretentious hypothesis. According to Berkowitz (1969), frustration only gives rise to an instigation to aggressive behaviour. Whether or not aggressive behaviour actually ensues is dependent on the presence of aggressive signals in the situation, and whether or not the person in question has developed strong aggressive habits. Berkowitz (1974) and Bandura (1973) are of the opinion that every increase in the level of physiological activation under these circumstances can lead to a higher level of aggression, whether or not frustration is present. Tannenbaum & Zillman (1975), in contrast, are of the opinion that physiological activation gives rise to such an effect only when there is an emotional situation of rage. Finally, Ekkers (1977) is of the opinion, on the basis of his research findings, that emotions other than rage can lead to a raising of the level of aggression.

That there is generally a high level of physiological activation both by sporting participants and spectators scarcely needs to be demonstrated. Emotions of rage and disappointment are often apparent. A great deal of sport practice is of an aggressive kind. Contact sports, for example, allow a certain amount of aggressive behaviour—such as barging—that can easily lead to higher forms of aggressive behaviour that fall outside the rules of the game, such as kicking, spitting and hitting. Often such behaviour is used in an instrumental way to prevent an opponent from scoring. Sometimes such behaviour serves as a means to intimidate an opponent so that he is unable to reach his normal level of performance. It is clear that behaviour of this kind can lead to spectators becoming irritated. Moreover, such sport practices provide a surplus of aggressive signals. The behaviour of fellow-spectators can also have a similar signal function.

Clearly, sport, both for the performer and for the spectator, provides many possibilities for violent behaviour because, generally speaking, there is a high level of activation, emotion and an excess of aggressive signals.

4.2.3. AGGRESSION AND LEARNED BEHAVIOUR

Bandura (1978), the most influential proponent of social learning theory, proposed that all behaviour—thus also aggressive behaviour—is learned by means of imitation and reward. According to him, people are not born with a repertoire of aggressive behaviours but they learn them. Some elementary forms of aggressive behaviour require little practice, but most aggressive behaviours are more complicated and require a process of learning. Aggressive behaviour can be learned through observation and by direct experience with such behaviour.

Bandura & Walters (1963) make the distinction between the acquisition and the establishment of a response. The establishment of a response follows the general guidelines of learning theory—in this case, the schedule of reinforcement. The acquisition of a response is not subject to these guidelines. Bandura (1965) also wishes to make a distinction between learning and performance. Particular forms of behaviour can be learned; that is to say that they can be added to a person's existing behavioural repertoire. The performance of the particular behaviour can be promoted by reward and inhibited by punishment. In agreement with the 'lawfulness' expressed in learning theory, the rewarding of aggressive behaviour in particular situations leads, via the process of stimulus generalisation, to similar behaviour in other situations (Lovaas, 1961). Other research (e.g. Geen & Pigg, 1970) demonstrates that the rewarding of physical aggression fosters the expression of verbal aggression and vice-versa (Parke, Ewel & Slaby, 1972).

For the application of these learning principles we can particularly think of social environments in which such (often) aggressive behaviour is apparent. This is particularly so when aggression is considered as a valued quality (Wolfgang & Ferracutti, 1967), such as in 'gangs' where aggression leads to a raising of one's status.

Figure 4.1. Aggressive behaviour commands respect. (ANP Foto.)

Aggressive behaviour commands respect, and will therefore be copied even if such behaviour is condemned by the rest of society. Certainly, there are clear indications that groups of supporters in England, Germany and Holland demonstrate the characteristics that might be attributed to such an aggressive sub-culture (Marsh, 1975). According to Bandura (1978), observation of aggressive behaviour can just as well lead to the appearance of aggressive habits as when one is, oneself, aggressive. (In many of these cases the so-called 'modelled' behaviour is learned in the same form.) Three of the most important sources for the learning of aggressive behaviour named by Bandura are: the family, the sub-culture and the mass media. Aggressive signals and frustrating circumstances are not, in social learning theory, considered to be causes of aggression. These lie in the success of the aggressive behaviour itself. Frustration leads to aggression only when people have learned, in such situations, to react aggressively. Both sport performers and fellow-spectators can function as models of aggressive behaviour.

One may think here of the adoption of intimidating language directed towards the referee or players of the opposing team, but also of rule-breaking carried out successfully. A behavioural strategy can also develop that goes beyond what is to be seen or heard. Bandura (1973) points out that people can learn to see violence as a solution to their conflicts, especially when the use of violence can be legitimised. People often exposed to violence can, moreover, become indifferent to its consequences. In the long run the reinforcement of aggressive behaviour and the observation of an aggressive model leads to the strengthening of aggressive habits and the extension of an aggressive behavioural repertoire. For the situation in The Netherlands, for example, these ideas are powerfully translated by Ekkers & Hoefnagels (1972) with respect to the relationship between the increasing rough play and the occasioning of violent behaviour by spectators of soccer matches. They are, moreover, of the opinion that a particular category of the public is attracted by violent soccer and the possibility for violence that surrounds it.

Since, in Europe anyway, many soccer matches are shown on television, the severe fouls also appear on the screen in an extensive way. Because, it would seem, young footballers regularly resort to these kinds of foul, increasing roughness of play is no longer limited to top-level soccer.

4.2. Disinhibiting influences

The significance of an aggressive signal for the development of an aggressive behavioural disposition has already been indicated. This phenomenon is mostly attributed to disinhibition. This idea is to be found in, amongst others, the publications of Bandura (1973) and Berkowitz (1969). Both sport participants and their fellow-spectators can, through their behaviour, be of importance for the reduction of inhibition.

Bandura (1973) has described how disinhibition can arise in the framework of a process of cognitive restructuring. This process implies that those against whom the hostility is directed become successively stripped of favourable characteristics until such time that an extremely objectionable person or group remains. Following this process, aggression becomes justified because guilt feelings have lost their inhibitory meaning. History can provide frightful examples of this process of cognitive restructuring—especially in situations of war. Sport situations can also provide examples: the way in which spectators sometimes abuse the referee speaks volumes. Fellow-spectators are, in this respect, of great significance, since comments and encouragements influence this process.

In addition to the phenomenon of cognitive restructuring, de-individuation is also of importance. Zimbardo (1969) considers de-individuation as a process by which particular influences can lead to changes in the perception of oneself and of others, and as a consequence thereof to a reduction in the functioning of behavioural controls. Elias (1969) developed an interesting theory about the function of watching sport competitions. This is connected to behavioural de-individuation as it becomes apparent in spectators. According to Elias, the social control for extreme agitation in public in recent centuries has increased greatly. Thus a need has arisen for circumstances in which such controls for emotional behavioural expression are less severe. In this way Elias explains the great interest in watching sport competitions. Whether this interest is, primarily, to be explained by increasing social control of violent agitation is, in our opinion, questionable, but the observation of Elias, that the behaviour of such spectators is partly determined by a norm that allows emotional behaviour, would seem to us to be correct.

4.4. Reactive and instrumental aggression

Three different psychological theories of aggressive behaviour have been discussed in this chapter. Moyer (1976) brings these approaches closer to one another by making a distinction, on the basis of the stimulus constellation and the reaction patterns, between different forms of aggression. In so doing he sets off stimulus-bound forms of aggression against instrumental aggression. The former becomes activated by specific stimuli and can be strengthened by anger and activation. Instrumental aggression, by contrast, is aroused by a broad variety of stimulus conditions. Behaviour that arises as a reaction to unpleasant, painful, stimuli (e.g. frustration) falls into the first category, while instrumental aggression is less specific and is learned. This form of aggression is controlled less by emotions and more by systematic considerations. In this respect, Moyer does not dismiss the importance of learning for the first indicated form of aggressive behaviour. He is also of the opinion that reactive aggression which is followed by reward also produces an increased chance of repetition. In sport, reactive aggression is seen as a reaction to a provocation by opposition players and frustrations that arise, such as losing a match. Instrumental aggression may comprise, for example, systematic activities designed to put opposition players off their game, or to deprive them of a certain chance of scoring. For a better understanding of aggression in sport, the distinction between reactive and instrumental aggression is of great importance.

4.5. Sociological theory-forming

For more complicated phenomena of an aggressive nature, such as the collective violence of groups of supporters at soccer matches, psychological theories are often insufficient. It then becomes unavoidable to consult, for example, sociological theory-forming and research. Often such theories are rather vague, which makes their empirical verification difficult. Nevertheless, we shall involve these more speculative approaches in our reflections. In England, in particular, (many) attempts have been made to account for the violence of spectators at football matches.

Taylor (1971) developed a sociological theory of violence in English soccer stadiums in terms of the loss of power of the sub-culture of the working class. Through commercialisation, and the turning of sport into a business enterprise, the supporters become alienated from their clubs. According to Taylor, the present hooliganism accompanying the sport of soccer must be seen as 'attempts by certain sections of the (working) class to assert some inarticulate but keenly experienced sense of control over the game that was theirs'.

The departure point for his speculation is the idea that soccer is an embodiment of values that, in the working class, enjoy prominence. According to Taylor, during the period of industrialisation there appeared life experiences that were influential in the rise of soccer as the central sport of the workers. These values were: manliness, active and collective participation and the urge to win. The values, following Taylor, can come to be expressed in the manner in which the game is played. Playing soccer is closely related to a culture of masculinity. The soccer player has to put up with all sorts of coarse behaviour, and this coarseness is connected to the toughness of everyday life. Taylor speaks of a soccer culture comprising workers with a common interest in the game itself, and for the local team in particular. The soccer clubs were, in this way, the symbolic representatives of the local identity. By means of soccer, expression could be given to the mutual rivalry between teams and regions.

The theory of Taylor was further elaborated by Clarke (1973) and Critcher (1973) to the idea that after the Second World War one could speak of a cultural crisis of the working class. The traditional behaviour patterns within the working class, that provided a certain identity for its members, had disappeared. The sub-cultural behaviour of the 'skinheads' and of groups of soccer spectators represent attempts to hold this culture in existence. Interest in professional soccer, following the Second World War, strongly increased in diverse segments of society, and soccer no longer was seen as the spectator sport of the working class. Moreover, in The Netherlands a great deal of commercialisation came to dominate professional soccer, leading to a growth in the social distance between players and supporters: the well-paid 'stars' became unreachable and often they had played the previous season in another association.

In order to understand crowd behaviour at soccer matches, Marsh (1975) considers it to be a ritualised form of aggression to which an important social function is to be attributed. He believes in the inevitability of aggression and in the need for society to provide appropriate channels for its discharge without the need for feelings of guilt. While the aggression of hooligans in the streets is not ritualised and, from a social point of view, damaging, there are few who are conscious of the fact that for violent behaviour by soccer fans sound rules hold. He makes the distinction between 'aggro' and 'violence'. Aggro, then, indicates ritualised forms of aggression that, in general, inflict no serious harm; but for violence this is certainly not the case. In fact, Marsh presents a strong argument to theories that draw upon ethological notions, such as those of Lorenz, who emphasises the positive biological significance of aggression, at least in so far as aggressive behaviour arises in a ritualised form. Marsh, Rosser & Harré (1978) conclude that in perpetrators of violence there lies at its base a striving towards self-respect in a social system which daily withholds this self-respect from them. Such a social system has no meaning for people who are treated as second-class citizens.

While the ideas of, amongst others, Taylor and Marsh are very interesting, their empirical basis is unfortunately weak. Taylor, Clarke and Critcher have not carried out any research, while the research of Marsh also gives rise to questions. He met with strong criticism, for example, from Nicholson (1978) in relation to his central thesis that 'aggro' (permissible 'violence') is the most effective means to sublimate aggression (unwanted violence). This theory has an ethological basis that retains the idea that ritualised aggression is an appropriate channel for the dissipation of aggressive energy. Nicholson contests the correctness of these possibilities, basing his argument on learning psychological principles indicating that aggression promotes aggression. Most research findings do, indeed, support the learning psychology vision. In addition, we find the difference between 'aggro' and violence rather artificial. We are of the opinion that violent behaviour at soccer matches and violent behaviour under other circumstances are structured by the same norms and values (see Section 4.6.2.).

4.6. Research into sport and aggression

From the theoretical overview presented, it would seem that the aggressive behaviours of sports performers and of spectators show, from some points of view, similarities. Moreover, there is also talk of reciprocal influences. Nevertheless, we choose here to address these behaviours separately, because in relation to these two forms of violence different research traditions have developed.

4.6.1. AGGRESSIVE BEHAVIOUR OF SPORT PERFORMERS

To begin with, then, we shall concentrate attention on the behaviour of sport performers themselves. In which sports is aggression manifested? What situational factors are of significance? Does the importance of the competition and the question of winning or losing play a role?

In relation to aggression in sport it would seem important at the beginning to distinguish between combat, contact and non-contact sports. This distinction is necessary because, for example, boxing offers more possibilities for aggressive behaviour than rugby, and rugby more than volleyball. In boxing aggression is, as it were, intrinsic, because in this sport the direct intention is to bring about pain or injury to the opponent. In contact sports some forms of aggression are normally allowed (for example the shoulder charge in soccer or the body-check in ice-hockey). Such contact, whether intended or not, often leads to violent retaliation. Moreover, aggressive behaviour in such sports is used as a means, for example, to prevent opponents from scoring. Aggression can also be carried to the extreme in that it is used to intimidate an opponent so that he is unable to attain his normal level of play. Finally, there are sports in which physically aggressive behaviour is seldom or never manifest because the players never come into bodily contact with one another. Yet the first gross distinction made between combat, contact and non-contact sports does not mean that within each category no differences will be apparent. These are related to the nature of the sport and the norms and values of the sport participants. The differences between soccer and rugby, for example — two sports related in origin — speak for themselves.

In addition to this categorisation, that has to do with the nature of the sport, it is useful to clarify the nature of the aggressive behaviour of sport performers. In the theoretical introduction we pointed out the importance of the distinction made between reactive and instrumental aggression. Top-level sport has become controlled by strategic considerations in which aggressive behaviours are considered as adequate means to attain goals. A pay-off analysis underlies such behaviour, according to the question of what advantages and disadvantages will ensue. These considerations can be translated into learning theory terminology, i.e. that reinforcement is apparent when such behaviour, on each new occasion, gives rise to more advantages than disadvantages. This implies, indeed, that such behaviour can become discouraged by changing the pay-off appropriately.

Ekkers (1977) points out, in this respect, that instrumental aggression can give rise to a fast escalation. This can happen in two ways:

1. In order to keep the odds reasonably equal, players may be forced to use instrumental aggression.
2. For the victim, instrumental aggression can be a very unpleasant experience giving rise to reactive aggression.

In this way a greater tolerance with respect to foul play can lead to an escalation in which emotions come to determine the player's behaviour.

A lack of insight into the possible origin of the aggressive behaviour can lead to a wrong interpretation of related events. Volkamer (1971), following his research into aggressive behaviour at football matches, concluded that the greater number of fouls by losing rather than winning teams was attributable to frustration. The results are reported in Table 4.1. The differences reported are statistically significant ($p<0.01$).

That the conclusions of Volkamer were premature was, to our mind, confirmed by Gaskell & Pearton (1979). Weak teams not only lose, but they tend to play defensively. Moreover, defensive teams commit more fouls than attacking teams. On the basis of these considerations there is just as much to be said for attributing the difference stated by Volkamer to a defensive strategy as to the appearance of frustrations. Winkler (1971) established, on the basis of statistical data spanning a period of years, that more than 75% of the infringements in soccer matches were committed by defensive players. Within the penalty area the reverse seemed to be the case—more infringements being committed by attacking players. It is not difficult to recognise that underlying these research findings is a 'weighing-up' procedure on the part of the sporting participant. Infringements within one's own penalty area produce serious risks; thus, behaviour of this kind is avoided. We cannot, in this connection, avoid challenging the statistical evidence presented by Winkler, without necessarily implying that his conclusions are incorrect. His research is about established infringements in which the role of the referee is, naturally, also of importance. It is dependent on his interpretation of play situations whether or not the whistle be sounded for an infringement. The referee also makes use of decision-making strategies in his functioning. The wisest approach for him is to ignore relatively minor infringements occurring in the penalty area, particularly when these are committed by defending players of the home team.

4.6.1.1. Aggressive behaviour and the nature of the sport

Many sports did not achieve their definitive form until towards the end of the nineteenth century. By organising competitions, first between schools

Table 4.1. Number (absolute and relative) of reprimands given to winning and losing teams[a].

	Number of matches	Number of reprimands	Number of reprimands per match
Matches won	1568	771	0.49
Matches lost	1568	980	0.62

[a] Matches ending in a draw are not included.
From Volkamer (1971); reprinted with permission of the publisher.

and later between teams and cities, it became necessary to formulate rules which would be of general application. In the course of the years such rule systems have been extended. One of the motives, in this respect, was to counter undesirable aggression.

Research in the area of sport and aggression has been directed primarily to contact sports. Under this category fall a number of the most practised sports, e.g. ice-hockey and basketball in America, soccer and varieties of indoor sports in Europe. In this connection reference must be made to the large number of injuries per year that arise as a consequence of participating in sport. In the Netherlands, for example (population *ca*. 13 million), this number amounts to 1.2 million injuries yearly (see Chapter 7). The extent to which physical contact is allowed is determined in the first instance by the rules of the competition. However, for particular sports, over the years 'informal rules' have arisen.

The distinction made between combat sports, contact sports and non-contact sports therefore needs to be further elaborated. A starting point, in this respect, is provided by the research of Voigt (1982). He related the structure of a number of sports to the infringements encountered. An important consideration for him was the fact that aggressive behaviour was normally associated with contact sports. For this reason his research addressed four such sports: soccer, ice-hockey, (inside) handball and basketball and one non-contact sport — volleyball. His research findings suggested that violent infringements were related to the current norms and values of the sport in question. These norms and values were partly determined by the nature of the sport. Important, in this respect, is that the interaction patterns during the game are primarily structured by the nature of the game, of which the rules form a part. On the basis of an analysis of 95 matches, Voigt proposed that the diverse sports differed with respect to the tolerance they permitted of the performer responsible for the infringement. To what is this tolerance related? The formal interaction structures of the sports analysed would seem to show remarkable differences. An important role is played by the occurrence of many or few individual encounters, as well as the space in which they occur. In volleyball, for example, opposition players never really come into bodily contact — a direct confrontation occurring only at the net. Handball, in contrast, is characterised by numerous individual encounters in a very limited space. Another difference between the four contact sports is the levity in interpretation of the rules of the game. In handball there is so much latitude in the rules that players have developed informal rules that promote infringements. The same holds, although to a lesser extent, for soccer. The rules of basketball are so circumscribed that little room is left over for differences in interpretation.

The values and norms of sport performers are influenced by both circumstances and ultimately determine the number of infringements. Moreover,

Figure 4.2. Close encounters. (ANP Foto.)

infringements in handball, and to a lesser extent soccer, are useful as compared to basketball. Positive results in handball and soccer go together with many infringements — in basketball with few infringements.

4.6.1.2. Situational factors

Wolf (1961) studied 1741 recorded reprimands of active soccer players of different levels in the season 1955−1956. What was notable was that the majority of these were recorded in the months towards the end of the competition. In addition, it is worth noting that players of teams who were due for promotion or relegation initiated a remarkable number of infringements. Drawing the conclusion that the importance of the competition is related to the number of infringements seems to us to be inescapable.

The already cited research of Volkamer (1971), based on match reports of the highest amateur leagues in Germany in the period 1963−1967, leads to the same conclusion. Volkamer restricted his analysis to warnings and instances in which players were sent off. In this case forms of unsportsmanlike behaviour served as the operationalisation of aggression. It is worth noting, therefore, that aggression is defined rather widely since an unsportsmanlike action is not necessarily aggressive. The importance of the competition was also a factor of great importance to him. This is confirmed by the fact that more infringements were committed by players in the first division amateur league than in the second. In addition, he found more infringements by losing than by winning teams. In Table 4.2 the number of reprimands is reproduced for home- and away-playing clubs in relation to the match results. All the reported differences are statistically significant ($p<0.01$). Volkamer could not resist analysing these findings in the context of the frustration−aggression hypothesis.

In the case of a match ending in a draw he was able to provide the necessary additional explanation of the difference. The fact that players of the visiting team committed more infringements than players of the home team was the consequence of the fact that visiting teams have to compete not only with their opponents, but also with the public. They react, then, indirectly by committing infringements against the home team players. In our opinion, however, this suggestion is contrary to predictions stemming from the frustration−aggression hypothesis. For players from the home team there are more reasons to expect a victory than for players of the visiting team, so that the hosts would more likely be frustrated by a drawn match. To our mind Volkamer's research results point to the fact that infringements are, to an important extent, strategies that are used in soccer. A defensive strategy is apparent both from the greater number of infringements by low classified teams and by the fact that visiting teams commit many infringements.

In Holland, van Galen (1986) investigated infringements and the consequent

Table 4.2. Number of reprimands for home- and away-playing clubs in relation to the result of the match (1971).

	Number of matches	Number of reprimands	Number of reprimands per match
Home-playing clubs	1986	1024	0.52
Visiting clubs	1986	1358	0.68
Victorious home clubs	958	433	0.45
Victorious visitors	610	338	0.55
Losing home clubs	610	353	0.58
Losing visitors	958	727	0.76
Home team drawn match	418	238	0.57
Visitors drawn match	418	297	0.71

From Volkamer (1971); reprinted with permission of the publisher.

Figure 4.3. Frustration−aggression? (ANP Foto.)

penalties in amateur soccer. As research material he used all the data from amateur competitions held in the County of Limburg during the 1980−1981 season. For each match a number of characteristics were set down. In addition, all the recorded 'penalty' (broadly conceived) reports were used in the analysis.

In almost two-thirds of the cases these had to do with incidents that occurred in the last half-hour of the match. The most striking observation was that many of these 'punishable events' had to do with the referee and the way in which he was controlling the game. Additionally, it appeared that more punishable incidents occurred in the higher divisions. A number of other factors played a more minor role:

1. The stage of the competition: in the early stages there were more punishable incidents.
2. The geographical distance between the clubs: the chance of punishable incidents was greater in matches between clubs geographically closer together.

3. The score difference in the particular match: a small difference being seen as an indication of tension, leading to more punishable incidents.

Widmeyer & Birch (1984) point to the conflicting findings of the various pieces of research into the relation between sport and aggression. In some cases the losing team perpetrated more infringements. In others it was the winning team that was shown to be more aggressive. A similar discrepancy is also to be found in this section. Volkamer, for example, reported more infringements by players from losing teams, while Voigt established that it was players from winning teams who committed more infringements! Such differences have perhaps to do with the fact that in this kind of research aggression is assessed in different ways. In the one instance use is made of an indirect measure, i.e. the number of recorded 'punishments', while in the other direct observations have been used. Another problem of research in which infringements of the rules is used as a measure of aggression is that not all aggressive acts are punished and that not all punishments are related to aggressive actions.

This particular problem can be clearly illustrated by the research carried out in Belgium by Lefebre & Passer (1974). As their measure of aggression they used the number of 'yellow cards' given out by the referee and the number of penalties awarded in the first and second divisions during the first half of the season 1973–1974. A considerably larger number of yellow cards were given to players from visiting teams and the number was higher in the first than in the second division. With respect to penalties, the reverse was the case: 40 penalties were awarded to visiting teams and 21 to home teams.

In their own research, Widmeyer & Birch used, as their measure of aggression, only those infringements that could clearly be designated as aggressive. A total of 1176 ice-hockey teams, distributed over four seasons, were involved in their research. They also distinguished between the different periods of a match and also between the beginning and end phases of the competition. No significant relationship was found between the average number of minutes in the penalty box per team and the number of points gained by the team in the competition. If account was taken only of the number of minutes in the penalty box in the first period of the competition, a positive relationship was apparent. Widmeyer and Birch interpret this result as support for the proposition that aggression is a good means of achieving success in sport.

In 1972, Naber, on the basis of 260 newspaper articles, investigated infringements in basketball. In the last five minutes of each of the playing halves he found 3.3 times as many infringements committed as between the sixth and tenth minutes of play. In this connection he reports three reasons. In the first place there were changes in tactics — zone defences being replaced by man-to-man. In the second place the course of the match led to increases

Figure 4.4. Reactive aggression.

in intensity of the play. As a third reason Naber cites tiredness leading to decreasing control over bodily movements. We doubt, however, if the latter has any real meaning.

There would appear, at the present time, to be a need for more research in which direct observation of aggressive behaviour is made and comparisons carried out with other, more indirect indices. In this way it would become clearer how far instrumental and reactive aggression are relevant to diverse playing situations, and what relationship there is between these forms of aggressive behaviour and the position of the player (attack or defence).

4.6.1.3. Socialisation processes

It has become clear to us from the relevant literature that violent infringements are related to the nature of the sport. In addition, it seems that in each sport there are variations in the number of infringements which, in turn, are related to situational factors such as winning or losing, playing at home or away.

In this section the attitude of the sports performer to the rules of the game is of central interest. How far are players prepared to make violent infringements of the rules, and what is the relation between this attitude and violent behaviour in sport? Do socialisation processes, in this respect, constitute the connection between social background and sport participation?

Originally, research in this area was directed to the significance of social background for infringements by sport participation. Smith (1974, 1975), for example, investigated the significance of social—economic status in relation to infringements. Moreover, the influence of significant others (coach, team-mates) in this respect was traced. Data were obtained from a youth ice-hockey competition at the highest level. The sample comprised 83 players differing in social—economic status. Interviews with players and official match reports formed the basis of the data. As a measure of infringement, use was made of the sum of the free hits awarded as a consequence of physical violence during a particular period. It seemed from this research that the social—economic status of neither the family nor the school had any major relationship with infringements made. Age and quality of play seemed to be the most significant predictor variables. Higher age and higher level of participation were positively correlated with the number of violent infringements. The attitudes of friends, team-mates and coach were determining factors in the selection of violent role-models. The more positively these reacted to such infringements, the greater the likelihood of violent models being chosen. While this research of Smith was concerned with ice-hockey at a relatively high level, Vaz (1974) reached similar conclusions following an investigation in which the sport performers were on a lower qualitative level. He based his conclusions on three methods of obtaining research data. In the first place he made (portable) tape-recordings, during a season, of players of all levels in a lower-level ice-hockey competition. Informal discussions with coaches, players and parents were recorded. Secondly, a series of semi-structured interviews with players from a lower class and from a professional youth class were carried out. Thirdly, an analysis was made of questionnaires ($N=1915$) of boys from a lower class.

According to Frogner & Pilz (1982), with the increase in age an aggressive norms pattern arises, and aggressive infringements in sport also increase. Aggressive behaviour that is consequent upon these norms is the result of a socialisation process that is limited to sport happenings alone. Aggressive behaviour in sport becomes socially acquired 'normal' behaviour. Frogner and Pilz base these conclusions on the results of a survey ($N=299$) with boys aged from 10 to 19 years. Their research findings agree not only with the earlier noted findings of Smith and Vaz for ice-hockey, but also with that of Heinilä (1974) for youth footballers. Heinilä was able to show that with increasing age the meaning of 'fair play' became less important and gave way to the norm 'try to gain as much advantage as possible for the team'. In this way the trainer—who is exposed to the social pressure that results must be achieved—becomes the central socialising figure for aggressive norms and aggressive behaviour.

One can agree with Heinilä that high-level sport has replaced the 'sacred ideology of amateurism' with a more instrumental value determined by the achievement of results. It hardly needs to be stated that such an orientation is particularly sensitive to instrumental aggression in which pay-off considerations predominate in significance.

4.6.2. AGGRESSION OF SPECTATORS

In our discussion of research into aggressive behaviour by sport performers no attention was paid to the question of whether participation in sport leads to an increase (or decrease) in aggressive behaviour. Research addressed to such questions has not produced any clear results. In most cases the research methods used (e.g. projective tests) have subsequently been shown to lack validity, and are no longer used. As far as the research relates to the effects of watching sport competitions on the aggression of the spectator, it will be discussed here, although the same reservations are expressed. Subsequently we shall address the influence of situational factors (such as the course of the match) on aggression by spectators. Finally, we will direct our attention to violent sub-cultures and the behaviour of spectators.

4.6.2.1 The effect of watching sport competitions on the aggression of the spectator

With respect to the question of whether the level of aggression increases or decreases after watching sport competitions, a number of research workers have been involved (e.g. Turner, 1970; Kingsmore, 1970; Berkowitz & Geen, 1966 and Schulz & Weber, 1979).

In his research, Turner made use of the TAT (Thematic Apperception Test) and a sentence-completion test. After watching basketball and American football, spectators showed an increase, but following observation of wrestling a decrease, in aggression. Kingsmore came to a similar conclusion. He also made use of the TAT but posed a series of questions. As with Turner, he found an increase in the aggression of basketball spectators and a decrease after watching wrestling.

Both researchers, on the basis of their findings, dismiss the catharsis hypothesis. Their research results, however, are not wholly indicative. The results with respect to the watching of basketball and American football are, it is true, in agreement with most of the findings about the relationship between the seeing of violence (mostly violent films) and aggressive behaviour by, for example, Bandura (1973) and Geen & O'Neal (1969), but both of these sets of authors leave undiscussed the watching of wrestling. This decrease, however, points precisely to the occurrence of 'catharsis', a phenomenon that forms a part of the theories of Freud, Lorenz and Vinnai about aggression.

Perhaps Turner and Kingsmore are correct in dismissing the catharsis hypothesis, but it would have been preferable if they had emphasised the lack of consistency in their own research findings.

Another comment about these investigations has to do with the fact that the TAT (a projective test) is known to be a relatively unreliable and invalid instrument for the measurement of aggression. These results, therefore, should be treated with the utmost caution.

An investigation in which another measure of aggression was used (the administration of electric shocks) did, indeed, produce the same result. Berkowitz & Geen (1966), for example, found that watching a violent sport (boxing) led to an increase in the level of aggression. This increase was shown, in this research, to be greater than that following watching a film thriller.

Schulz & Weber (1979) administered a questionnaire to supporters of the German soccer association F.C. Stuttgart, relating to aggressive behaviour before the start of a match. The average scores were shown to be higher following the match than before the start. The above studies, naturally, do not allow a definitive answer to be given to the question of whether or not aggression increases following the watching of sport competitions. Most do, however, indicate that it leads to an increase in aggression.

The widely mooted and extremely popular 'catharsis' hypothesis is not supported by any of the studies reported here. However, in this connection it needs to be noted that the investigations discussed here had to do with a direct effect following the completion of a match. The society-critical theory of Vinnai (1970), for example, has to do with more long-term effects. He developed the idea that aggression during the watching of a match becomes channelled and no longer directed to the source of the aggression—namely, unfavourable working conditions.

In addition to the question of the raising or lowering effect on aggression it is also important here to pay attention to the problem already addressed in the theoretical exposition on aggression, namely that it is caused by a high level of physiological and/or emotional activation, or by the cue-function of violent stimuli (these two variables mostly cannot be strictly distinguished). Unfortunately there is little meaningful research in this connection. Goldstein & Arms (1971) found, as the result of a field investigation, that spectators of American football were more aggressive after watching a match while others who watched gymnastics were not so affected. Aggression, in this investigation, was measured with three sub-scales of the 'Buss—Durkee Inventory' (Buss & Durkee, 1957). Goldstein & Arms concluded, on the basis of the differences between the aggression of spectators at American football and gymnastics, that these differences were to be attributed exclusively to the cue-function of aggressive stimuli. According to Goldstein and Arms, watching gymnastics is just as exciting as watching American football. Unfortunately, they did not verify whether or not this was, in fact, the case.

Thus, whether or not watching gymnastics excites spectators as much as watching American football remains an open question. Moreover, a troublesome self-selection factor has to be indicated. Fans of American football are different from fans of gymnastics. Perhaps fans of gymnastics are not more aggressive after watching American football, and American football fans are more aggressive after watching gymnastics! Finally, the comment needs to be made with respect to this research that in an investigation by Leibowitz (1968), the Buss—Durkee Inventory showed no significant correlation with a measure of aggression operationalised as the administration of electric shocks. Thus, the usefulness of the Buss—Durkee Inventory for the measurement of aggression should not go unchallenged.

Leith & Orlick (1975) reported an increased inclination by boys of junior-school age towards aggression following the watching of a 3-minute round of heavyweight boxing between Muhammad Ali and Joe Frasier. Other children who watched gymnastic exercises for a similar length of time showed no change in their scores for aggression; but, here also, there are alternative explanations possible for this finding.

Neither of these investigations can, as they stand, be considered as providing empirical support for the hypothesis that aggressive signals emanating from a sport competition 'cause' increased aggression in spectators. Indeed, the results of the earlier-discussed investigations of Turner and Kingsmore do not point in this direction. Watching wrestling did not, in either investigation, lead to a raising of the level of aggression while a different sport, with

Figure 4.5. The cue function of violent stimuli. (ANP Foto.)

probably fewer violent signals — for example basketball — certainly did. Other facts also do little to clarify the picture. For example, Lewis (1975) produced, for the situation in the United States, the overview of riotous behaviour reported below. His findings were based on reports in six newspapers between the years 1960 and 1972. In total, 312 incidents were noted — 17 with fatal consequences — in this period; an average of 26 per year. Categorised according to the nature of the sport, the incidents shown in Table 4.3 were recorded.

Most noticeable, from this overview, is the great variety of sports that can give rise to disorderly behaviour. Violent sport does not necessarily lie at the root of such behaviour. In baseball, for example, the opportunities for violent behaviour are extremely limited. Nevertheless, this sport gave rise to the largest number of incidents, probably because baseball is the number one sport in the U.S.A. The number of spectators at professional team sports in 1970 in the U.S.A. amounts to 28.5 million in baseball, 9.5 million in football and 6.9 million in basketball (Guttmann, 1978). Given the differences in the number of spectators, the number of incidents reported for baseball compared to football and basketball is not exceptionally high. Since it can be concluded that in the period 1960—1974 at least three times as many attendances were recorded than for football, and five times as many as for basketball, the number of incidents for baseball matches is rather on the moderate side. On the basis of these figures the number of incidents at basketball matches is, relatively, the greatest. This, in itself, is contrary to the idea that it is primarily violent sports that give rise to violent behaviour of spectators.

Table 4.3. Incidents, recorded in six newspapers in the U.S.A. between 1960 and 1972.

Sport	Incidents
Baseball	97
American football	66
Basketball	54
Ice-hockey	39
Boxing	19
Horse racing	11
Motor racing	10
Motor-cycle racing	10
Golf	4
Football	3
Wrestling	3
Athletics	2
Tennis	2
Other	2

Adapted from Lewis (1975).

Figure 4.6. Aggressive signals. (ANP Foto.)

The practice of violent sport is not a necessary condition for the generation of violent behaviour in spectators. In spite of these indistinct research findings the most plausible assumption remains that violent sport has a reinforcing effect on the readiness of spectators to be aggressive.

4.6.2.2. Situational factors that have an influence on the aggression of spectators

In this section the influence of situational factors on the level of aggression of spectators is discussed. One of these factors is frustration. A number of studies have addressed the influence of this factor on the aggression of spectators, mostly making use of the following lines of thought. If frustrations are, indeed, important for the behaviour of spectators, then it will mostly be supporters of losing teams that become angry and use violence, because of the way in which they negatively appraise the match. Surprisingly enough, a number of research findings that have to do with the public at sporting

Figure 4.7. The influence of situational factors. (ANP Foto.)

competitions are incompatible with this theoretical standpoint. This remarkable fact is a good argument for examining, on the basis of our own research, the meaning of frustration on aggression.

In the research of Goldstein & Arms (1971) it seemed, for example, that supporters of the losing team were no more aggressive than supporters of the winning team. This falsification of the frustration–aggression hypothesis gives rise to a number of questions. The conviction of Goldstein and Arms that the Buss–Durkee Inventory is an instrument with sufficient sensitivity for establishing situationally determined aggression does not sound convincing enough. Perhaps such a questionnaire is able to register very gross effects of situational influences but, in general, it would seem to be more suitable for the assessment of more stable behavioural characteristics, such as habits. The earlier-reported research of Schulz & Weber (1979) also failed to establish a connection between winning/losing and the scores obtained by supporters of F.C. Stuttgart on their questionnaire. Notable in this research is that the authors, in their theoretical reflections, point to the importance of expectations with respect to the end-result as an important factor for the onset of frustration in spectators. However, in the interpretation of their results they seemed to forget this aspect. Their investigation had mainly to do with a total of nine matches of F.C. Stuttgart, of which seven home matches were won while two away matches, against the strong opponents Bayern Münich and F.C. Saarbrücken, ended, respectively, in a defeat and a draw. The fact that the supporters of F.C. Stuttgart were not significantly more aggressive following these 'lost' matches than following the victorious home matches was interpreted by Schulz & Weber as incompatible with the frustration−aggression hypothesis. This in spite of the fact that it is well known that German first division home matches are more often won than away matches, so that the expectation pattern of the supporters of home and away matches will differ.

In contrast to the findings of Goldstein & Arms, and of Schulz & Weber, the meaning of frustrations for the way in which a match will be appraised, and for the extent to which anger and consequent violent behaviour of spectators will ensue, is clearly demonstrated in our own research (van der Brug, 1983). In one experiment we carried out, 112 pupils of lower technical school level from Amsterdam were required to watch a summary of an English soccer match between Queen's Park Rangers and Stoke City. The summary lasted 25 minutes and Queen's Park Rangers won 3−2, after a goal in the last minute. A week before the experiment was carried out, a questionnaire was completed by potential subjects in order to discover if they were sufficiently interested in soccer and, by means of a series of questions about aggression, to control if the inclination towards aggression, before the experiment, was the same for all conditions. Following the end of the summary film, subjects were required to complete a further questionnaire in which their opinion was asked about different aspects of the match. Three experimental conditions were used in the experiment:

1. Size of group: small group (six pupils), large group (16 pupils).
2. Composition of group: homogeneous (supporters either of Stoke City or of Queen's Park Rangers; heterogeneous (supporters of both clubs together).
3. Winners or losers: losers (supporters of Stoke City), winners (supporters of Queen's Park Rangers).

In total, this gave rise to the eight conditions reproduced in Table 4.4. Subjects were paid (approximately two English pounds) for participating in the experiment. At the Baschwitz Institute (University of Amsterdam) where the experiment was carried out, they were asked once again if they would like to participate. Moreover they were informed that it would be fun to watch an exciting occasion, such as a real match. In order to realise this aim, lots were drawn. If 'Queen's Park Rangers' was drawn it implied that if this

Table 4.4. Experimental design with eight conditions, based on three independent variables: winning/losing, group composition and group size.

	Large		Small		
	Homogeneous	Heterogeneous	Homogeneous	Heterogeneous	
Winners	16	16	2×6	2×6	56
Losers	16	16	2×6	2×6	56
	32	32	24	24	112

club won they would receive approximately 3.50 English pounds, and if they lost only approximately 75p. The same applied if they drew 'Stoke City'. Subsequently, they were asked if they had problems with this procedure. This did not appear to be the case. The lottery procedure was carried out in such a way that it was possible to randomly distribute subjects over the diverse conditions. In order to avoid unwanted interaction effects, each subject sat next to two other subjects from other schools.

Supporters of the losing team appraised the quality of the match more unfavourably than supporters of the winning team. The scores continually differed significantly for appraisals on an adapted version of the semantic differential for the dimensions 'good—bad', 'interesting—boring' and 'varied—monotonous' (Kruskall—Wallis test; $p<0.05$). The referee was also more unfavourably appraised by supporters of the losing team on the dimensions 'good—bad' and 'biased—unbiased' ($p<0.05$).

Finally, it seemed that supporters of the losing team found it less pleasant to watch the match than supporters of the winning team ($p<0.01$). These results demonstrate clearly that the result of a match has a great influence on the way in which the match, in retrospect, is appraised. Very important, however, in this experiment was the finding that supporters of the losing team, in retrospect, showed more anger towards both the referee ($p<0.05$) and supporters of the opposing team than supporters of the winning team ($p<0.05$). This research finding demonstrates that frustration has an influence on the generation of an emotional state—such as anger—while anger, as was shown in Section 4.2.2, is a factor raising the level of aggression.

In a subsequent investigation (van der Brug, 1986), use was made of incidents reported in newspaper articles arising from matches in Dutch professional soccer. The analysis was carried out on articles in three daily papers in which, in general, elaborate reports of sport occasions are reported. The manner of reporting was not an object of the study. These daily papers, then, were used exclusively for their information value in relation to the objectives of the investigation. The period over which the investigation was carried out encompassed the seasons from 1970 to 1980. The manner in which this was done was relatively simple. For those matches in which incidents occurred a number of special features were established. To this end every reported disorderly occasion caused by spectators was considered as an incident. Disorderly conduct caused by the sport performers themselves was therefore not considered, except when spectators were also involved. Verbal aggression in the form of provocative chants and slanging-matches were also outside the realm of the investigation. The study looked at violent behaviour directed towards the referee, the sport performers or the supporters, the destruction of material and the throwing of objects inside or outside the stadium as a sign of displeasure.

The following factors constituted the departure points for the investigation: the result of the match, the situation at the moment the incident occurred, the point of time at which the incident occurred, the expectations and preference of the aggressors and the target of the aggressive behaviour. The newspaper articles provided the possibility of establishing the significance of frustrations for the violent behaviour of spectators. As an operationalisation of the concept frustration, use was made of the result of the match in terms of lost, drawn or won when the incident occurred after the end of the match. If the incident occurred during the match then a score arrear was considered to be frustrating. In Table 4.5 the results of the investigation are reported; a distinction is thereby made between incidents that occurred either during or after the match.

From the table a clear connection is to be seen between incidents and (threatened) loss of the match. The most concrete evidence is naturally provided by incidents after the match. The majority of these were, indeed, committed by supporters of the losing team. Threatened loss also seemed to have explanatory value since, during the game, it was supporters of the team in arrears who committed violent acts. It would not seem unreasonable to suppose that, in most cases, defeat is already foreshadowed during the game. This supposition again finds some support in the fact that most incidents during the match occurred during the last part of the second half. Losing is thus clearly an important explanatory factor for the occurrence of

Table 4.5. Characteristics of the state of affairs, the moment at which the incident occurred and riotous consequences.

	Lost match goal arrears	Drawn match equal score	Won match goal advantage	Total
Incident occurred during match	33 (40.7%)	28 (34.7%)	20 (24.7%)	81 (100%)
Incident occurred after end of match	29 (49.2%)	18 (30.5%)	12 (20.3%)	59 (100%)
	62 (44.3%)	46 (32.9%)	32 (22.8%)	140 (100%)

incidents but, in itself, is not a sufficient explanation. In the great majority of matches no incidents occur. Losing is also not a necessary condition, since not all incidents occur on the basis (also) of (threatened) defeat. This holds in particular for incidents that have already occurred before the start of the match and, for this reason, remain outside the consideration of the analysis.

In the experiment arising from the match between Queen's Park Rangers and Stoke City (above), it was also considered whether, in addition to frustrations, there were other situational factors significant for the arousal of anger in the spectators. In that experiment, in addition to winning–losing, the number of spectators (six or 16) and the composition of the groups (supporters of one or other of the teams and of both teams) was also varied. We elaborate now on the significance of this number for anger in spectators at football matches. While it is generally held that a positive connection exists between the number of participants and aggression, there is little psychological theoretical basis to provide a framework for this idea. However, with goodwill it is possible from the contagion theory of Blumer (1969) and the de-individuation theory of Zimbardo (1969) to make such a connection. The theory of Blumer in its simplest form reduces to emotions becoming strengthened in interaction with emotional others. The possibilities in this respect are enhanced if one is a member of a large group of people rather than a smaller group. In the de-individuation theory the observer's perception of himself and of others stands central. Impulses and emotions that are ordinarily under strong cognitive control become more easily expressed. This happens whenever self-observation and self-evaluation are reduced and, moreover, there occurs a certain indifference towards being criticised by others. Watching football generally satisfies the following conditions for de-individuated behaviour distinguished by Zimbardo: (1) a high level of motivational and emotional arousal; (2) a large number of fellow-spectators. To these, in our opinion, can be added the fact that amongst spectators at soccer matches there is mostly a norm that allows emotional and impulsive behaviour. Our supposition is that the large-group condition satisfies the condition for the occurrence of behavioural de-individuation more strongly than does the small-group condition. In the large group the identification of diverse behavioural aspects is less than in the small group. In one way or another this leads to the prediction that, in the large-group condition, more anger towards the referee and players will be expressed than in the small-group condition. The results do not support the supposition arising from the contagion and de-individuation theories. In reaction to an adapted version of the semantic differential, subjects in the large-group condition showed, after the end of the match, no more anger towards the referee ($p > 0.10$), towards players of the opposition ($p > 0.10$) or players of own team ($p > 0.10$) than did subjects in the small-group condition. There was therefore no evidence of a difference between the conditions in the extent to which emotions were strengthened or that disinhibition was of importance. The significance of behaviour-contagion and/or de-individuation of spectators at sport competitions is, with this finding, brought into question. In the first place there are naturally reasoned doubts if the number of subjects in the large-group condition is sufficiently large to give rise to a situation of de-individuation. In the second place, additional findings from this experiment give rise to further questions. In the large-group condition spectators had the impression that their fellow-spectators became more aggressive ($p<0.05$) and more excited ($p<0.01$) than in the small-group condition. This was apparent from answers to questions related to whether subjects found that people with whom they had viewed the summary were aggressive or excited. This research finding is precisely in agreement with the contagion or de-individuation theories. Ostensibly, this last finding is incongruent with the former. There are two possible explanations for this. The first is that differences may indeed have occurred *during* the watching of the match but not *after the end*. This would not be contrary to either theory. The explanation of this phenomenon could be in the extinction of the effect of behaviour contagion and/or de-individuation; but there is also another plausible explanation. In this connection this points to the idea of Turner & Killian (1972) about behavioural uniformity in crowds. According to them this phenomenon rests, for a large part, on an illusion caused by the fact that the observer of crowd behaviour is inclined to attribute the characteristic behaviour of a conspicuous minority to the greater majority. The fact that in our larger-group condition more aggressive behaviour occurred than in the small-group condition speaks naturally for itself. A large collection of people increases the possibility for aggressive behaviour to occur. This does not mean that as a group they were necessarily more aggressive but, perhaps, that incorrectly this impression was confirmed. Unfortunately the experiment we carried out does not provide an unequivocal interpretation of the relationship between number of spectators and aggression. It is not, therefore, absolutely clear if our findings are contrary to the predictions from the contagion and de-individuation theories. The ideas of Turner and Killian provide, for their part, an excellent alternative explanation of the research findings.

In our experiment attention was also paid to another situational factor that can be important in relation to aggressive behaviour of spectators. We refer to the composition of the group: homogeneous (supporters of one of the teams) and heterogeneous (supporters of both teams). In the heterogeneous group condition there are two competitive groups with opposing interests being put together. It is proposed that this, in itself, has an influence on the behaviour of the spectators in this condition. This proposition is supported by the research of Deutsch (1960, 1973) who, following a series of group experiments, was able to establish that the relations in the cooperative groups were more friendly than those in the competitive groups. At soccer matches group identification often plays a leading role. There occurs what, in sociology, is referred to as the formation of 'ingroups' and 'outgroups'. According to Sherif, Harvey, White, Hood & Sherif (1961), quite often in such situations unfavourable stereotypes of the 'outgroup' arise. In contrast, ideas about the 'ingroup' are often based on strong feelings of group identification and the feeling of belonging. In some cases this feeling of oneness becomes characterised by positive exaggeration with respect to the group members. On the basis of the above considerations we propose that members of the heterogeneous group condition have become more angry towards players in the opposition, while members of the homogeneous condition become more angry towards their own team members. In the small-group condition this certainly seemed to be the case: both differences were significant ($p<0.05$). In the large-group condition there was no difference in the degree of anger between the homogeneous and heterogeneous group members. We feel that this can probably be attributed to the fact that members of the large heterogeneous group can more easily come into contact with people of a like mind (supporters of the same team) than those with an unlike (supporters of the opposition). In the small heterogeneous group it is equally possible to make contact with like-minded people as with unlike. For this reason members were probably more angry than in the small homogeneous group.

4.6.2.3. Violent sub-cultures and attendance at sport competitions

From the previous section it is apparent that situational factors can contribute towards aggression at sport competitions. We have also noted that, for example, experimental research can provide insight into the significance of fostering and inhibiting factors. Such an approach, however, has shortcomings when we wish to discover which factors are influential in making the decision to behave aggressively (Ekkers, 1977). It is also not possible by this means to explain why particular groups of young people in England, Germany and The Netherlands are repeatedly involved in incidents that occur at soccer matches. Still, the need for explanations of such behaviour is great, not only from the point of view of scientific curiosity, but also to carry out responsible policy-making based on research findings.

In earlier times, riots at soccer matches seemed to occur only in Latin-American countries. The example (cited previously) of the notorious soccer war arising from the match between Honduras and El Salvador in 1969 is well known. Before that time, competitions between Peru and Argentina had already (in 1964) accounted for 350 fatal casualties and a further 500 wounded. But also in Great Britain, as early as the end of the nineteenth century, there were already serious disorders at football matches (Dunning, Murphy, Williams & Maguire, 1984).

Soccer hooliganism in its present form manifested itself initially in England in the 1960s. Later, the same phenomenon emerged in The Netherlands and in Germany. At the present time violence occurs almost weekly on and around sports fields in The Netherlands.

Such violence can be directed against the players, the referee and other supporters, but also against bystanders. Considerable destruction is also caused, in which buses and trains carrying supporters bear most of the consequences. Diverse notions exist as to the causes of soccer hooliganism. Initially it was thought that rough play on the field lay at the root of the violent behaviour of spectators. Later the emphasis was placed more on the existence of violent sub-cultures amongst particular youth groups.

The bonds between family and neighbourhood become weaker and this, accompanied by the improved financial position of young people, leads to a greater social, economic and cultural freedom compared to their parents. This relative freedom of the youth of the working class lay at the basis of different youth sub-cultures of working-class youths, such as 'Teds', 'Mods' and 'Skinheads'.

This implies, at the same time, in addition to a fall-off in the traditional value pattern, a decrease in social control. Undoubtedly there is both a direct and an indirect effect. Many activities occur outside the reach of supervisory observers while, moreover, there is a lack of clarity about desirable and undesirable behaviour. This crisis is not limited to young people from the working class, although it is possible that, in England, it is most clearly visible.

In our own research (van der Brug & Marseille, 1983) an attempt was made to discover, for the situation in The Netherlands, what the causes are of violent behaviour of groups of young people at soccer matches. A large number of questions were posed to specific youngsters in order to gain more insight into the experiences, forms of behaviour and social backgrounds of regular spectators at soccer matches from the so-called 'sides'. The total sample comprised 268 respondents from four first division supporters' clubs whose supporters were often involved in violence in connection with soccer matches. The respondents were, for the greatest part, younger than 20 years. Violent spectator behaviour reaches its peak in the age group 16—18. A low level of schooling is characteristic. This tendency has, indeed, been less considered than might have been expected. Also, the educational level of the father—as an indication of social background—was considerably more differentiated than had been surmised. These research findings are, therefore not in agreement with the descriptions of the homogeneous workers' culture of Taylor with respect to the situation in England. This gains more

Figure 4.8. Social control. (ANP Foto.)

prominence given the fact that in our research no statistically significant relationship could be established between level of schooling and participation in fights within the stadium. In the opinion of the respondents themselves those involved in violence at soccer matches are less happy at school than others. The problems that they claim to have lie more in the sphere of conflicts with teachers than with difficulties in learning *per se*. It is true that for one of the (sub)samples, the members of which were asked about their completion of schooling, this was less the case for those who participated in fights at soccer matches, than for others. Also, violent respondents were less inclined to follow further education. The social control exercised by parents

Figure 4.9. Sublimation of aggression? (ANP Foto.)

is very limited. To some extent this is attributable to the style of upbringing but, in addition, many of these young people do not care at all for their parents, an attitude which manifests itself particularly in the more violent soccer spectators. The notion of, for example, Taylor and Marsh that pretending to be self-assured and taking risks to which danger is attached, constitute important values for violent supporters is clearly confirmed by our own research. What are less important for our respondents, in particular for the more violent, are values that enjoy esteem elsewhere, such as being good at school and being knowledgeable about politics.

In general, subjects were very tolerant of behaviour by friends which exceeds the norm, such as housebreaking, abusing because of skin colour or leaving a café without paying. It is sometimes asserted that hooligans are not active in sport. This idea agrees with the proposition that these violent youngsters form a group, alienated from society, that is interested in becoming integrated anywhere, including sporting life. In our research the majority of the respondents (86.6%) did indeed participate in sport and, amongst these, no less than 61.8% in soccer! What is now the comparison, in this respect, between soccer hooligans and others? Those who often participate in fights take part in less sport than those less involved in combat ($X=13.57$; df=4;

$p<0.01$). There is no connection between participation in fights in the stadium and participation in soccer (tau$=-0.06$; $p<0.01$). This last observation restrains us, perhaps, from popular propositions such as the idea that the practice of soccer fosters violent behaviour as a spectator. In connection with the lower participation in sport of those who are often involved in fights, we would remark that the idea about the lesser integration of stadium fighters in society applies, anyway, to them.

Finally, we would like to report that it is a mistake to assume that violence at soccer matches is an isolated phenomenon unrelated to behaviour in other situations. This is apparent, for example, from the relationship between those scales that purport to measure a more general preparedness to aggression and those that provide a measure of violence by spectators at soccer matches. This relationship is shown in Table 4.6. This table also reports the relationships found in two pieces of research using a somewhat different questionnaire than was used for the sample 'sides', for young people from Amsterdam ($N=68$) and spectators of the club F.C. Utrecht ($N=89$). (The measure of association was Kendall's tau.)

The correlations reported above suggest that those who demonstrate violent behaviour as spectators also do so under other circumstances. Physical aggression in particular seems to be consistently highly correlated in all three samples.

What is the situation with respect to violence as a sport performer? In this connection two scales have been constructed that are related to such violent behaviour — namely, a scale for 'instrumental aggression in sport' and a scale for 'reactive aggression in sport'. The respective relationships are reproduced in Table 4.7. Large differences are not apparent. The relationships do, however, point in the same direction — namely, a more violent attitude as sport performer by those involved in fights in the stadium, than by others. On the basis of our research we are led to conclude that Marsh's idea, that soccer violence can be considered as a non-dangerous ritualised form of violence, is incorrect. Violent behaviour at soccer matches and violent

Table 4.6. Relations between scales for general aggression and violence at soccer matches as spectator.

	Violence at soccer matches as spectator		
	Amsterdam young people	F.C. Utrecht	Sides
Physical aggression	0.35**	0.31**	0.45**
(Hot) temper	0.17*	0.11*	0.19**
Expressions of rage	0.19**	0.20**	0.19**

From van den Brug and Marseille (1983); reprinted with permission of the authors.
* $p<0.05$; ** $p<0.01$.

Table 4.7. Relationships between aggression by sport performers and violence as spectator.

	Violence at soccer matches as spectator		
	Amsterdam young people	F.C. Utrecht	Sides
Instrumental aggression in sport		0.17*	0.27**
Reactive aggression in sport	0.08ª (n.s.)	0.21**	0.28**

From van der Brug and Marseille (1983); reprinted with permission of the authors.
ª For the Amsterdam young people, instrumental and reactive aggression formed a single scale.
* $p<0.05$; ** $p<0.01$.

behaviour under other circumstances are structured by the same values and norms. This is also apparent from half-structured interviews carried out using a standardised questionnaire, with a sub-sample of the respondents from the sample 'sides'. From this research it was clear that possible inhibiting factors lay scarcely in the normative plane, as Marsh proposed, but rest on an estimation of negative consequences. Regrets for particular behaviours are primarily dictated by similar considerations.

In a later publication (van der Brug, 1986) a report appeared of the newspaper analysis for the period 1970–1980. This analysis was based on newspaper articles in which reports appeared of disorderliness caused by spectators at soccer matches. These data were analysed from three different angles. In the first place a distinction was made between groups of followers who more or less often cause incidents to occur. The central question in this connection is whether differences between the two categories exist with respect to the question of the course of play being significant in the generation of incidents. Secondly, the idea was entertained if any changes, over time, in the nature of the incidents occurred. In this respect a distinction was made between the periods 1970–1975 and 1975–1980. Thirdly, an analysis was made of the different targets: the referee, the players, other supporters, destruction within and outside the stadium and misconduct in trains.

The results were quite unequivocal. Supporter groups which frequently caused incidents did so less in response to the score, and less directed against the referee than the less violent supporter groups. They also often caused destruction both inside and outside the stadium. They often started the incidents before the match began, or in the first half, while the less violent groups of spectators, relatively speaking, often came into action during the second half or after the finish of the game.

In the period 1970–1975 there were many fewer incidents than in the later period. The pattern also changed drastically: in the second period the relationship to incidents in the match was considerably reduced. The score was less important and the referee was less often the target of violence. The incidents also occurred at an earlier point in time, and more destruction outside the stadium was apparent.

The separate analyses of targets also gave rise to interesting conclusions. Violence against the referee was, in the first instance, exclusively confined to supporters of the losing team. Later this was also apparent when the scores stood even. The referee was, later, also chosen in relation to other targets. Practically all the incidents in which the referee was the target were related to the result of the match: disputed penalty shots, offside or disputed goals. Sometimes, in connection to the actions of the referee, the behaviour of the players was important, e.g. in the deception by a penalty kick or, by a major infringement, preventing an opponent from scoring. Players in the first instance also contributed to a lesser degree to the creation of incidents — also, in some cases, coaches — by entering into heated debate with the referee as a consequence of a disagreeable decision.

With respect to the players the pattern changed markedly. Initially, players were the victims of violence only if they became involved in incidents directed towards the referee. The incidents were never caused by supporters of the winning team: they had a reactive character. Later, however, incidents sometimes occurred in the first half aimed directly at the players, and these were caused by supporters of both the winning and the losing teams. Mostly, the easy-to-reach goalkeeper was the target. The above thesis would appear to be in contrast to the hypothesis that it is the violent behaviour of players themselves that has particularly led to the tradition of soccer hooliganism. The beginning of the development of soccer hooliganism was primarily characterised by reactive violence arising from referees' decisions that had important consequences in terms of winning or losing. Also, the behaviour of players gave rise to violence when this had affected the result of the match.

Van der Brug (1986) also reported the development of an explanatory model for participation in soccer hooliganism. Survey research amongst young people known that to be involved in violence at soccer matches ($N=$ 171) provided the evidence. This model was tested using a *Lisrel* procedure.

A number of theoretical considerations were at the root of this model. Two variables were included that fit in with Hirschi's social control theory (1972). Within this theory three elements are distinguished:

1. Close ties with conforming groups, for example the parents, brothers, teachers, etc. Their influence is two-fold: (a) 'internal control', in the form of support; and (b) interest, involvement, control and 'external support' in the form of a direct influence on activities.
2. Dedication within social sub-systems. This concerns the orientation towards socially accepted aims and conventional aspirations with regard to school and work.

3. Functioning in social sub-systems. This concerns the way in which somebody functions within sub-systems, such as his family, his school, his work and his leisure environment.

Research has shown that direct control of the conduct of children by their parents correlates with the frequency of delinquent behaviour. The significance of this aspect was greater than other aspects of social control (Junger-Tas, 1976). Besides this, functioning in terms of school results, disciplinary measures and playing truant shows a much stronger correlation with delinquent behaviour than, say, integration in the family. The hypothetical model finally predicts the diffuse effects of 'effective parental social control' on the intervening variables 'school career', 'aggressive perception', 'discrimination' and 'unsocial behaviour'. 'School career' is expected to be directly significant for 'unsocial behaviour'. The above three variables — 'unsocial behaviour', 'aggressive perception' and 'discrimination' — were determined by means of the construction of a scale (Mokken method). 'Unsocial behaviour' includes norm-transgressions such as stealing bicycles, walking away without paying, stabbing with a knife, etc. 'Aggressive perception' includes abusing the referee, being angry with the players of the opposing team, etc. 'Discrimination' includes prejudices against immigrant workers. These three scales proved to be important for explaining soccer hooliganism in Dutch society.

It is beyond the scope of this chapter to go into the methodological details of Lisrel analyses. However, using this model it has been possible to explain more than 60% of the variance of the dependent variable — football hooliganism. The polychoric correlations, starting point for the construction of an explanatory model, are reproduced in Table 4.8. The final model can be constructed as shown in Figure 4.10. This model meets the requirements very well, both in an empirical and theoretical sense. As an assumption the expected diffuse influence of parenthood in this model still holds completely. The fact that the significance of 'school career' proceeds entirely via 'unsocial behaviour' is in agreement with the results of criminological research. As a

Table 4.8. Polychoric correlations between the variables included in the model[a].

		X1	Y1	Y2	Y3	Y4	Y5
X1	Social control of parents	—					
Y1	Running away from school	0.42	—				
Y2	Unsocial behaviour	0.68	0.75	—			
Y3	Discrimination	0.45	0.15	0.44	—		
Y4	Aggressive sympathy	0.29	0.28	0.52	0.49	—	
Y5	Soccer hooliganism	0.49	0.35	0.66	0.58	0.69	—

From van der Brug (1986); reprinted with permission of the publisher and author.
[a] All correlations are significant at at least $p<0.05$.

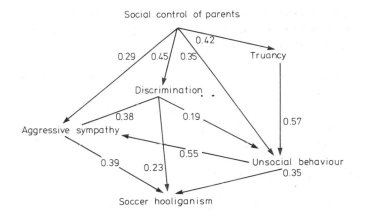

Figure 4.10. Explanatory model for participation in soccer hooliganism. From van der Brug (1986); reprinted with permission of the publisher and author.

short comment, the observation should be made that on the basis of theories from criminology a model has been tested of which the causal effect proceeds from 'school career' to 'unsocial behaviour'. In our opinion this idea is very uncertain. Such an effect would be plausible on the basis of learning problems; however, in this case we are dealing with conflicts, which can also be explained by the fact that the youngsters are part of a circle of friends, in which norms and values dominate that are opposite to a career in school. In that case the causal effect is just the reverse. It should also be mentioned that a study of Dutch supporters at the European Championship in Germany gave the same results with respect to the significance of parental control and school career for football hooliganism (van der Brug & Meijs, 1988).

Integration of research about soccer hooliganism

Finally, the question arises as to how our research findings about soccer hooliganism in The Netherlands can be seen in a meaningful, coherent, way. In this connection the concept 'configuration' of Elias can serve as a departure point for a global thesis. Configurations can best be considered as a phenomenon with a certain internal coherence. The relationships within and between such configurations are only to a limited degree the result of the activities of individuals, and have their own unpredictable dynamics. Professional soccer in The Netherlands can be conceived as such a configuration partly as a consequence of the great cultural diversity that exists. Within this configuration 'the result' became, at the beginning of the 1970s, a dominating value to which normative limitations are subordinated. 'Fair play' is replaced by a more instrumental value in which only success counts.

This was apparent from the behaviour of members of managing councils, coaches and players as well as that of the public. Rinus Michels (coach to the Dutch team at the World Championship) in 1974, expressed this excellently with the statement 'soccer is war'. In fact, in so doing he translated what was essential for the behaviour of all concerned: for the member of the managing body who presses for the discharge of the trainer when results are not being achieved, for the coach who presses the players to go for results and for the players who, sometimes, use rough forms of instrumental violence in the service of achieving a result. The behaviour of particular groups of the public can also become dominated by this value. It is unrealistic to suppose that this holds exclusively for so-called soccer hooligans. It is not only these young people who greet the players before the start of a match with a whistle concert in place of applause, and it is not exclusively the hooligans who subject the referee to verbal abuse.

Our investigation has shown that the public, over the years, have increasingly resorted to similar behaviour. People have also become more complacent with respect to violent infringements by players. Moreover, it has become clear that spectators who are particularly guilty of hooliganism find it more important that their club win than that they play a good game.

The experimental investigation showed that a disappointing result of a match frequently gave rise to vehement anger in spectators, while on the basis of the content analysis of newspaper articles it can be concluded that the beginning of the tradition of soccer hooliganism was characterised by important referee decisions not being accepted by particular groups of spectators.

During the 1970s soccer hooliganism became increasingly detached from the progress of the game. A causal pattern arose which showed many similarities to other forms of hooliganism and delinquent behaviour. In the meantime, soccer hooliganism showed a strong relation to diverse forms of unsocial behaviour, such as delinquency. While those spectators who watch from the 'sides' are not more strongly prejudiced than the minority of their age-group confederates who are not interested in soccer, it is a fact that the more violent of them have, at the same time, the strongest prejudices. This last factor can best be interpreted in terms of 'hostility to others'. Such 'others' can be minority groups but also 'different-minded' or representatives of another interest group, such as supporters of the opposing team. Two attendant circumstances are the absence of effective social control by parents and an unfavourable school career.

It is tempting to judge the development of professional soccer in terms of the disintegration of society. This disintegration is seen as a consequence of an increasing cultural diversification, implying that different sectors of our society, with their matching norms and value systems, continue to separate themselves out from one another. Within professional soccer there will arise, in this vision, a norms-and-values pattern that is separate from similar societal systems.

While it is undoubtedly true that the development of professional soccer is characterised by serious erosion in the area of social values and norms, such considerations do not in the least take into account a similar blurring of moral principles in various other sectors of society. Moreover, two circumstances remain unexplained. In the first place why is it that traditions of soccer hooliganism have come into being in England, Germany and The Netherlands, and only to a lesser extent in other West European countries where professional soccer has developed in a similar way. In the second place, it remains unclear why traditions of hooliganism are apparent in some clubs and not in others.

4.7. Conclusions

For those who expect a definitive answer to the questions formulated at the beginning of this chapter: 'does sport promote aggression?' or 'is the aggressive drive removed by means of sport?', our conditional answers are, perhaps, disappointing. We may well state, however, that the idea that after the end of a match the drive towards aggression is reduced brings with it little empirical support.

In all fairness, it must be reported here that in this chapter we have restricted our attention to the significance of catharsis for spectators. From general psychology, however, it is known that there are scarcely any examples of research that subscribe to the significance of catharsis for aggressive behaviour. It is undoubtedly true that such research refers to direct effects after the end of a match. Long-term influences have seldom been the subject of such studies. The different theories that emphasise the cathartic working of sport probably lead a tenacious life. They come back anew in diverse variations. One of the variants that relates to the canalising significance of sport has been treated in some detail in this chapter. For the canalising significance of fights between groups of supporters (Marsh) there is, however, no supporting research material, at least, not if we use our own research as a yardstick. Sport provides obvious possibilities for learning aggressive behaviour. Given this bold assertion, some qualification has to be made. There are many sports in which aggressive behaviour is hardly ever apparent while, on the other hand, there are sports in which aggression is, as it were, inbred. In connection with this suggestion a tentative distinction is often made between combat sports such as boxing, sports in which bodily contact can occur (such as rugby) and sports that do not provide possibilities for such contact (such as volleyball). A further consideration of this categorisation, however, indicates that this distinction is still too gross. Within the category of contact sports there are notable differences in the possibilities for aggressive behaviour. In handball, for example, numerous personal encounters within a very limited area take place before they lead, or not, to direct scoring chances. A similar circumstance is highly conducive to infringements. What is also important is whether the rules of the game leave space for infringements or not. If, on weighing up the pros and cons, the balance is in favour of the perpetration of infringements, it need occasion no surprise that such infringements are committed. The instrumental aggression that is a consequence of these considerations can be mitigated by altering the pay-offs in an appropriate way via changes in the rules of the game.

In addition to the nature of the sport, we also find a reflection of developments in society in aggressive behaviour during sport performance. We think, in this connection, of the norms and values passed on from one generation to another via the socialisation process. The meaning of 'fair play' appears, in most sports, to be repressed in favour of a more technocratic morale. This cannot, indeed, be seen as separate from society, and it also embraces specific components that are coupled to the nature of the sport. Sports that provide abundant opportunities for aggressive behaviour generally lead, in consequence, to norms that are extremely complacent from the point of view of such behaviour. The extent to which this is the case is not, or is scarcely, related to the social background of the sports performer, but has a lot to do with the experience that people have of this area and the level at which they play.

The violent behaviour of groups of young people at soccer matches in England, Germany and The Netherlands has received special attention. Most of the theory-forming in this area is speculative in nature. In this connection we have rather liberally cited our own research findings. Explanations of such violent behaviour connect to theory-forming that has been developed for hooliganism. A reduction in social control in different directions appears to be of significance. It is also the case that a negative school career must be considered as an indication of acts of outrage at soccer matches. Violent behaviour at soccer games, and behaviour under other circumstances, is structured by the same norms and values. Acting in a self-assured way, showing pluck, and the taking of risks to which danger is attached are of central significance. The repelling of such violence is no simple exercise. In England, as well as in Germany and The Netherlands, efforts in this direction have not led to any demonstrable results. The causes of such violence are too strongly enmeshed in social changes and processes. To a large extent, these do not lend themselves to measures that remain limited to what happens in soccer.

References

Bandura, A. (1965). Influence of model's reinforcement contingencies on the acquisition of imitative responses. *Journal of Personality and Social Psychology*, **1**, 589–595.

Bandura, A. (1973). *Aggression, a Social Learning Analysis*. Englewood Cliffs, NJ: Prentice-Hall.

Bandura, A. (1978). Social learning theory of aggression. *Journal of Communication*, **28**, 12–29.

Bandura, A., & Walters, R.H. (1963). *The Social Learning of Deviant Behavior: a Behavioristic Approach to Socialisation*. New York: Rinehart & Winston.

Berkowitz, L. (1969). The frustration–aggression hypothesis revisited. In L. Berkowitz (Ed.), *Roots of Aggression*. New York: Atherton Press.

Berkowitz, L. (1974). Some determinants of impulsive aggression; role of mediated association with reinforcements for aggression. *Psychological Review*, **81**, 165–176.

Berkowitz, L. (1975). The contagion of violence: an S-P mediational analysis of some effects of observed aggression. In W.J. Arnold and M.M. Page (Eds), *Nebraska Symposium on Motivation*. Lincoln, NA: University of Nebraska Press.

Berkowitz, L., & Geen, R.G. (1966). Film violence and the cue properties of available target. *Journal of Personality and Social Psychology*, **3**, 525–530.

Blumer, H. (1969). *Symbolic Interactionism. Perspective and Method*. Englewood Cliffs, NJ: Prentice Hall.

Brug, H.J.H. van der (1983). Situationele faktoren die van invloed zijn op agressie bij toeschouwers van voetbalwedstrijden (Situational factors affecting aggression in spectators at soccer matches). In J.E. Hueting and H. van der Brug (Eds), *Sport Wetenschappelijk Onderzocht (Research in Sport)*. Haarlem: De Vrieseborch.

Brug, H.J.H. van der (1986). *Voetbalvandalisme: een Speurtocht naar Verklarende Factoren (Soccer Hooliganism: In Search of Explanatory Factors)*. Haarlem: De Vrieseborch.

Brug, H.J.H van der, & Marseille, N. (1983). Achtergronden van Vandalisme bij Voetbalwedstrijden (*The Background of Hooligansim at Soccer Matches*). Haarlem: De Vrieseborch.

Brug, H.J.H. van der, & Meijs, J. (1988). *Dutch Supporters at the European Championship in Germany*. Rijswijk: Ministerie van WVC.

Buss, A.H., & Durkee, A. (1957). An inventory for assessing different kinds of hostility. *Journal of Consulting Psychology*, **21**, 343–348.

Clarke, J. (1973). *Football Hooliganism and the Skinheads*. Centre for Contemporary Cultural Studies, University of Birmingham.

Critcher, C. (1973). *Football Since the War: a Study in Social Change and Popular Culture*. Centre for Contemporary Cultural Studies, University of Birmingham.

Deutsch, M. (1960). The effects of cooperation and competition upon group processes. In D. Cartwright and A. Zander (Eds), *Group Dynamics*. London: Tavistock.

Deutsch, M. (1973). *The Resolution of Conflict: Constructive and Destructive Processes*. New Haven, CT: Yale University Press.

Dollard, J., Miller, N.E., Doob, L.W., Mowrer, O.H., & Sears, R.R. (1939). *Frustration and Aggression*. New Haven, CT: Yale University Press.

Dunning, E., Murphy, P., Williams, J., & Maguire, J. (1984). Football hooliganism in Britain before the first World War. *International Review for Sociology of Sport*, **19**, 3–4.

Ekkers, C.L. (1977). *Activatie en Agressie (Activation and Aggression)*. Leiden: WJPG/TNO.

Ekkers, C.L., & Hoefnagels, G.P. (1972). *Agressie en Straf op het Voetbalveld (Aggression and Punishment in Soccer)*. Meppel: Boom.

Elias, N. (1969). *Ueber den Prozess der Zivilisation (The Process of Civilisation)*. Bern and München: Franke.

Freud, S. (1946). Triebe und Triebschicksale. In *Gesammelte Werke*, Vol. 10. London: Hogarth Press (1957). Instincts and their vicissitudes. In J. Strachey (Ed.), *The Standard Edition of the Complete Psychological Works of Sigmund Freud*, Vol. XIV. London: Hogarth Press.

Frogner, E., & Pilz, G.A. (1982). Untersuchung zur Einstellung von jugendlichen Fussballspielern und -spielerinnen zu Regeln und Normen im Sport (Investigation into the attitudes towards norms and rules in sport of young male and female soccer players). In G. Pilz (Ed.), *Sport und Gewalt (Sport and Violence)*. Schorndorf: Verlag Karl Hofmann.

Galen, W.C.C. van (1986). *Overtredingen en Strafzaken in het Amateurvoetbal (Fouls and Punishment in Amateur Soccer)*. Haarlem: De Vrieseborch.

Gaskell, G., & Pearton, R. (1979). Aggression and sport. In J.H. Goldstein (Ed.), *Sports, Games and Play*. Hillsdale, NY: Erlbaum.

Geen, R.G., & O'Neal, E.C. (1969). Activation of cue-elicited aggression by general arousal. *Journal of Personality and Social Psychology*, 11, 289−292.

Geen, R.G., & Pigg, R. (1970). Acquisition of an aggressive response and its generalisation to verbal behavior. *Journal of Personality and Social Psychology*, 15, 165−170.

Goldstein, J.H., & Arms, R.L. (1971). Effects of observing athletics contests on hostility. *Sociometry*, 34, 83−90.

Guttmann, A. (1978). *From Ritual to Record*. New York: Columbia University Press.

Heinilä, K. (1974). *Ethics of Sport*. University of Jyvaskyla, Department of Sociology and Planning for Physical Culture, Research Reports No. 4, Jyvaskyla.

Hirschi, T. (1972). *Causes of Delinquency*. Berkeley, CA: University of California Press.

Junger-Tas, J. (1976). Verborgen jeugddelinquentie en gerechtelijke selectie (Hidden youth delinquency and legal selection). SCJM Publicatie No. 38. Brussels.

Kingsmore, J.M. (1970). The effect of a professional wrestling and a professional basketball contest upon the aggressive tendencies of spectators. In G.S. Kenyon and T.M. Grogg (Eds), *Contemporary Psychology of Sport*. Chicago, IL: Proceedings of the Second International Congress of Sport Psychology.

Klapp, O.E. (1972). Currents of unrest, an introduction to collective behavior. In *Proceedings of the Second International Congress of Sport Psychology*. New York: Rinehart & Winston.

Lang, K., & Lang, G.E. (1961). *Collective Dynamics*. New York: Crowell.

Lefebre, L. & Passer, M.W. (1974). The effects of game location and importance on aggression in team sport. *International Journal of Sport Psychology*, 2, 102−110.

Leibowitz, G. (1968). Comparison of self-report and behavioral techniques of assessing aggression. *Journal of Consulting Clinical Psychology*, 32, 21−25.

Leith, L.M., & Orlick, T.D. (1975). The effect of viewing aggressive and non-aggressive sport models on the aggressive predispositions of the young audience. In J.M. Cagigal (Ed.), *Psicologia del Deporte*, Vol. 2. Madrid: Instituto Nacional de Educacion Fisica.

Lewis, J.M. (1975). Sports riots: Some research questions. Paper presented at the

American Sociological Association Meetings, San Francisco, CA, August.

Lorenz, K. (1963). Das sogenannte Böse: zur Naturgeschichte der Aggression. Wenen: Borotha-Schoeler; (1966) *On Aggression*. New York: Harcourt, Brace & World.

Lovaas, O.J. (1961). Effect of exposure to symbolic aggression on aggressive behavior. *Child Development*, **32**, 37−44.

Marsh, P. (1975). Understanding aggro. *New Society*, **32**(652), 7−9.

Marsh, P., Rosser, E., & Harré, R. (1978). *The Rulers of Disorder*. London: Routledge & Kegan Paul.

Mokken, R. (1970). *A Theory and Procedure of Scale Analysis*. Den Haag: Mouton.

Moll, H. (1977). De vreugde van het voetbalvandalisme (the pleasure of soccer hooliganism). *Tijdschrift voor Criminologie*, October, pp. 255−261.

Moyer, K.E. (1976). *The Psychobiology of Aggression*. New York: Harper & Row.

Naber, F. (1972). Verteilung der Fouls während der Dauer eines Basketballspiels (Distribution of fouls during a basketball match). In M. Volkamer (Ed.), *Experimente in der Sportpsychologie (Experiments in Sport Psychology)*. Schorndorf: Verlag Karl Hofmann.

Nicholson, J. (1978). 'Put the boot in'. *New Society*, **45**, 201−202.

Parke, R.D., Ewel, W., & Slaby, R.G. (1972). Hostile and helpful verbalisations as regulators of non-verbal aggression. *Journal of Personality and Social Psychology*, **23**, 243−246.

Parsons, T. (1951). *The Social System*. New York: Free Press of Glencoe.

Schulz, J., & Weber, R. (1979). Bedingungen aggressiver Handlungen von Fussballzuschauern (Conditions of aggressive actions in soccer spectators). *Sportwissenschaft*, **3**, 290−302.

Sherif, M., Harvey, O., White, B., Hood, W., & Sherif, C. (1961). *Intergroup Conflict and Cooperation: the Robbers Cave Experiment*. Norman Institute of Group Relations, University of Oklahoma.

Singer, R.N. (1975). *Myths and Truth in Sports Psychology*. New York: Harper & Row.

Smith, M.D. (1974). Violence in sport: a sociological perspective. *Sportwissenschaft*, **4**, 164−173.

Smith, M.D. (1975). The legitimation of violence, hockey players perception of their preference groups saction for assault. *Canadian Review of Sociological Anthropology*, **12**, 72−80.

Tannenbaum, P.H., & Zillmann, D. (1975). Emotional arousal in the facilitation of aggression through communication. *Advances in Experimental Social Psychology*, **8**, 149−192.

Taylor, I.R. (1971). Football mad: a speculative sociology of football hooliganism. In E. Dunning (Ed.), *The Sociology of Sport*. London: Cass.

Turner, E.T. (1970). The effect of viewing college football, basketball and wrestling on the elicited aggressive response of male spectators. In G.S. Kanyon and T.M. Grogg (Eds), *Contemporary Psychology of Sport*. Chicago, IL: Proceedings of the Second International Congress of Sport Psychology.

Turner, R.H., & Killian, L.M. (1972). *Collective Behavior*. Englewood Cliffs, NJ: Prentice-Hall.

Vaz, E.E. (1974). What price victory? *International Review of Sport Sociology*, **34**, 33−55.

Vinnai, G. (1970). *Fussballsport als Ideologie (Soccer as an Ideology)*. Frankfurt: Europäische Verlagsanstalt.

Voigt, H.F. (1982). Die Struktur von Sportdisziplinen als Indikator für

Kommunikationsprobleme und Konflikte (The structure of particular sports as an indicator for communication problems and conflicts). In G. Pilz (Ed.), *Sport und Gewalt (Sport and Violence)*. Schorndorf: Verlag Karl Hofmann.

Volkamer, M. (1971). Zur Aggresivität in konkurrenz-orientierten sozialen Systemen. Eine Untersuchung an Fussballpunktspielen (Aggression in rivalry-oriented social systems. An investigation into soccer). *Sportwissenschaft*, 1, 33–64.

Widmeyer, W.N., & Birch, J.S. (1984). Aggression in professional ice hockey: a strategy for success or a reaction to failure? *Journal of Psychology*, 117, 77–84.

Winkler, T. (1971). Paper presented at the meeting of the British Sociological Association, Study Group on Sport.

Wolf, P.G. (1961). Die Kriminalität bei Fussballspielern (Delinquency in soccer players). University of Freiburg (unpublished).

Wolfgang, N.E., & Ferracutti, F. (1967). *The Subculture of Violence*. London: Tavistock.

Zimbardo, P.G. (1969). The human choice: Individuation, reason and order versus de-individuation, impulse and chaos. In W.J. Arnold and D. Levine (Eds), *Nebraska Symposium on Motivation*. Lincoln, NA: University of Nebraska Press.

5 MOTOR LEARNING

5.1. Introduction

From birth onwards people start developing a broad range of motor skills. Already in babyhood they are able to grip, point, throw, turn themselves over, roll and crawl—to name but a few of such skills.

In infancy they learn skills such as hopping, skipping, jumping over a rope, riding a scooter or bicycle without requiring very much instruction. At a later age very complex movement patterns can be learned—such as somersaults and other complicated leaps performed in gymnastics and ballet.

Questions as to how people learn motor skills are central to almost everyone active in sport. For example, how important is the role of demonstrations and instructions in the acquisition of a new motor skill? Is it helpful to provide feedback, for example, by way of video? At what stage in the learning process should this type of feedback be provided, and is it suited to young children? Why is it extremely difficult to change an existing, inadequate movement pattern? What is meant by 'mental training', and is it possible to learn a new skill without actually carrying it out?

In this chapter the learning processes involved in the acquisition of motor skills will be discussed. This will lead to the following subjects. In Section 5.2 general characteristics of motor learning processes will be described. The learning of motor skills by techniques derived from operant conditioning will be discussed in Section 5.3. Section 5.4 will be devoted to social learning theory; in the latter, learning on the basis of imitation is a central issue. Section 5.5 will be concerned with an information-processing approach to motor learning, and Section 5.6 with the importance of a specific form of information, namely, feedback about performance.

In Section 5.7 a form of training known as mental training or mental practice will be addressed. In Section 5.8 a very short consideration will be made of the relationship between scientific psychological research into motor skills and the everyday practice of sport.

In handling the different psychological theories in the area of motor learning an attempt will be made to signal those learning and instructional processes that have practical relevance.

5.2. General characteristics of the learning process

Learning is a process that leads to relatively durable changes in behavioural potential as a result of specific environmental experiences. If, and to what degree, learning has occurred is deduced from changes in behaviour. In this respect it is necessary to be aware of the fact that what is learned does not always manifest itself in performance; in the absence of motivation or because of tiredness, performance may be worse than might be the case under optimal circumstances. Those closely associated with sport training will recognise this phenomenon all too well. After an hour's volleyball training, for example, a player may well have a new volleyball smash under control despite the fact that a significant number of smash attempts are doomed to failure. If, after an interval of a few days, the same smash once again forms part of the training session, it is likely that some players will perform better than they did at the end of the previous training period.

This phenomenon of improved performance after a period without practice (known as 'reminiscence') has been documented not only in practice, but in the scientific literature also (see for example Schmidt, 1982). This demonstrates that actual performance does not always reflect what has in fact been learned, and that learning may therefore be better defined in terms of changes in behavioural *potential* that in terms of changes in behaviour *per se*.

In this respect it should also be realised that similar levels of performance may be due to different learning processes. A simple example will suffice to make this clear. A child's correct answer to the sum 17×17 can be the consequence of having rote-learned the squares of the numbers between 1 and 25 or of having learned the general principle of multiplication. The same, observable, performance is here the consequence of completely different behavioural potentials.

In the description of learning provided above, reference was made to *relatively durable* changes in behavioural potential; if someone, for example, makes a very good 'spike' in volleyball on one occasion and thereafter consistently fails in his 'spike' attempts we are not inclined to say that he has learned the 'spike' shot.

In relation to learning there is generally reference to 'specific environmental experiences'. On the one hand, a statement such as this excludes pure maturational effects (we don't talk, for example, about a kitten learning to open its eyes). On the other hand, talking of 'specific environmental experiences' instead of practice serves to suggest that learning can sometimes occur without actual practice, leaving the possibility that, for example, a specific movement pattern may be learned after having seen it performed one or more times. Finally, learning processes may well occur without any particular intention to learn being present. In the latter case the term 'incidental learning' is used. All the faults that creep in during the learning of movement patterns, and which later seem very difficult to eradicate, are in themselves examples of incidental learning. Also, the fact that some tennis players bounce the ball two or three times before they can serve properly is the consequence of an incidental learning process (dubbed sometimes in the literature as 'superstitious behaviour').

The traditional method of establishing the progress of a motor learning process is the graphical reproduction of the scores obtained on performance tests administered after regular intervals. Such a curve is often referred to as a 'learning curve', although, as the reader will by now be aware, it is always a performance curve. An example of a learning curve is presented in Figure 5.1.

The form of this curve is typical for motor learning, with an initial sharp increase in performance giving way to gradually reducing increases in

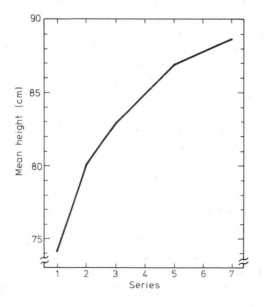

Figure 5.1. Characteristic course of the performance curve during a motor learning process: mean height jumped by 26 children learning mini-trampoline jumping. Each series consisted of five jumps and the inter-series interval was three minutes. From Bakker (1981); reprinted with permission of the author.

performance, the curve eventually becoming asymptotic.* According to Schmidt (1982, p. 566) the relatively large increase at the beginning of the learning process is, to a large extent, to be attributed to cognitive factors (the learner comes to realise what is required of him) rather than motor factors, so that the movements themselves are not carried out any better or more efficiently. Generally speaking, motor learning is characterised by increasing automation. Where, initially, there is a large measure of cognitive involvement in the skill to be learned, and the movements to be carried out demand all the attention of the learner, towards the end of the learning process, this is much less the case. While, during the first dancing lesson, attention is directed towards the performance of the steps and movements — often under visual control — during the last lesson this is scarcely necessary any more. The dancers can then, with impunity, limit their attention to the conversation with their partner — the dance movements themselves seeming to have become to a large extent automated. Within sport many of these apparently automatically performed movements are known. One has only to think about the routinised basketballer who, when dribbling, hardly needs cognitively to monitor the dribble itself and in consequence is able to direct more attention to his immediate environment in order to make his actions that much more appropriate.

Finally, it must be pointed out that motor skills, in the practical situation, can vary along two different dimensions of complexity. To begin with, strong or less strong demands can be placed on motor coordination — the attunement of sub-movements to each other. Next, the decision to carry out a particular motor action can be the consequence of more or less complex perceptual and decision processes. If, on the basis of the first criterion, a double somersault with a full twist be designated more complex than a square-pass in football then, on the second criterion, the square-pass can probably be said to be the more complex. The decision, in this respect, is dependent on a large number of factors, such as position of players of one's own side and those of the opposition, weather and pitch conditions, and probably also the score in the match and the stadium in which the match takes place (see Chapter 6).

Depending on the nature of the complexity, a continuing improvement in performance will have to be attributed to differing causes. An increasing capacity to process environmental information quickly, and to anticipate changes will, for the cross-pass in particular, lead to improvement in performance. Related to this is the increasing compatibility between signals

---

* This is not to dispute the fact that performance may keep improving over very long periods. A classical example of such improvement has been offered by Crossman (1959), noticing that cigar makers were still increasing their speed of performance after 7 years (and more than 10 million cigars) of practice.

from the environment and the actions they demand, i.e. the actions seem to follow more 'naturally' from the signals 'triggering' them.

Improving performance of the somersault has less to do with the anticipation of environmental events than with increasing ability to coordinate the (sub)movements and to integrate them into the intended total pattern, a process which has to be realised by continual repetition and 'drill'.

5.3. Classical and operant conditioning

In traditional, behaviouristic theories little concern was paid to cognitive processes enacted in the learning organism. Theorists restricted themselves to overt behaviour (hence the term behaviourism) that could be described in relation to objectively recorded events in the surrounding environment. With respect to behaviour and surroundings the terms used were *responses* and *stimuli* respectively. Within the behaviouristic tradition two fundamental learning processes were distinguished — classical and operant conditioning.

Briefly, according to *classical conditioning*, an already available response (R) is coupled to a stimulus (S) that otherwise would not give rise to that response. The most well-known name in this area is that of Pavlov, whose experiments with dogs are the most well known (see, for example, Pavlov, 1960 — originally 1924). The classical example is that in which dogs learn to secrete saliva in response to the ticking of a metronome. Initially reflexive secretion of saliva (unconditioned response, UCR) is evoked by applying powdered meat (unconditioned stimulus, UCS) to the tongue of the animal. After a number of simultaneous presentations of powdered meat and the ticking of a metronome, the latter stimulus (conditioned stimulus, CS) will have acquired the capacity to evoke the secretion of saliva when presented alone. The response in question is then designated the conditioned response (CR).

Less well known than the experiments of Pavlov are those of Twitmyer (1902), who worked with human subjects. He combined the sound of a bell with a tap to the tendon of the knee and discovered that after a large number of such simultaneous presentations the sound of the bell also gave rise to an 'involuntary' stretching of the knee in the absence of the tap. An often-used application of classical conditioning is to be found in the 'bell and buzzer method' used to help children to avoid bed-wetting. To achieve this it is necessary that the child reacts to the increasing pressure in the bladder by waking up. In order to promote this end, an electric circuit is provided that becomes closed (activated) as soon as the first drops of urine become released. This leads to an alarm bell going off and the child is startled into waking up. In classical conditioning terms the alarm bell would be considered as the UCS and the waking response as the UCR. The increasing pressure in the bladder is the CS. Because this occurs repeatedly, together with the alarm bell, the bladder pressure in itself (that is to say without the alarm bell needing to sound off) becomes sufficient to cause the child to wake up (waking up now being the CR).

The fact that classical conditioning consists of coupling *already available* responses to new stimuli implies that this conditioning process is not suited to learning *new* behavioural patterns. As a consequence the relevance of this form of conditioning to motor learning is marginal. That it can, nevertheless, play a role has to do with the fact that classical conditioning can lead to the coupling of emotional responses — such as anxiety responses — to stimuli that initially were neutral in this respect. By this means, for example, anxiety reactions evoked when a child, unexpectedly during a swimming lesson, slips underwater and is unable to breathe, can become coupled to (neutral) stimuli in the swimming bath surrounds; anxiety reactions can subsequently interfere with the motor learning in question namely, learning to swim (Whiting, 1970).

Contrary to classical conditioning, operant conditioning can be applied when *new* patterns of behaviour have to be learned. With this form of conditioning the name of Skinner, one of the most radical of present-day behaviourists, is irrevocably associated.

A typical example of the way in which Skinner went about things is the conditioning of the pressing of a lever by a white rat in a so-called Skinner-box by repeatedly providing a food reward each time the animal presses the lever. This food serves as a reinforcer (reinforcing stimulus S^r) of the pressing of the lever. Initially, the animal will come to press the lever now and again by chance alone. By reinforcing these 'chance' responses they come to occur more frequently or, put in another way, the chance of their occurrence increases. Such behaviour can be brought under stimulus control by selective or differential reinforcement, i.e. the responses in question become reinforced under particular conditions (for example, when a green light is on) and not under others (for example, when a red light is on).

In such a case the animal quickly learns to respond only when the green light is present, and refrains from responding in the presence of the red one. The green light would, in this example, be designated the discriminative stimulus (S^D), which has to be discriminated from the red light, referred to as S-delta (S^δ). This process of stimulus discrimination may serve to counteract an opposite process, called stimulus generalisation. By this is meant that behaviour that becomes reinforced in a particular situation will also exhibit the tendency to occur in similar situations, a tendency which is stronger the closer the two situations resemble each other. The following example will serve as an illustration of the processes of stimulus generalisation and discrimination. A beginner tennis player, who was sometimes successful in surprising his opponents running up to the net by producing a lob shot, may be strongly inclined to use this ploy when similar situations occur. This stimulus generalisation can be brought to a halt if the lob in a number of instances does not lead to the desired result; the player will then learn to discriminate between that situation (stimulus pattern) for which a lob to a player approaching the net is appropriate and other situations where this should not be done.

With respect to the description of operant behaviour, or instrumental behaviour, as it is often called, Skinner (1969) remarked:

> *An adequate formulation of the interaction between an organism and its environment must always specify three things: 1. the occasion upon which a response occurs, 2. the response itself, and 3. the reinforcing consequences. The interrelationships among them are the contingencies of reinforcement* (p. 7).

An explanation of behaviour, according to Skinner, consists of a description of these 'contingencies of reinforcement', and behaviour can be changed by manipulating these contingencies, a procedure that has been designated 'contingency management'. By this means the reinforcement procedures become changed. Skinner does not pose the question *why* a particular stimulus or event is reinforcing, he only establishes *that* this is the case if the behaviour that preceded the reinforcement, in similar situations, appears more often. Thus, an explanation of behaviour is looked for in an accurate description of the conditions under which it appears, and not in a description of hypothetical or non-hypothetical internal processes in the organism. With respect to the latter, Skinner can be seen as a-theoretical, he does not believe that such knowledge will lead to better predictions or improved control of behaviour.

In contrast to Pavlov, Skinner pays no attention to physiological processes as possible explanations of overt behaviour. Such explanations, however, are not dismissed by him on fundamental grounds, and he proposes that a complete description of observable behaviour and its related physiological processes would lead to the conclusion that: 'The organism would be seen to be an unitary system, its behavior clearly part of its physiology' (Skinner, 1969). For the time being, however, he considers physiological techniques as too limited as to make an adequate description of the relevant physiological processes possible (Skinner, 1969, p. 202).

In the light of the above, it is perhaps not surprising that operant conditioning has sometimes been denied the status of a theory, as Harzem & Miles (1978) indicate when they remark that:

> *It is perhaps less misleading to think in terms of operant* techniques, *and our thesis is that such techniques can help psychologists, whatever their interests, to do their job better* (p. 71; emphasis ours).

In addition to the reinforcement of the required responses it is possible to provide 'punishment' following unwanted responses, and hence try to suppress them. In this respect it needs to be emphasised that 'punishment' in itself is not a suitable technique for learning new behaviour, as is the case with reinforcement. Punishment is a means to eliminate undesirable responses, and therefore a combination with reinforcement of the wanted response may be necessary. In order to produce long-lasting effects the punishment must be administered consistently, and follow immediately on the behaviour that is to be overcome.

Complementary to the definition of reinforcement in terms of increasing the frequency of occurrence of the preceding response, punishment is defined by Azrin & Holz (1966) as follows:

> *Punishment is a reduction of the future probability of a specific response as a result of the immediate delivery of a stimulus for that response. The stimulus is designated as a punishing stimulus; the entire process is designated as punishment* (p. 381).

As will be seen later, it is not essential that the punishment, in order to be effective, has an intrinsically unpleasant and aversive character.

Before giving examples of the applications of operant conditioning in the field of sport, two important phenomena will be indicated, namely, that of *secondary conditioning* and that of *shaping*.

Secondary conditioning is used when a stimulus that is presented at the same time as a reinforcing stimulus comes, itself, to acquire reinforcing characteristics. By means of such a form of 'higher-order conditioning', particular stimuli, if they are associated with many primary reinforcers, become generalised conditioned reinforcers. Example of this are money or social stimuli such as attention.

'Shaping' is used to describe what has taken place when a particular behaviour, which is not in the behavioural repertoire of the organism, becomes learned as successively better approaches to the required behaviour become selectively reinforced. The final criterion behaviour is approached in this stepwise manner ('successive approximation') — a technique that can be applied in the training of new skills.

For example, if it is required that a dog learn to dance, a reward is promptly presented each time the animal transfers its weight to one or the other front paw. Once this response has been established, reward is only given when two successive transferences of weight occur, and thereafter, for example, only if a particular rhythm is apparent. Consequently, the reward is presented only if two rhythmical movements are followed by an attempt to turn towards one side. Gradually, turning of a complete circle by means of such 'shaping' can be achieved. The dog has then learned to follow its dance steps by turning in a circle; the two responses become linked to one another and form, for the dog, a new behavioural sequence.

It must be pointed out that during 'shaping', more use is made of secondary reinforcers than primary reinforcers such as food. In principle, a stimulus (such as a snapping of the fingers or the speaking of a word) can serve as a secondary reinforcer if, before the 'shaping' process begins, it is presented simultaneously with the primary reinforcer a number of times. Its reinforcing quality then is attributed to the process of classical conditioning. That shaping procedures can lead to surprising results will not be doubted by anyone who has ever attended a circus performance.

Techniques based on operant conditioning used to bring about changes in the behaviour of humans have been designated 'applied behaviour analysis'. With respect to the learning of movement patterns this kind of approach has especially been used in the rehabilitation of patients with neuromuscular disorders and in the learning of self-care by mentally handicapped children. In the context of sport, rather less research has been carried out into the applications of the principles of operant conditioning than in the areas indicated. In 1976 a book was published in which a number of aspects of sport were described within a reference framework derived from operant conditioning, but in which not one example of empirical research in the field of sport was to be found (Dickinson, 1976). Nevertheless, at least some research has been carried out in this area and a number of such investigations will be reported below.

Rushall (1975) reports successful attempts to improve behaviour in sport situations via operant conditioning. He was able, for example, within the course of 60 lengths, to correct a faulty leg stroke in an inexperienced swimmer by, immediately following its appearance, shining a light in the eyes of the swimmer. A particular length was counted only if it satisfied a particular criterion with respect to the number of faulty leg strokes allowed, the number being made successively smaller when learning progresses ('shaping').

Another application outlined by Rushall (1975) had to do with learning to stabilise a rowing shell. He was able to reduce the learning process in this respect from around two months to a few days by making use of an alarm system mounted on the rowing shell that automatically came into operation when the boat tilted beyond a previously established angle. This critical angle was made smaller and smaller during the course of the learning process ('shaping'). When these two examples (Rushall reports more in his article) are taken into consideration, it becomes apparent that shining a light in the eyes of the swimmer and activating the alarm system on the canoe qualify as punishments in terms of the definition provided by Azrin & Holz (1966), since the behaviour that immediately precedes their presentation diminishes.

It should be remarked, here, that in a large number of training procedures more stringent requirements are placed on the actions to be learned as training progresses (initially, the coach is satisfied if the volleyball passes over the net, subsequently only if the ball falls within the court, thereafter only if it achieves a particular speed, and so on). Nevertheless, it would not appear correct to categorise such procedures, without further qualifications, as 'shaping'. This term should be used only if the criterion that the actions have to satisfy is, both systematically and on the basis of previous performances, raised.

Such a systematic approach is characteristic of the work of Rushall and of other sport psychologists who base themselves on operant conditioning techniques. An example of its usefulness in American football was presented by Komaki & Barnett (1977), who demonstrated that consistently applied reinforcement, in which checklists and verbal praise were used, led to improved performance. It is interesting that Rushall (1975), on the basis of an analysis of the way in which a coach trained his swimmers, developed a programme based on operant conditioning techniques by which to improve the coach's training methods.

Previously it was pointed out that favourable effects of punishment do not necessarily have to be attributed to the intrinsic aversive qualities of a punishing stimulus. An earlier investigation in which this was empirically demonstrated was carried out by O'Brien & Azrin (1970). In order to get people who walked with a bent back to walk in a more upright position they developed a piece of apparatus that their subjects could wear on their backs, and that automatically administered a tactile stimulus to the back or shoulder if the subject walked in too bent a posture.

O'Brien & Azrin first showed that subjects did, indeed, learn to walk in a more upright position if a bowed posture was punished by a tactile stimulus to the back. Subsequently they carried out another experiment in which subjects had to learn to walk in an upright position but, in this case, a tactile stimulus was administered to the one shoulder if they walked in a bent posture and a similar stimulus to the other shoulder if they walked correctly (i.e. not bent). Also in this case, subjects learned to walk in an upright manner. This indicates, according to the authors:

> that the slouching was not reduced because of the aversiveness of the consequence, since the level of tactile stimulation was constant whether or not the subjects slouched. This finding shows that simple informational feedback will reduce an undesired behavior and suggests that feedback procedures could be used more generally as a behavior modification procedure for patients who are known to be motivated toward eliminating their undesired behavior (p. 239).

The fact that a stimulus that, intrinsically, is neither pleasant nor unpleasant (because of its informative quality), can either reward or punish behaviour, is explained by O'Brien & Azrin in the same way as was done by Skinner (1953). According to the latter author such a stimulus is considered as a secondary reinforcer or punisher that owes its effect to having, earlier, been associated with a primary reinforcer or punisher.

Several authors have included techniques based on operant conditioning principles in 'behavioural packages' for the use of coaches. Because demonstration of correct behaviour to be imitated by athletes often forms part of such packages, the presentation of two such examples will be postponed until the end of the next section, which is devoted to learning by imitation.

Informational feedback will be further discussed in Section 5.6.

5.4. Social learning theory

Bandura's (1976) social learning theory emphasised that many learning processes are socially mediated in the sense that the learning of particular behaviours does not always occur purely on the basis of experience with the responses to be learned, but also by the observation of the responses of others. Often in sport there is talk of movements needing to be imitated by learners.

Skinner tried to interpret learning by imitation within his operant conditioning framework. The *discriminative stimulus* (S^D) is provided by the behaviour of the model (behaviour of the teacher, coach or other model that is to be imitated) and the 'matching responses' (the attempts by the learner to 'copy') are then so reinforced that they gradually become more and more like the behaviour of the model. There is thus talk of a 'shaping' process. Finally, when such imitative behaviour has been reinforced in many situations, a generalised tendency to imitate will have developed. Learning by means of imitation (sometimes designated 'observational learning' or 'modelling') is thus explained here by the typical operant conditioning schema $S^D - R - S^r$ (in which S^D, R and S^r refer to stimuli arising from the model behaviour, the imitation responses of the learner and the reinforcing stimuli consequent on these responses, respectively).

This Skinnerian explanation of learning through observation is not without its critics. Bandura words his criticism as follows:

> The schema ... does not appear to be applicable to observational learning where an observer does not overtly perform the model's responses in the setting in which they were exhibited, reinforcements are not administered either to the model or to the observer, and whatever responses have been thus acquired are not displayed for days, weeks or even months. Under these conditions, which represent one of the most prevalent forms of social learning, two of the factors (R, S^r) in the three-element paradigm are absent during acquisition, and the

third factor (S^D, or modelling stimulus) is typically missing from the situation when the observationally learned response is first performed (Bandura, 1976, p. 6).

In short, Bandura emphasises the fact that observational behaviour can be *learned* before it is actually *carried out*; via operant conditioning an account can be provided of the performance of behaviour but not of the way in which it was learned.

According to Bandura, explanations of such learning processes ('observational learning' or 'modelling') cannot avoid invoking cognitive functions that mediate between the model stimuli and the imitated behaviour later to be carried out.*

Because verbal instructions are not sufficiently precise about the motor skills to be learned, demonstrations are often used as a training device in sport. In spite of this, there is only a small amount of scientific research in this area which, furthermore, does show conflicting results.

With regard to video demonstrations, Burwitz (1981) suggested that positive effects are only to be expected if the subjects are required to pay attention to what are considered to be essential aspects of the movement.

From a literature overview, Gould & Roberts (1982) come, amongst others, to the tentative conclusion that model behaviour can better be imitated if: (1) the model, in the eyes of the learner, has a high status; (2) the model is of the same sex as the learner; and (3) the model behaviour is also, either symbolically or verbally, repeated by the learner. At the same time it would seem that modelling can have a favourable effect on the anxiety experienced by some people in being required to learn what, for them, is an unfamiliar skill.

An investigation carried out by Jordan in 1977 confirmed that it makes a difference if the model is seen from the front or from the back. Subjects, in this experiment, were required to learn the basic steps of an American dance (the cha-cha), half the subjects being allowed to view a model from the back and the other half from the front. In the latter case, performances were worse than in the former (fewer correct steps and irregular timing). The author's interpretation of his finding was that looking at the model from the back did not require transformations of the visual image to be made which, in itself, made the information easier to process.

Carroll & Bandura (1982) found evidence to suggest that, when learning a

---

* It is worth emphasising that almost all modern behaviourists, contrary to Skinner, ascribe an important role to cognitive processes in the explanation of behaviour. What they do deny, however, is the existence of essential differences between these processes and the externally observable ones. They posit a continuum between the types of behaviour (Mahoney, 1974) and contend that they are subject to the same conditioning principles (Wolpe, 1978).

pattern of arm movements by means of observation, a cognitive representation of this pattern became established, but it remains unclear how such an internal model is formed and what information is picked up by the learner from the behaviour of the model.

Such questions are central to ongoing research in the authors' laboratory in learning slalom-ski type movements on a so-called ski simulator with the help of a video model of an expert. In contrast to the usual experimental design in this area, the model was available *while* the subjects were training, so that it could be observed while they themselves were attempting to learn the movements. The three dependent measures used in the first experiment (Whiting, Bijlard & den Brinker, 1987) were frequency, amplitude and fluency of the movement of the ski simulator platform. Subjects who had the advantage of a video model during training showed better mean fluency scores, which in turn were also less variable, and produced a more consistent movement frequency.

In the light of the frequency with which examples of movement patterning are used in gymnastics and other sport coaching, it would seem evident that the above research and, more generally, theory-forming with respect to learning through observation, are, from a didactic point of view, extremely important developments.

As mentioned earlier, learning principles based on modelling and on operant conditioning have sometimes been combined in behavioural packages for the use of coaches. Allison & Ayllon (1980) developed such a package and evaluated its effectiveness for American football, gymnastics and tennis. When an error occurred the coach shouted 'freeze', and the athlete was required to hold the position he or she was in at that moment. The coach then gave feedback with respect to the error being made, and demonstrated the correct behaviour. Finally the athlete was allowed to relinquish the frozen position and instructed to imitate the correct one. It was shown that this procedure led to clearly better results than the usual coaching methods in all three sports. Koop & Martin (1983) investigated a coaching procedure to decrease persistent errors in swimming strokes (back stroke, breast stroke and freestyle) in five young swimmers. The procedure consisted of several elements, including instructions, demonstrations, punishments and reinforcement. An example of the punishment following incorrect performance was a tap on the swimmer's shoulder. Each time an error on the target behaviour occurred, the trainer immediately gave such a tap with the padded end of a stick. Reinforcements, following correct performance (defined as two or fewer errors on the target behaviour per lap), consisted of verbal praise and approving feedback regarding the swimmer's performance. The strategy was shown to be effective in reducing errors, an improvement which was limited to the stroke being trained. After training two of the swimmers, who did not receive any or scarcely any further response-specific feedback, showed a performance deterioration. The authors conclude that:

> *Behaviors that have not reached a level of acquisition high enough to be maintained by existing reinforcement contingencies in the natural environment will show performance decrements unless additional sources of reinforcement are supplied* (Koop & Martin, 1983, pp. 458, 459).

For further reading about the usefulness of behavioural techniques for coaching the reader is referred to Martin & Hrycaiko (1983a,b). Recently Ziegler (1987) conducted a study in which the focus of intervention was not on the addition of feedback or reward to the performer, but on the actual focus of the performer at the time of skill execution. The author demonstrated that beginning tennis players profited from attentional training, by means of stimulus cueing, in learning both forehand and backhand returns. Without going into further detail it may be suggested that training athletes in 'self-cueing' is a promising complement to techniques based on cueing provided by the coach.

5.5. Information processing

While in the preceding sections cognitive processes were addressed, and the concept of information was also used, it is only now, in this section, that an approach will be sketched in which these concepts play a central role. In this kind of approach, man is explicitly conceived as an information-processing system such as is reproduced in Figure 5.2. From this figure a number of different processes can be differentiated:

1. Receptor processes — the afferent sensory sub-systems which receive information (these include the sensory organs and the nerves that travel from these to the CNS).
2. Effector processes — efferent motor sub-systems subserving overt responses (muscles and the nerves that unite them with the CNS).
3. Translatory processes — that mediate between receptor and effector processes in order to ensure optimal tuning of the one to the other.

In addition, memory processes play an important role both in the processing of incoming information (one has learned, for example, that the rhythm being heard is that of the tango and not of the waltz) and in the sending of commands to the effectors (tango steps are carried out and not those of the waltz). Feedback processes also have a role to play: proprioceptive (internal) and visual or acoustic (external) information about the effects of its motor actions are fed back to the system. The external information can be either

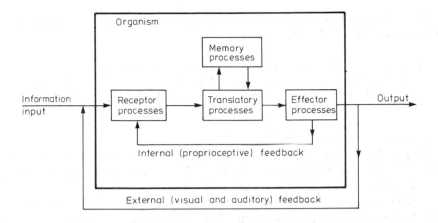

Figure 5.2. Schematic reproduction of man as an information-processing system.

intrinsic or extrinsic in nature (Holding, 1965). Intrinsic feedback is feedback that is always available when a particular task is carried out. Extrinsic feedback, in contrast, is a form of 'extra' feedback provided during the learning process (for example by the coach), and which is known as either 'knowledge of results' (referring to the 'outcome' of the movements) or 'knowledge of performance' (referring to the movements themselves). Under normal circumstances this information would not be available, and eventually the learner would have to learn to operate without it. Research into the effects of feedback variables on the learning process will be discussed further in Section 5.6. In Figure 5.3 the different types of feedback are distinguished.

Welford (1952) put forward what he termed a 'single-channel' hypothesis according to which the pathway from 'input' to 'output' is seen as a simple channel with a limited capacity within which information has to be *successively* processed. Evidence for such an idea is found in experiments in which stimuli which follow one another in rapid succession have to be responded to — for example, having to depress a key with the left index finger when a lamp comes on and subsequently to depress another key with the right index finger on a given auditory signal. Now, if the second stimulus follows the first after a very short interval of time there is a delay in the reaction time to the second stimulus, a phenomenon that has become known as the psychological refractory period (PRP). The delay in reacting to the second stimulus increases as the inter-stimulus interval becomes smaller and the reaction to the first stimulus requires more time. The PRP is interpreted to be indicative of the fact that the processing of the second stimulus is delayed until the (central) processing of the first has been completed.

A number of researchers have attempted to establish precisely what is the

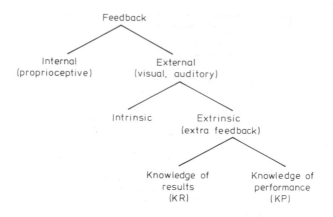

Figure 5.3. Different types of feedback in learning motor skills.

capacity of the human information processing channel. The information value (h) of the occurrence of one of 'n' *a priori* equally — probable events has been defined as $h = \log_2 n$ bits. If a subject is required to react to such an event, this amount of information has to be processed. From a large number of choice reaction time experiments it seems that the reaction time to a stimulus is a linear function of the information value h of the stimulus, as is apparent from Figure 5.4. This figure was presented by Posner (1966) in an article summarising the results of a number of choice reaction time experiments.

From this figure it would, at the same time, appear that the slopes of the curves are to a large extent determined by stimulus—response codes used. The more compatible these codes, i.e. the more 'naturally' they are related to one another, the less steep the slope of the curve in question — indicating that the processing of extra information is requiring less time. It is important in connection with the motor-learning process that the S—R compatibility is not fixed, but increases as the task becomes more familiar. The limitations imposed on human information-processing capacity can, to a large extent, be overcome by practice. The more often a particular stimulus is reacted to, the faster the response in question can be initiated (Marteniuk, 1975). Ultimately, control will be automated, as has been described by Schneider & Shiffrin (1977) and Shiffrin & Schneider (1977), i.e. that particular stimuli, dependent on the context in which they occur, automatically actuate particular responses. As an example of contextual influences the authors quote the reaction to a red traffic light; when driving a car this leads, almost automatically, to stopping — but such a reaction may not occur when one is walking.

Another reason that reactions will become faster has to do with the fact

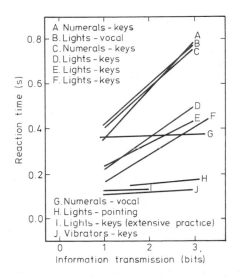

Figure 5.4. Choice reaction time as a function of stimulus−response compatibility. The letters A−J give an indication of the stimuli and responses used. From Posner (1966); reprinted with permission of the AAAS and author.

that events in the environment show specific relations which are discovered during the learning process. This discovery of 'redundancy' enables one to predict certain events on the basis of the occurrence of other ones, resulting in a decrease in their subjective uncertainty (or information value), and a corresponding decrease in time needed to react to them. A real-life illustration of the importance of such 'anticipation' is offered by Muhammad Ali (1975), where he reports on a fight against Jeff Merritt. Initially Ali is in trouble because he finds no defence against Merritt's dangerous left cross. After some time, however, Ali's problem was solved:

> *I had his movements so catalogued and timed that I knew the meaning of the slight twitch that would involuntarily appear in his throat when he was about to smash the bomb. Then I would cut over his blow* (p. 321).

Anticipations like this abound in many sport games, and we leave it to the reader to come up with other examples.

The constraints to which the information processing system is subjected are important to the way in which motor skills are to be learned. Thus, one of the authors remembers very vividly how much difficulty it cost him, during his first tennis lessons, in returning a ball played to him, to respond to the following instructions:

1. move racquet backwards,
2. step into the ball
3. bring racquet forward into a vertical position
4. follow through having contacted the ball.

The information couched in these instructions, although cognitively process-able, did not seem to be — motorically speaking — realisable; following one instruction resulted in neglecting the others.

Undoubtedly, the fact that the stroke had, in this case, to be adjusted to an oncoming ball played a role. For this reason some trainers prefer to train the stroke first without the ball, until it is reasonably under control. An example of such an (albeit disputed) approach is to be found in a tennis instruction book by Willis (1976).

Ungerer (1973) reports experimental investigations into the capacity of subjects to follow verbal instructions. To this end he established the 'sensory-motor quotient' (SQ) of his subjects. This measure was defined as that part of the information couched in the instructions that can become realised by the learner while carrying out the movement.* Amongst other things, the experiments were concerned with learning a particular technique of long-jumping, namely, the 'hitchkick'. The instruction for this purpose comprised the following set of instructions: (1) take-off; (2) kick, at take-off, the free-leg, forward; (3) bring it back behind; and (4) follow-on by bringing it forward again before landing; (5) together with the take-off leg; (6) after which both arms should be thrown forward. Even for adults the actual realisation of such a long list of instructions during the early stages of the learning process proved to be impossible. They could, at the start, only carry out sequences of around four of the instructions. If more had to be achieved then the SQ became smaller or equal to 0.7, resulting in a complete failure to achieve the required movement pattern. In children the SQ dropped under this critical value earlier; teenagers were able to follow only three and still younger children only two instructions at the same time. These data have obvious consequences for the provision of instructions during the early phase of a motor learning process: the trainer should be aware of the problems, partly determined by age, in the 'translation' of verbal information into the corresponding movements. According to Ungerer (1973) research into the relative efficiency of verbal instructions and demon-strations indicates that the former turn out to be the best. As was remarked earlier, verbal instructions in many cases will not be accurate enough, and in

---

* For the way in which Ungerer quantified the information contained in the instructions and in performance the reader is referred to Ungerer's (1973) publication itself. Because of the important role played by cognitive processes the Hungarian sport psychologist Rokusfalvy (1980) prefers to speak about 'cognitive-motor quotient' instead of 'sensory-motor quotient'.

practice use will also be made of demonstrations. The learning process involved ('observational learning') was addressed in Section 5.4 and will not be further developed here. Undoubtedly, as Volpert (1973) remarked, demonstrations (for example by means of film or video) and verbal instructions can be combined in practice, whereby the latter can be used to direct the attention of the learner to the essential characteristics of the demonstrated movement pattern.

In relation to the 'single-channel' hypothesis mentioned earlier, yet another comment is in order. A number of different authors have justifiably proposed that such a theory, in a strict sense, is patently incorrect. In this connection Legge & Barber (1976) point out that the information-processing necessary for the regulation of vegetative functions such as heart beat and blood pressure occur simultaneously with all the different behaviours of the individual. Legge and Barber conclude from this that particular classes of information are processed in special channels. These 'special-purpose' channels are specialised in the processing of specific forms of information. They are laid down genetically and their development does not rely on learning processes. Legge and Barber, however, propose that there are also 'special-purpose channels' that, to a greater or lesser degree, are dependent on learning and that are arranged in a hierarchical fashion under a 'super-channel'. In the latter channel information is, indeed, processed successively, i.e. it functions like the single-channel earlier discussed. This has to do with attention-demanding, conscious processes: 'It is in this channel that problem-solving is accommodated — at least when it is accomplished at the level of conscious awareness' (Legge & Barber, 1976, p. 131). This channel is very flexible, but processes specific information less quickly than 'special-purpose channels' specialised in processing the specific information in question. Such channels, which allow for parallel processing of information, are developed during the automatisation of skills.

Thinking in terms of the usual computer analogy invoked in information theory, the 'super-channel' can be conceived as the channel via which the executive programme or 'master routine' is carried out while the 'sub-routines' of that programme become realised via the 'special-purpose' channels.

That the replacement of a form of automatised control (realised by means of a sub-routine or 'special-purpose' channel) by conscious control (via the 'master routine' or 'super-channel') can have a negative effect is apparent from the problems experienced when, in climbing stairs, for example, attention is paid to what the feet are doing (Legge & Barber, 1976).

Without going further into that matter, it is mentioned in passing that the information-processing approach to motor skills has recently been challenged by authors who are influenced by Gibson's (1979) ecological theory of perception on the one hand, and the physics of self-organising biological systems on the other hand (see for example Kugler & Turvey, 1987). A discussion of the latter approach is outside the realm of this book. Readers interested in the theoretical controversies between the two conflicting views are referred to Wade & Whiting (1986) and Meijer & Roth (1988).

5.6. Feedback

In many instances trainers or coaches provide feedback for their pupils about their performances. When this information relates to the *result* of a particular action (for example, the distance jumped) the term 'knowledge of results' (KR) is used. Where the information relates to the way in which the movement pattern is carried out, the term 'knowledge of performance' (KP) is used.

There is a considerable body of literature concerning the effects of varying the way in which KR is given on motor learning processes. Unfortunately, almost all this work is restricted to the learning of simple laboratory tasks, of which the relevance for the learning of skills within sport is at least arguable (see, for example, Fowler & Turvey, 1978). We will therefore refrain from discussing this literature and refer the reader to a recent overview article on the topic by Salmoni, Schmidt & Walter (1984).

More recently, increasing use has been made in sport of KP. The use of film and video recordings of learners come particularly to mind while 'on-line' feedback of (aspects of) movement patterns carried out by means of computer also fall under this category. With respect to the use of video recordings as KP an overview article by Rothstein & Arnold (1976) showed that many of the earlier studies can be criticised on the grounds of methodo-logical shortcomings, and that their results are inconsistent. What was clear, however, is that the trainer continues to play an important role: he serves to direct the attention of the student to specific aspects of the recorded move-ment patterns. In particular he must be able to indicate faults in the perform-ance of the movements, since learners themselves are rather 'blind' in this respect (Robb, 1972). The latter point is apparent from Bakker's (1981) investigation into learning a running extended jump with the help of a trampette. Learners (around 12 years of age) were required to appraise, in total, six such jumps. They did this by indicating, directly following a jump, which of eight aspects of the jump (such as, for example, distance at take-off, height reached during the free-flight phase and whether or not the legs were fully extended) were, or were not, effectively carried out.

Deviations between their answers and the actual jumps carried out (which were filmed) demonstrated that the learners ran into great difficulty in making the required judgements. What was surprising was that the appraisals did not improve as the learning process progressed. Having carried out more and more jumps their evaluations became more positive, but that was just as likely with respect to those aspects that indeed were carried out well, as to those that were still relatively poorly carried out. Thus, learners were of the opinion that their jumps were becoming better even with respect to aspects that did not show actual improvement.

An approach in which an active role was reserved for the trainer was followed in an investigation by den Brinker (1979) into speed skaters participating in competitive selections for the Dutch championships. Half of these were trained without feedback while the other half had the benefit of seeing video recordings of their own events — these being discussed with the trainer. By the end of the season the latter procedure appeared to have contributed to the significantly better improvement in skating technique as compared to those who trained in the normal way. This greater improvement in performance, however, did not lead to greater benefit in times — perhaps the improved technique has to become further automated before such an effect can be expected.

In a study by Emmen, Wesseling, Bootsma, Whiting & van Wieringen (1985), the effect of video feedback on the learning of the tennis service by beginners was investigated. While there were indications that the use of video feedback in training did, indeed, lead to a better service technique, the results were not statistically significant. It is worth reporting that at the start of the study no significant relationship was apparent between the service technique and the service outcome. After five training sessions (each of 45 minutes), however, there was evidence that a better technique was accompanied by a better outcome. This points to the validity of the earlier suggestion that it can take some time before improved technique results in improved performance.

To conclude this section we would like to refer briefly to an investigation (different from the one already mentioned in Section 5.4) into learning to make slalom-type ski movements on a so-called 'ski simulator'. In this study, 'on-line' feedback was provided for subjects about the frequency, amplitude or fluency of their movements, while they were training on the ski simulator, by means of a TV screen. Subjects were required to pay particular attention to that movement parameter about which they received feedback, while performing the movements required. After four days of training — a total of 10 minutes each day — it was apparent that the condition in which feedback about the amplitude was provided led to the best learning: the amplitude was larger than under the other conditions while the frequency and fluency did not differ significantly among the three conditions. The increased amplitude, then, was not at the cost of one or other of the other parameters. Feedback about movement frequency, it is true, led initially to a higher movement tempo, but this was at the cost of the amplitude — an effect that was still present at the end of the four days of training. For further details of this study the reader is referred to the publication in question (den Brinker,

Stabler, Whiting & van Wieringen, 1986) which is particularly important since it has to do with the learning of a complex motor skill, a skill that, unlike the usual laboratory tasks, may serve as a model for 'real-life' sport activities.

5.7. Mental training

That cognitive processes can also play an important role in the learning of motor skills is apparent from the results of mental training. By the latter is meant the systematic and intensive mental rehearsal of an action without actually carrying it out.

In the everyday practice of dance and sport it is commonly accepted that mental training can have a positive effect on performance, and many sports performers make use of it (Suinn 1980).

From an overview of 60 studies into the effect of mental training on motor skills it would seem that, in general, performance can be improved as a consequence (Feltz & Landers, 1983). That is to say, subjects who use mental training tend to do better than control subjects who do not train mentally in the great majority of cases; however, the results of mental training *per se* are inferior to the results of physical training. The largest effect of mental training seems to be with those skills having a substantial cognitive component. With 'pure' *motor* skills, or skills in which strength plays the most important role, the effects in general are smaller. Moreover, the greater the cognitive component, the more quickly are the favourable effects of periods of mental training likely to occur. The latter has implications for the learning and instructional process. As previously indicated, the first phase of the motor learning process is to a large degree cognitive in nature. This implies that with relatively short-term mental training relatively large effects can be achieved. At the same time, this does not mean that positive effects of mental training can be established only with beginners: advanced learners also seem to be able to profit from mental training.

With respect to the favourable effects of mental training, three explanations have been put forward:

1. An explanation in terms of symbolic learning.
2. An explanation in terms of attention and activation (arousal).
3. An explanation in terms of muscular excitation.

5.7.1. SYMBOLIC LEARNING

The explanation via symbolic learning assumes that, by means of mental training, different strategies at a cognitive level can be tried out, the possibilities of preventing and correcting faults can be explored, the sequencing of movements can be established, the consequences of particular actions can be considered, and so on.

It is proposed that the learner is actively working on the attainment of a correct idea of the movement which forms the basis for the designing of an action plan. Reflecting on the spatial and temporal regularities in the skill to be learned promotes the tuning of different 'sub-routines' (sub-skills) to each other, and thus contributes towards an adequate action plan.

For this kind of explanation much empirical support is available. The fact that advanced learners can also profit from mental training is, however, not so easy to explain in this way. The second explanation proposed offers, in this respect, a better perspective.

5.7.2. ATTENTION AND ACTIVATION

The explanation in terms of attention and activation assumes that mental training brings the level of activation to an optimum and concentrates attention on the skill in question.

The learner prepares himself, optimally, for the actions to be carried out, amongst other reasons because he is able, from the start, to pay attention to the relevant cues and because he knows what information to expect. Support for this explanation comes from research which has shown that during mental training action potentials in particular muscle groups are apparent. This is an indication that the person is preparing himself for the skill to be carried out.

5.7.3 MUSCULAR EXCITATION

The third explanation proposes that the action potentials referred to above are so specific to the mentally trained skill that they constitute, as it were, a weak reflection of the muscle activity that goes hand-in-hand with the skill in question. The previously named author Suinn is of the opinion that this explanation, according to which mental training can in fact really be considered as a very weakened form of physical training, is correct. He reports in this respect that he is able, on the basis of electromyograms derived from the leg muscles of skiers engaged in mental training, to deduce to what part of the slalom trajectory their attention is directed (Suinn, 1980). Feltz & Landers (1983), however, are of the opinion that such anecdotal evidence cannot be decisive: they point to investigations from which it would seem that during mental training not only the muscles involved in the movements concerned, but also very different muscles, become activated — which provides more support for the explanation put forward under item 2, above.

Feltz & Landers (1983) quote research in which the variables that play a mediating role with respect to the relationship between mental training and the actual carrying out of a movement have been investigated. In this respect the work of Pijning (1982) deserves mention. He distinguished two kinds of motor learning strategies — a 'fault-analysing strategy' and a 'moment strategy'. Subjects following the former strategy are inclined to identify and analyse their mistakes, and try to use the results of this analysis for improving their performance. Subjects with a 'moment approach' do not relate the different learning trials to each other, directing themselves to immediate results only. Pijning refers to empirical evidence demonstrating that the 'fault-analysing strategy' is the more adequate, leading to better motor learning results than the 'moment strategy'. The importance of this finding in the present context lies in the fact that the 'fault-analysing' behaviour may be considered a form of mental training. Pijning concludes his paper by drawing attention to some educational implications of his analysis, noticing that:

> *Either in the normal physical education lessons, or in a special motor remedial teaching program, the teacher can try to change the inadequate strategies by instructing in a behaviour-centred way. If the teacher does not succeed in changing the learning strategy because it is fixed, a goal-centred method of instruction seems to be more suitable than a behaviour-centred method* (Pijning, 1982, p. 63).

5.8. Conclusion

In this chapter, as its title suggests, an attempt has been made to relate a number of lines of psychological theory-forming about motor skills to the practice of sport. As has been shown, this leads to problems that have to do with the kind of research on which the theory-forming is based. Until recently this research involved relatively simple laboratory tasks such as reaction time and movement positioning. Generalising the results found in this way to complex everyday skills is often a very difficult and hazardous enterprise.

This problem cannot be circumvented by carrying out research in everyday practice; the number of uncontrolled variables is, in general, so large that it becomes impossible to say which variables are responsible for the results found. The best perspective for practical relevancy is provided by scientific research into learning processes in skills that, on the one hand, arise from the practice of sport and, on the other, lend themselves to analyses of the movement patterns involved in relatively standardised situations. Until recently such approaches encountered many problems, problems that go together with the fact that the recording and analysis of relatively complex movements could rarely be carried out. More recently, however, much progress has been made in this area. The use of fast films and SELSPOT systems, by means of which an infra-red camera can register the positions of

'LEDs' (light-emitting diodes) attached to the body, makes possible, in combination with computer processing, very detailed analyses of complex movement patterns. It would seem possible, at least in principle, that, thanks in part at least to such technical developments, the gulf between theory and practice can in the near future be reduced (see also Chapter 7).

References

Allison, M.G., & Ayllon, T. (1980). Behavioral coaching in the development of skills in football, gymnastics and tennis. *Journal of Applied Behavior Analysis*, **13**, 297–314.

Azrin, N.H., & Holz, W.C. (1966). Punishment. In W.K. Honig (Ed.), *Operant Behavior*. New York: Appleton-Century-Crofts.

Bakker, F.C. (1981). Persoonlijkheid en motorisch leren bij kinderen (Personality and motor learning in children). Doctoral dissertation, Free University, Amsterdam.

Bandura, A. (1976). Social learning theory. In J.T. Spence, R.C. Carson and J.W. Thibaut (Eds), *Behavioral Approaches to Therapy*. Morristown, NJ: General Learning Press.

Brinker, B.P.L.M. den (1979). Extra feedback bij het aanleren van bewegingen (Extra feedback in the learning of movements). In H. Nakken (Ed.), *Psychomotorische Leerprocessen (Psychomotor Learning Processes)*. Haarlem: De Vrieseborch.

Brinker, B.P.L.M. den, Stabler, J.R.L.W., Whiting, H.T.A., & Wieringen, P.C.W. van (1986). The effect of manipulating knowledge of results on the learning of slalom-type ski movements. *Ergonomics*, **29**, 31–40.

Burwitz, L. (1981). The use of demonstrations and video-tape recorders in sport and physical education. In I.M. Cockerill & W.W. MacGillivary (Eds), *Vision and Sport*. Cheltenham: Stanley Thornes.

Carroll, W.R., & Bandura, A. (1982). The role of visual monitoring in observational learning of action patterns: making the unobservable observable. *Journal of Motor Behavior*, **14**, 153–167.

Crossman, E.R.F.W. (1959). A theory of the acquisition of speed skill. *Ergonomics*, **2**, 153–166.

Dickinson, J.A. (1976). *A Behavioral Analysis of Sport*. London: Lepus Books.

Emmen, H.H., Wesseling, L.G., Bootsma, R.J., Whiting, H.T.A., & Wieringen, P.C.W. van (1985). The effect of video-modelling and video-feedback on the learning of the tennis service by beginners. *Journal of Sport Sciences*, **3**, 127–138.

Feltz, D.L., & Landers, D.M. (1983). The effects of mental practice on motor skill learning and performance: a meta-analysis. *Journal of Sport Psychology*, **5**, 25–57.

Fowler, C.A., & Turvey, M.T. (1978). Skill acquisition: an event approach with special reference to searching for the optimum of a function of several variables. In G.E. Stelmach (Ed.), *Information Processing in Motor Control and Learning*. New York: Academic Press.

Gibson, J.J. (1979). *The Ecological Approach to Visual Perception*. Boston, MA: Houghton Mifflin.

Gould, D.R., & Roberts, G.C. (1982). Modelling and motor skill acquisition. *Quest*, **33**, 214–230.

Harzem, P., & Miles, T.R. (1978). *Conceptual Issues in Operant Psychology.* New York: Wiley.

Holding, D.H. (1965). *Principles of Training.* Oxford: Pergamon.

Jordan, F.R. (1977). Meaningful motor learning and cognitive structure: The experimental facilitation of imitation learning of a complex motor task. Unpublished M.Ed. thesis, University of Sydney.

Komaki, J., & Barnett, F.T. (1977). A behavioral approach to coaching football: improving the play execution of the offensive backfield on a youth football team. *Journal of Applied Behavior Analysis,* **10**, 657–664.

Koop, S., & Martin, G.L. (1983). Evaluation of a coaching strategy to reduce swimming stroke errors with beginning age-group swimmers. *Journal of Applied Behavior Analysis,* **16**, 447–460.

Kugler, P.N., & Turvey, M.T. (1987). *Information, Natural Law, and the Self-assembly of Rhythmic Movement.* Hillsdale, NJ: Erlbaum.

Legge, D., & Barber, P.J. (1976). *Information and Skill.* London: Methuen.

Mahoney, M.J. (1974). *Cognitive Behavior Modification.* Cambridge MA: Ballinger.

Marteniuk, R.G. (1975). Information processing, channel capacity, learning stages and the acquisition of motor skills. In H.T.A. Whiting (Ed.), *Readings in Human Performance.* London: Lepus Books.

Martens, R. (1971). Anxiety and motor behavior: A review. *Journal of Motor Behavior,* **3**, 151–179.

Martens, R. (1974). Anxiety and motor performance. In J.H. Wilmore (Ed.), *Exercise and Sport Sciences Reviews,* Vol. 2. London: Academic Press.

Martin, G.L., & Hrycaiko, D. (1983a). Effective behavioral coaching: what's it all about? *Journal of Sport Psychology,* **5**, 8–20.

Martin, G.L., & Hrycaiko, D. (Eds) (1983b). *Behavior Modification and Coaching: Principles, Procedures, and Research.* Springfield, IL: C.C. Thomas.

Meijer, O.G., & Roth, K. (Eds) (1988). *Complex Movement Behaviour: 'The' Motor-Action Controversy.* Amsterdam: North-Holland.

Muhammad Ali (1975). *The Greatest: My Own Story* (with R. Durham). New York: Ballantine Books.

O'Brien, F., & Azrin, N.H. (1970). Behavioral engineering: control of postures by informational feedback. *Journal of Applied Behavior Analysis,* **3**, 235–240.

Pavlov, I.P. (1960). *Conditioned Reflexes: An Investigation of the Physiological Activity of the Cerebral Cortex (Lectures Delivered in 1924).* New York: Dover Publications.

Pijning, H.F. (1982). Effective learning strategies in the acquisition of psychomotor skills. *Sportwissenschaft,* **12**, 56–64.

Posner, M.I. (1966). Components of skilled performance. *Science,* **152**, 1712–1718.

Robb, M.D. (1972). *The Dynamics of Motor-skill Acquisition.* Englewood Cliffs, NJ: Prentice-Hall.

Rokusfalvy, P. (1980). *Sportpsychologie (Sport Psychology).* Bad Homburg: Limpert.

Rothstein, A.L., & Arnold, R.K. (1976). Bridging the gap: Application of research on video-tape feedback and bowling. *Motor Skills: Theory into Practice,* **1**, 35–62.

Rushall, B.S. (1975). Applied behavior analysis of sports and physical education. *International Journal of Sport Psychology,* **6**, 75–88.

Salmoni, A.W., Schmidt, R.A., & Walter, C.B. (1984). Knowledge of results and motor learning: A review and critical reappraisal. *Psychological Bulletin,* **95**, 355–386.

Schmidt, R.A. (1982). *Motor Control and Learning: A Behavioral Emphasis.* Champaign, IL: Human Kinetics.

Schneider, W., & Shiffrin, R.M. (1977). Controlled and automatic human information processing: I. Detection, search and attention. *Psychological Review*, **84**, 1–66.

Shiffrin, R.M., & Schneider, W. (1977). Controlled and automatic human information processing: II. Perceptual learning, automatic attending, and general theory. *Psychological Review*, **84**, 127–190.

Skinner, B.F. (1953). *Science and Human Behavior.* New York: Free Press.

Skinner, B.F. (1969). *Contingencies of Reinforcement.* New York: Appleton-Century-Crofts.

Suinn, R.M. (1980). Body thinking: psychology for Olympic champs. In R.M. Suinn (Ed.), *Psychology in Sports.* Minneapolis MN: Burgess.

Twitmyer, E.B. (1974). A study of the knee jerk. Ph.D. thesis, 1902. Reprinted in *Journal of Experimental Psychology*, **103**, 1047–1066.

Tyldesley, D.A., & Whiting, H.T.A. (1975). Operational timing. *Journal of Human Movement Studies*, **1**, 172–177.

Ungerer, D. (1973). *Leistungs- und Belastungsfähigkeit im Kindes- und Jugendalter (Performance Capability and Work Capacity in Children and Adolescents)*, 3rd edn. Schorndorf: Karl Hofmann.

Volpert, W. (1973). *Sensumotorisches Lernern (Perceptual Motor Learning)*, 2nd edn. Frankfurt am Main: Limpert.

Wade, M.G., & Whiting, H.T.A. (Eds) (1986). *Motor Development in Children: Aspects of Coordination and Control.* Dordrecht: Martinus Nijhoff.

Welford, A.T. (1952). The 'psychological refractory period' and the timing of high-speed performance—a review and a theory. *British Journal of Psychology*, **42**, 2–19.

Whiting, H.T.A. (1970). *Teaching the Persistent Non-swimmer.* London: Bell.

Whiting, H.T.A., Bijlard, M.J., & Brinker, B.P.L.M. den (1987). The influence of a dynamic model on the acquisition of a complex cyclical action. *Quarterly Journal of Experimental Psychology*, **39A**, 43–59.

Willis, D. (1976). *Learn to Play Tennis at Home.* New York: McGraw-Hill.

Wolpe, J. (1978). Cognition and causation in human behavior and its therapy. *American Psychologist*, **33**, 437–446.

Ziegler, S. (1987). Effects of stimulus cueing on the acquisition of groundstrokes by beginning tennis players. *Journal of Applied Behavior Analysis*, **20**, 405–411.

6 DECISION-MAKING IN SPORT SITUATIONS

6.1. Introduction

Sporting activities are closely allied to other activities of daily life in the sense that they have mutual effects on both immediate and long-term decision-making. One of the reasons for a failure to take account of this close relationship is the very narrow interpretation which is often placed on the concept 'skill'. The term is generally restricted to the particular *movements* that a player is making at any one time. But, as Aspin (1977) confirms, most sport activities involve what might be termed 'simple' and 'complex' *actions*. To take the game of cricket as an example, while the movements of both batsman and bowler may have become so routinised as to no longer require active attention in their performance, success in taking wickets involves the bowler in: 'taking into account, as an act of theorising, such disparate factors as the state of the game, the placing of the fielders, the condition of the pitch, etc.' Carr (1980), in distinguishing 'human' from 'animal' skill, points out that the teaching and learning of human skills involves the communication and transmission of complex rules, the grasp of which requires that capacity to perform mental acts which we call rationality.

On this basis it must be recognised that any skilled performance is part of a larger whole—the event, culture and society at large. Thus the skill of controlling an ice-hockey puck in a game has to be seen in relation to: the particular competition, the ice-hockey culture in general and, if it happens to be within, say, the Olympic Games, society at large, in the sense that any of these wider contexts may have an influence on the player's/coach's/team manager's decision-making and performance. To extend the concept further, the player may in turn be an 'amateur' concerned primarily with the pleasure of participation, or a professional for whom part of the commitment, at least, is that of earning a living. Situations provide what Gibson (1979) terms

154

different 'affordances' for each of these different points of view, where an 'affordance' is conceived of as what a particular environmental feature or event has to offer a person in both a positive and a negative sense.

The kind of skill structure being stressed here is of a *nested* or *telescoped* kind. For example, in a ball game it is possible to think of individual skill in ball control which contributes to skill in a particular playing unit (e.g. line-out play in rugby football), which in turn is part of a particular team strategy (which demands skill in its innovation and development) which contributes to skilfulness in the game itself (Figure 6.1). In addition, it has to be appreciated that players do not necessarily make the same decision when confronted with similar situations. Such decisions are affected by factors such as the stage of competition, whether they are winning or losing, what is to be gained or lost (since most decisions involve risk).

In developmental terms, as a person progresses in acquiring skill in sport, he is concerned not only with mastering the specifics of the movement skill itself, but with, for example, how the culture expects one of his age, sex and background to perform (Cratty, 1975). Thus he is always sensitive about the extent to which his level of performance measures up to cultural expectations. The younger and less experienced the person, the less elaborate the affordance structure to which he has access. The possibilities for educating attention, for exploring and adjusting, for extracting and abstracting information (to use Gibson's words) from the sport environment as a basis for decision-making are potentially unlimited. However, in practice a person is constrained in what information he is able to pick up by the restricted nature of his exposure to different situations and his limited contact with significant others, which reduces the scope of his affordance structure. One of the important tasks of the coach is not only to facilitate the acquisition of the appropriate movement skills, but to extend the affordance structure by making the developing sportsman aware of possibilities—a procedure that has been referred to by Whiting (1969) as *social facilitation*.

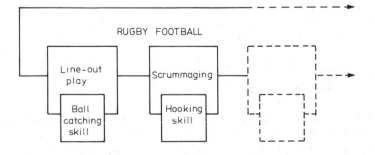

Figure 6.1. Schematic skill telescoping—rugby football.

It is necessary to think in terms of such an expanded and hierarchically organised skill structure in order to come to terms with the kinds of question for which sport participants and spectators are seeking answers. With respect to the heterogeneous nature of skill already outlined, for example, to what extent is it possible to speak about the outcome of sporting competitions being determined by the skilfulness of the players? It is commonplace that teams or individuals, apparently with superior skill in one or other of the senses being outlined, prove to be unsuccessful in competitive situations. Recourse is then often made to such unscientific terms as 'they were unlucky'. Unfortunately this sort of explanation does not lead far, because it is precisely such unexplained variance that is of interest to the sport psychologist. Of course, it is always possible to generalise the definition of skill to encompass such explanations in terms of, for example, 'the ability to bring about a predetermined objective...where the objective is defined as defeating another opponent or team'. While this kind of approach is, again, in practice not very helpful, it has the advantage that it may lead to a reconsideration of the whole concept of skill in the hierarchical manner already loosely outlined. Such considerations, for example, might pre-empt the naive questions of the spectator to the effect 'why did such and such a player make such a pointless move'? Not only do such spectators not realise that they see the situation *literally* from a different point of view, but their affordance structures may differ considerably from those of the players. The situation is most marked when spectators observe an event from high up in the 'stands'. They not only see more of the pattern of the event than any participant actually on the field, but their advantageous viewpoint allows them to see openings and possibilities that are not apparent to the participant from his less advantageous but nevertheless 'real' viewpoint. The contention that the spectator sees more of the game is a truism! This fact is utilised by some coaches in American football who may have a 'scout' high in the stands who can relay situation changes before they are apparent from the 'touch-line'.

An almost universal question in sport centres around the advantages occasioned by playing on the home ground. To what extent is this true and why? What kind of interactive effect does this have on the decision-making of the players? What particular 'affordance(s)' does it provide? In the first place it is of course necessary to check on the validity of the statement, and whether it is generalisable or needs to be qualified by reference to particular kinds of sport or particular levels of attainment. It would certainly be expected that its effects on decision-making would have far-reaching consequences. Since it is normal to play 50% of a season's games on the home ground and the other 50% on a variety of different grounds, it must be assumed that extended experience with the affordances alone might prove to be a considerable advantage. In what sense this might operate would need to be worked out.

The latter consideration relates to another common question in sport. Since many sport competitions take place in the presence of fast-moving objects and people, is speed of decision-making a characteristic of better players and, if so, on what does this depend? Is it in some way intrinsic to the make-up of a person, or is it acquired? Such decision-making processes, it must be remembered, involve the detection of appropriate information from the environment and the planning of actions to meet contingencies. To what extent are such abilities situationally determined and to what extent are they characteristic of the person himself? Or is there an interactive effect?

Questions of this nature lead naturally to a consideration of anticipation in sport. Some players, according to popular comment, seem to have a *natural* ability in this respect. Once again, claims of this kind have to be pursued in more depth before a meaningful explanation is forthcoming which might provide valuable evidence to those involved in the training of sports people. Not the least of these lines of enquiry relates to the information available from other players — both fellow-players and opponents — and the way in which this might be used as an anticipatory strategy.

Many questions raised from the field of sport focus on the concept of *risk*. Such a concept needs to be broadly conceived since it relates to the risk of winning or losing, risk of incurring injury, risk of gaining or losing promotion, risk of scoring against that of making a bad pass, etc. Since all sport involves risk of one kind or another, it is natural to speculate on the determinants of risk-taking behaviour and why some players are prepared to take more risks than others.

It would be possible to go on with an extensive list of questions relating to decision-making in sport, but this would be beyond the scope of a single book chapter. Rather, it is considered that an attempt to find empirical answers to some of the questions already posed will provide an interesting framework which might lead to further ecologically valid experimental approaches. However, before attempting to provide possible answers to these and similar questions, it is interesting to consider the way in which psychological theory has tackled the problem of decision-making in order to examine the extent to which it provides a possible source of application to a phenomenon such as sport. There is a difference in this respect between utilising an extant psychological theory in an attempt to find an answer to a problem generated from within the field of sport and trying to develop a theoretical system and methodology which is sport-oriented — the recipient/generated knowledge problem of Wilberg (1973) already referred to.

Figure 6.2. Underestimated probability. (ANP Foto.)

6.2. Psychology and decision-making

Since the problem of decision-making is central to any theory of human action it is not surprisingly that it should have received attention from psychologists. While some of the central concepts which have emerged in psychological decision theory have general applicability, research work in this area has tended to be laboratory-based and its application to more practical situations a questionable enterprise.

Decision theory (Edwards & Tversky, 1967) is an attempt to describe, in an orderly way, the variables that influence choices among alternatives. Two major classes of variable are generally specified:

1. Utility—specifying the relative attractiveness of one alternative rather than another.
2. Probability—that such an alternative will occur.

The basis of such theorising stems from the field of economics and, as Edwards (1954) suggests, has been largely an 'armchair' method, theories being developed which presumably could be, but seldom are, tested. Not only are such theories static in the sense that they are addressed to single choices among courses of action rather than with a sequence of such choices, but their utilisation of the concept *economic man* is of dubious psychological value. Such a fictitious person possesses the properties of being 'completely informed', 'infinitely sensitive' and 'rational'! In the real world, of course, one is seldom completely informed and often insensitive to particular sources of information (particularly for example in the early stages of acquiring a skill) so that all decision-making incorporates risk.

6.2.1. SIGNAL DETECTION THEORY

A more interesting psychological approach to decision-making arose in the early 1950s as a development from the more mechanistic models of statistical decision theory and electrical engineering (directed towards the performance of *ideal* sensing devices). This was the so-called theory of *signal detectability* (Tanner & Swets, 1954) addressed to decision-making in the context of human perceptual processing, e.g. the detection of faint sounds against background noise or faint visual signals on an illuminated background constituting visual 'noise' (Welford, 1968). The theory attempted to distinguish two, normally confounded, aspects of human performance:

1. The observer as a signal detector.
2. The observer as a decision-maker, in the sense of the effect of his values and expectations on his responses.

Basically, the theory is concerned with a comparison of two cortical states (evidence) — that due to 'noise' (broadly conceived as anything that interferes with the pick-up of that information in which interest lies) and that due to the information (signal) on which interest is focused, plus noise. In the present context it is perhaps easier for the reader if Coombs, Dawes & Tversky's (1970) example is adopted, whereby 'players in American football are trying to detect quarterback signals when the stadium is in uproar'. Two possible distributions of cortical states of any particular player at any one time are illustrated in Figure 6.3.

Such distributions, and the overlap between them, will differ in form and parameters over time and over situations, so that the difference between the mean of the 'noise' distribution and that of the 'signal plus noise' distribution — the so-called d' (d prime) — will vary accordingly. The value of d' sets the detection possibility, i.e. if the signal strength (for example, information about what the quarterback is going to do) is much more dominant than the noise signal, d' will be large — there will be little overlap between the two cortical distributions. But the more interesting facet of the theory is the

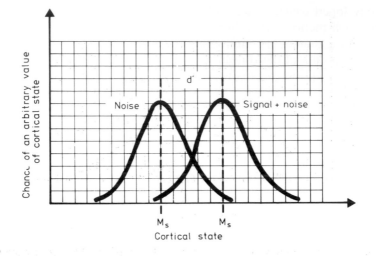

Figure 6.3. Hypothetical distributions of 'noise' and 'signal + noise'.

contention that there is no fixed sensory threshold which determines a person's decision. Instead, it is postulated that he establishes a *response* criterion which is determined by a number of considerations (perceived risk, pay-off, etc.). Figure 6.4 illustrates two possible positions of such a hypothetical variable criterion K (K_1 and K_2). Shifting the criterion—from K_1 to K_2 for example—affects the likelihood ratios of 'false-positives' (saying that the quarterback gave a signal when he did not) and 'false-negatives' (saying that the quarterback did not give a signal when he did). For position K_1 the likelihood ratio is given by XZ/YX and for position K_2 by AC/BC. The position at which a person establishes the hypothetical criterion is a measure of his cautiousness in the situation.

While this kind of approach is interesting, and has generated considerable laboratory experimental work, Cohen & Christensen (1970) draw attention to the restricted utility of the theory, pointing out its statistical rather than psychological nature. In a similar way, Broadbent (1971) refers to 'unsolved problems' in signal detection theory as follows:

1. Can the evidence received by the observer be arranged on a single dimension of sensory evidence?
2. Even if such 'evidence' does form a single continuum, can it be assumed that the subject knows the likelihood of each separate value on the continuum?
3. Even if it is the case that both a single dimension of likelihood ratio and perfect knowledge of its value by the subject are available, can it be assumed that the subject will behave rationally?

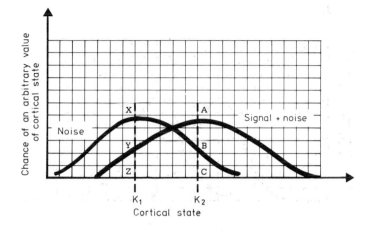

Figure 6.4. Two hypothetical positions of the criterion (K_1 and K_2) set by the player.

The latter critical point relates to the relatively mechanistic nature of the model. In the real world, decision-makers — as has been stressed — are seldom completely informed and are often insensitive to particular sources of information, so that all decision-making involves risk. In response to Broadbent's particular point, the fact that man is not always rational or guided by information pertaining to the situation is confirmed by Meredith's (1966) statement:

> *Any day you can witness men exposed to information who make decisions manifestly not necessitated by the information and often, indeed incompatible with it. It is information selected and often transmuted and further augmented from our internal source, which shapes the decision.*

It is also possible to distinguish *actual* and *perceived* rationality. Wilberg (1975) raises an interesting possibility in this respect.

> *While your opponent may appear to be playing irrationally, he may in actual fact be laying a trap for you, a trap from which you may not recover. Consequently, it is usually assumed that even though irrational play may arise it is in effect a disguise for well considered and successful rational play.*

6.2.2. BEHAVIOURAL DECISION THEORY

Not surprisingly, when psychologists began to take a deeper interest in decision-making in real-life situations, they wished to introduce the term *subjective* probability into their models. Cohen & Christensen (1970), for example, draw a distinction:

The task of the psychology of decision-making, by contrast with that of decision theory, is to study the subjective elements that enter into decision-making, partly for their intrinsic interest and partly because only when their nature is understood will it be possible to improve and control them, and remove, or at least be on guard against, their erratic features. This approach to decision-making is inspired by a desire to extend our self knowledge so as to understand how, so to speak, we make up our minds.

While one of these elements is subjective *probability*, it is not the only element. This trend towards a recognition of the essential importance of subjectivity in human performance has become not only more acceptable, but more necessary (Coombs, Dawes & Tversky, 1970) in an attempt to come to terms with the limited explanatory possibilities in classical theoretical positions. Considerations of man — the decision-maker — as an information-processing system have become less mechanistic in outlook and more concerned with the way in which such information is *actively organised* by the person not only in terms of information pick-up *per se*, but in terms of related parameters such as 'perceived risk' and 'utility value'.

The latter concepts have also received attention from contemporary psychologists under other guises. Gibson's (1979) term 'affordances' has already been introduced, and this can be considered for present purposes to carry a similar meaning to that of 'utility value'.

Whether one is dealing with classical decision theory or the behavioural decision theory approach, the concept of modelling is implicit. In the classical approach an ideal solution or model can be established on the basis of certain 'key factor' information which can be provided by the theorist, i.e. given this and this information, and assuming that the person behaves in a rational manner, the following is the logical solution — there is no risk, because within the constraints provided it will be the right decision. Unfortunately, humans are more often ill-defined systems and this sort of information is either not available or not generalisable across situations. In contrast to the classical approach, behavioural decision theory assumes that a person's experience within a particular recurring kind of situation (such as might be encountered in any sport) will lead to the build-up of his own conceptual model of the system which enables him to appreciate the interaction of the main parameters in the system and to predict the consequences of any control action he may take (Whitfield, 1967). Such conceptual models will not only be in terms of what leads to what, but also in terms of the formulating of variable options, an appreciation of the uncertainty pertaining to the prediction of events and the relevance of feedback and decision-making of other people involved. Further, as Luce (1963) proposes, the presentation of similar choices, again and again, leads over the course of time to a person acquiring considerable statistical information about an event. This is reinforced by Moray & Fitter (1973) in proposing that:

> *extensive practice must be given if attention is efficiently to function, since only with such practice can the statistical properties of the source be incorporated into an internal model.*

Marteniuk (1976) takes a similar stand in pointing out that one of the characteristics of highly skilled individuals is that they can, with considerable accuracy, make predictions about which events are most probable.

Further operationalisation of the idea of a player building up, over time, a 'knowledge base' about a particular game which, as well as being specific, may be organised in a hierarchical manner, is implicit in the work of de Groot (1965, 1966) with respect to the game of chess. The ability of chess masters to recall a chess position once having been exposed to that position for a brief interval of time (five or 10 seconds) was later shown by Chase & Simon (1973) not to be due to a superior visual short-term memory. As Chase & Chi (1980) elaborate in their recent extended analysis of the organisation of spatial knowledge:

> *In theory, the Chess Master is seeing familiar patterns of pieces that he recognises from experience, patterns that simply do not exist in the minds of less experienced and less skilled players.*

Masters, for example, were estimated to have a store of some 50 000 hours of looking, and the good club player 1000 to 5000!

The essential subjectivity of such models is implicit in Whitfield's (1967) elaboration:

> *[people's] use of these conceptual models seems to be more effective in many cases than the attempts of the design engineer to control the process, presumably because of complex interactions which cannot be predicted from theoretical formulations.*

Such knowledge is acquired only by 'acquaintance'. Gibson (1979) might talk about the detection of 'invariances' in the situation, and Polanyi (1958) about 'tacit knowledge' which, he also maintains, is not definable. For example, people ride bicycles and use skateboards without being able to verbalise about the rules which have to be followed in carrying out such a skill. These ideas seem to have been equally implicit in the minds of Cohen & Dearnaley (1962) when they wrote:

> *skill, in whatever form it is manifested, including skill in football, may be regarded as the exercise of connoisseurship, the ingredients of which cannot all be made explicit.*

Figure 6.5. International Grand Master Boris Spasski. (Benelux Press.)

6.2.3. DECISION-MAKING IN SPORT

In spite of considerable attention over the past 25 years to a psychology of decision-making, it would appear true to say that its practical relevance has been less than obvious. It may be that the complexity of the information which determines decision-making in real-life situations precludes the application of simplistic laboratory-derived information. Certainly, the possible relevance for decision-making in sport, outlined in the early part of this chapter, makes the formulation of a meaningful and comprehensive model a rather daunting prospect. It is not surprising, therefore, that moves in this direction from the field of sport have been both tentative and rather simplistic. Nevertheless, a start has to be made somewhere, and it is significant that meaningful questions are being asked and tackled, sometimes in laboratory paradigms and at others in more naturalistic settings.

In the first place it should be acknowledged that decisions based purely on the available information within a particular sport are not the only, or even the most necessary, determinants of success in sporting situations. Cohen (1975), for example, points out that there is more to winning and losing than skill factors alone:

> There is confidence and the will to win which may be crucial. Such considerations emphasise the need to take cognisance of other factors in the decision-making process under risky conditions which in sport always prevail.

Cohen's point is an important one in as far as such parameters, while being recognized by sport psychologists, have seldom been utilised within a sport-oriented paradigm.

6.3. Uncertain outcomes

The fact that there are no certain outcomes in sport competition is obvious to any gambler. The clearest manifestation of this statement is the existence in many countries of so-called 'football pools', which owe their existence to the fact that the outcomes of football matches are of a probabilistic nature. Not only are the probabilities in predicting the outcome of a single match low, but they reduce considerably when predictions have to be made about groups of matches — so much so that amateur gamblers are inclined to argue that sticking pins into lists of team pairs is just as likely to produce a successful prediction of a *pattern* of results as are more detailed analyses of the previous games. For such 'punters' the outcome of a series of games — if not each single game — is a 'chance' determined, in the sense that the explanation of the variance which would make prediction more certain is beyond their possibility of obtaining.

The idea that the outcome of a match may in fact be 'chance' (in the manner here described) determined rather than based on factors such as skill superiority is an interesting one. Such an idea has been entertained by Goldstein (1979), who is critical of circular reasoning of the following kind: 'How does one know whether team A is better than team B?' 'Because A defeats B!' 'Why does A defeat B?' 'Because it is better!' The sceptic, Goldstein maintains, might want to dispute such a contention, preferring the view that winning and losing are random events. Goldstein (1979) presents evidence to the effect that in the games of American football and basketball — for which there is a professional draft (i.e. teams with the worst win–lose record from the previous year are allowed the first draft choice for the following year) — equilibration, in terms of at least the physical characteristics (height, weight, etc.) of the players in the respective teams is reached. Why then, even with such equality in physical characteristics, do team successes in these sports differ markedly? The sceptic would want to say that they do not! If, for example, the season, instead of consisting of around 20 games, were extended over say several hundred games (the results for a number of seasons), it might be expected that the win/loss ratio would approximate at 50% split. If such evidence could be provided, what factors might be invoked in explanation thereof? Goldstein (1979) suggests as possibilities team morale, attitudes of the home-team crowd and playing at home or away, i.e. situational variables.

In its turn, team morale might be operationalised in terms of two independent variables: (1) winning or losing the previous game; (2) location of present game. It would not be difficult to agree with Goldstein that a higher probability of winning would be attributed to a team that: (1) had won its previous game; (2) was playing opponents who had lost their previous game; (3) was playing on home ground.

6.3.1. THE HOME-FIELD ADVANTAGE

Whether or not there is an advantage in playing on the home field, there is no doubt that players *believe* this to be the case. In fact such a contention is part of the mystique of most sports. What evidence is there to this effect? To begin with, it is useful to discover whether or not home teams do, in fact, win more often than away teams.

Edwards (1979), in a survey of the results of American football games during the seasons 1974, 1975 and 1976 ($N=349$ professional games), for example, reported that more games (54.4%) were won by the home teams than by visiting teams. Although the overall result showed no significant advantage to the home team, the average *margin* of victory for the home team was 14.47 points and for visiting teams 11.48. The home team showed both defence (conceded on average 1.68 points fewer) and offence (scored on average 1.58 points per game more) advantage over visiting teams. The situation was, however, somewhat different for college teams, the home team showing 58.6% success overall—a highly significant result compared with successful visiting teams. Moreover, the points spread could be attributed more to offence than defence.

Although such analyses have not been reported in detail for other sports and/or at varying levels of peformance, it does seem, even from the limited evidence available, that statements about the home field advantage would need to be qualified both with respect to the kind of sport and to the level of competition. An interesting side-issue is the extent to which players of differing standards and different sports hold this kind of viewpoint, i.e. are subjective probabilities about home field advantage part of their modelling of the sport? This particular point does not appear to have been investigated, although questions about other subjective probabilities have been researched.

6.4. Subjective probability

The fact that the statistical properties of events form a part of the conceptual model that a player builds up of the sport in which he operates has already been suggested. It might also be expected that the more experienced the sporting player, the closer the relationship which might exist between his subjective predictions and the actual outcome of events. Cohen & Dearnaley (1962) researched this possibility in the context of soccer. Players from two (at that time) first division professional English clubs, a university amateur club and a school amateur club were asked to make judgements about their ability to score goals from different distances away from the goal. Such subjective probabilities are given in Table 6.1. A few surprising factors are apparent from the table. For example, the grammar school players thought that they could successfully score 1 in 100 attempts or 1 in 5 attempts from distances further away than the players from either of the first division clubs! The university players, on the other hand, (except for the 1 in 100 prediction) were always more conservative in their judgements. While such discrepancies are likely to be mediated by different lengths of experience with the game of football, other possible individual difference parameters must not be overlooked—particularly given the unequal numbers of players in each of the teams.

Figure 6.6 shows the relationship between the *estimated* success of the players and the objective outcomes when they were required actually to shoot goals from the distance specified. These findings confirm the ability of experienced players to match subjective to objective probabilities of events, but at the same time to differ in the degree of risk which they are prepared to take.

Table 6.1. Average distance to the goal, in feet (and metres), corresponding to variations in expected success in attempts to score goals of football players from two first division (professional) clubs, a university (amateur) club, and a grammar school (amateur) club.

Players	Expected success						
	1 in 100 attempts	1 in 5 attempts	2 in 5 attempts	3 in 5 attempts	4 in 5 attempts	99 in 100 attempts	N
Manchester United	106 (32.3)	67 (20.4)	50 (15.2)	39 (11.9)	29 (8.8)	19 (5.8)	12
West Bromwich Albion	96 (29.3)	68 (20.7)	55 (16.8)	46 (14.0)	36 (11.0)	28 (8.5)	8
University	96 (29.3)	59 (18.0)	45 (13.7)	36 (11.0)	28 (8.5)	17 (5.2)	5
Grammar school	116 (35.4)	71 (21.6)	55 (16.8)	45 (13.7)	33 (10.1)	19 (5.8)	8
Mean	104 (31.7)	67 (20.4)	53 (15.8)	42 (12.8)	31 (9.4)	21 (6.4)	—

From Cohen & Dearnaley (1962); reprinted with permission of British Journal of Psychology.

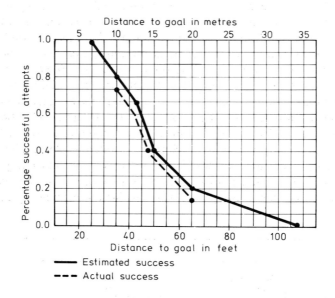

Figure 6.6. Estimated and actual success in scoring from various distances of the goal. From Cohen & Dearnaley (1962); reprinted with permission of British Journal of Psychology.

While this particular study is an interesting approach to the topic of subjective probability, the findings in relation to the game of football *per se* have to be viewed with caution, since a meaningful validation study, although attempted, was not conclusive. Considerable criticism of the methodology could also be made (e.g. players competed against goalkeepers from their own teams; not all players from a team participated in the analysis reported in Table 6.1, so that the samples might well be biased). Decision-making in soccer (or other sports), it might also be contended, is seldom so simplistic. As Hueting (1977) points out, by deciding to shoot from a greater distance away, the attacking player brings a greater element of surprise with his shot (since goalkeepers also have subjective probability models of the distance from which they expect players to shoot), but at the same time the shot is not likely to be as strong as from a shorter distance. On the other hand, if he waits until he is closer his shot will most probably be harder and more accurate, but the 'surprise' value will be decreased. It would not be unusual to find that decisions of this kind were affected by the particular stage of the game, winning or losing, etc. Hueting (Figure 6.7) proposes a useful pay-off matrix to cover the possible decisions.

Using terminology already introduced, this information can, following Hueting (1977), be presented in a more fundamental way. Suppose that an attacking player is able to pick up the relevant information very easily (i.e. there are no perceptual problems) — for example, he makes a good estimate of the number of metres to the goal, accurately perceives the number of opponents, etc. In such a case, d' is relatively large. However, given this information, there are many other constraints on how cautious he is in his decision-making as to whether or not to shoot. For example, in Figure 6.8 the units on the abscissa are used to represent decision inclination in the direction 'yes' or 'no' (shoot). A player who sets his criterion at K_3 has a high chance of scoring and a small chance of missing (the double-hatched area to the right of the criterion line). However, he lets many possible chances go by, i.e. he needs to be relatively sure of scoring before he will shoot. On the other hand, the player who sets his criterion at K_1 takes more

		Action	
Signal		Successful shot (scored)	Ought to have shot but did not (hesitated)
		Unsuccessful shot (too much haste)	Ought not to have shot and, in fact, did not (patient)

Figure 6.7. Pay-off matrix showing two types of correct and two types of incorrect actions. Each of the four actions carries a chance factor that is more or less probable. From Hueting (1977); reprinted with permission of De Tijdstroom, Lochem.

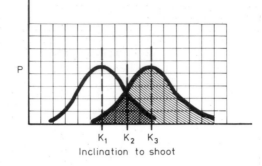

P

K_1 K_2 K_3
Inclination to shoot

Figure 6.8. The effect on decision-making of various hypothetical positions of the criterion.

chances, with the corresponding risk of more misses. The break-even point, i.e. 50/50 chance of a score or a miss, occurs when the criterion is set at K_2.

To return once again to a more applied approach, it is useful to consider the work of Alain and his co-workers with respect to the racquet games — squash, badminton, racquetball and tennis. In their 1978 study Alain & Proteau were concerned with the assignment of probabilities to their opponents' shots during such racquet games. Rallies in normal games were filmed without the players being aware of which particular rallies were being selected. After each filmed rally the game was stopped, and players were asked questions about the shots used during the rally. In particular they were asked: What was the probability that you, as a defensive player, assigned to the shot of your opponent? Answers were to be based on a five-category scale — 10%, 30%, 50%, 70% or 90%.

From the filmed sequences the relation between the total body displacement of the defensive player and the direction of his opponent's shot, i.e. the degree of anticipation, was also worked out.

Figure 6.9 shows the relation between the proportion of anticipatory movements and the subjective probabilities assigned to the opponent's shot. The higher the probability the defensive player subjectively attributed to an event, the higher the proportion of anticipatory movements which accompanied it. Alain and Proteau draw attention to the sharp increase in the proportion of anticipatory movements when the subjective probability shifts from 0.5 to 0.7. This, they suggest, represents a threshold point when the advantages accompanying an anticipatory movement overcome the occasional negative pay-offs associated with it.

In a subsequent study (Alain & Girardin, 1978), the finals of the 1976 Montreal Open Racquetball Championships were videotaped. From the analysis, four positions were identified (Table 6.2) from which more than

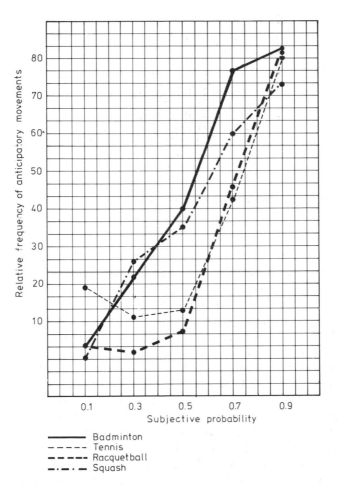

Figure 6.9. Subjective probability and anticipatory movements. From Alain & Proteau (1978); reprinted with permission of the authors.

3% of all shots were driven. The relative frequency of 'kill' and 'drop' shots from these four positions were computed. The table indicates that for each of the categories of final (A, B and C) offensive shots were used more often from positions 2 and 6 than from positions 7 and 8.

Table 6.3 shows the same results expressed in terms of the amount of uncertainty conveyed by these types of shot. This can be seen to increase systematically with the distance separating the striker of the shot from the front wall, i.e. the player did not maximise uncertainty *irrespective* of the situation at hand.

Table 6.2. Percentage use of offensive shots (kill shots and drop shots) as a function of positions 2, 6, 7 and 8 for each player category.

	2	6	7	8
Class A	59.5	55	35	25
Class B	58	50	43.5	24
Class C	48.5	54.5	40.4	22

X = author of shot; O = opponent.
From Alain & Girardin (1978); reprinted with permission of the authors.

Table 6.3. Amount of uncertainty conveyed by use of offensive shots (kill and drop).

	2	6	7	8
Class A	0.75	0.86	1.5	2.0
Class B	0.76	1.01	1.2	2.1
Class C	1.10	0.90	1.3	2.2

X = author of shot; O = opponent.
From Alain & Girardin (1978); reprinted with permission of the authors.

The amount of uncertainty was computed in 'bits' using the formula:

$$\log_2 \frac{1}{p^1}$$

The results of these experiments, deriving from real-life situations, illustrate the cognitive involvement of players and the kind of modelling and decision-making in which they are likely to be involved. In the last experiment of Alain and Girardin it would be possible to speak in terms of *affordances* of the situation to the players. It would then be necessary for the player to appreciate which situational information affords which particular action. The detection of such affordances would be dependent on what the player had in his repertoire as well as the particular stage of a game. Thus, while a particular situation might afford a 'kill' shot, the player might prefer to prolong the duration of the rally in the interest of tiring his opponent.

6.5. Ballistic actions

In so far as most of the actions carried out in sport situations are ballistic in nature — in the sense that they take such a short period of time ($\pm$ 150 ms) that feedback can have no steering function — it is not possible for a player to wait until his opponent's action is under way before he makes a decision as to his own course of action. Inherent limitations in his own reaction and movement times would result in the decision being made too late to provide an effective counter. These limitations have not unnaturally led to a series of experiments directed at the discovery of the amount of information, or the time which is necessary to pick up and/or process such information, in order to make particular decisions, and the way in which this might differ dependent on the experience of the player.

Typical of the paradigms used in this respect is that of Jones & Miles (1978). Using samples of professional lawn tennis coaches ($N=32$) and undergraduates ($N=60$) as subjects, they presented them with cine-film 'clips' showing an international player in the act of serving. Subjects were required to indicate on a diagrammatic representation of the court the place, from amongst three possibilities, where they thought the ball would land. Three conditions were utilised. In condition A the film was cut off 336 ms after the impact of the ball on the racquet: in condition B, 126 ms after impact, and in condition C, 42 ms before impact. The result for coaches (divided into two categories) and undergraduates are given in Table 6.4. Significant differences between coaches and undergraduates were shown under conditions B and C. While the differences between the top-grade and other coaches were in the direction that might be predicted (in terms of experience), they did not reach an acceptable level of significance.

Further analysis demonstrated that at least some of the coaches scored significantly better than 'chance' under condition C, indicating that the use of information from the movements of an opponent before the moment of

Table 6.4. Means and standard deviations of percentage of correct responses for three groups of subjects

	Condition A	Condition B	Condition C
Top trainers	75.40 (12.93)	78.41 (12.61)	42.38 (26.18)
Other trainers	78.30 (9.70)	75.00 (16.77)	38.06 (16.30)
First-year student	74.35 (12.56)	68.75 (15.35)	27.01 (12.66)

From Jones & Miles (1978); reprinted with permission of Journal of Human Movement Studies.

impact is at least possible. While the inexperienced players produced very successful results when the ball could be seen until shortly before it landed, their performance deteriorated markedly when information was cut off shortly before impact (condition C).

In a related study addressed to visual cues in ice-hockey goal-tending, Salmela & Fiorito (1979) required subjects to observe filmed sequences of an ice-hockey player approaching the net and directing a shot to one of the four target (12-inches square) corners of the goal. The player skated along the middle of the rink and made the required shot to the designated corner in a manner that neither camouflaged nor exaggerated the normal shooting action. In addition to indicating verbally to which of the targets they believed the ball to be directed, subjects were required to indicate their degree of response confidence on a $1-5$ Likert scale in both the horizontal and vertical axes. The film sequences were edited so that two, four or eight images ($\frac{1}{12}$ s, $\frac{1}{6}$ s, $\frac{1}{3}$ s, respectively) were occluded prior to the impact of the stick on the puck. Thirty-four young (mean age 15.8 years) goal-tenders comprised the sample which viewed the three film 'clips' presented in random order. For the analysis, four gradations of response success were used:

TS total success, i.e. correct target selected
HS correct side (left or right), incorrect target
VS correct height (upper or lower), incorrect target
NS both side and height incorrect.

Table 6.5 gives the overall distribution of results for these possibilities. Analysis indicated that the pattern of results was significantly different from that which would have been achieved by guessing at random. Table 6.6 gives the results for the three occlusion conditions (two, four, or eight images). While the ratio TS/NS decreased (3.2, 2.4 and 2.1, respectively) across conditions, the ratio HS/VS (1.5, 1.2 and 1.6, respectively) remained more stable. Analysis of the confidence ratings showed subjects to be more confident in the horizontal than in the vertical plane; the response confidence decreasing, as might be expected, with increased periods of occlusion.

Table 6.5. Overall distribution of response alternatives for success in goal-tending predictions.

Response category	Frequency	Percentage
Total success	944	38.6
Horizontal success	666	27.2
Vertical success	466	19.0
No success	372	15.2

From Salmela & Fiorito (1979); reprinted with permission of the authors.

Table 6.6. Distribution of response alternatives as a function of period of occlusion for goal-tending predictions.

Moment of stopping film	Measure of success				Relation	
	TS	HS	VS	NS	TS/NS	HS/VS
− 2 frames	345	217	147	107	3.2	1.5
− 4 frames	304	214	173	125	2.4	1.2
− 8 frames	295	235	146	140	2.1	1.6

From Salmela & Fiorito (1979); reprinted with permission of the authors.
Abbreviations are explained in the text.

That use of information from a player, prior to the shot being taken, may be necessary for successful goal-tending in ice-hockey is apparent when, it is known for example, that the average speed of the puck shot by a professional player from the blue line will be many times faster than the human reaction time (Drouin & Salmela, 1975). The finding of superior performance in the horizontal plane when compared to the vertical is interesting and deserves further attention, particularly as success is relatively unaffected by changes in the occluded periods. This may indicate — as Salmela & Fiorito propose — that goal-tenders make sequential judgements with the left−right decision occurring earlier in time.

While individual differences are less marked in this study than in the Jones & Miles (1978) work, since the sample was relatively more heterogeneous, they were still apparent. Souliere & Salmela (1979) returned to this problem in a partial replication study on volleyball players, smashing to one of three widely separated targets. In the so-called non-stressed condition, subjects were required to dive to the simulated target position marked on the floor of the laboratory within a time interval before the ball on the film would have touched the floor. Four occluded conditions of the film were used — complete (approach, ball contact and trajectory) or partial (either approach to contact or to two, or four images before contact). Figure 6.10 shows the percentage of correct responses under the four conditions for the three ability groups. Significant differences between the three groups were found, with experienced players being able to make their predictions from cues much earlier in the filmed sequence than inexperienced players. Absence of information about the trajectory was the most important cause of performance decrement. The effect of time-stress (Figure 6.11) was devastating, reducing the rate of success to less than 10%.

One of the problems about the series of experiments presented is that while it is true that the amount of information available to subjects can be varied, no answer is provided to the question of what information is actually used and if, for example, all the available information is made use of. One method of extending this kind of approach is to check on the sampling

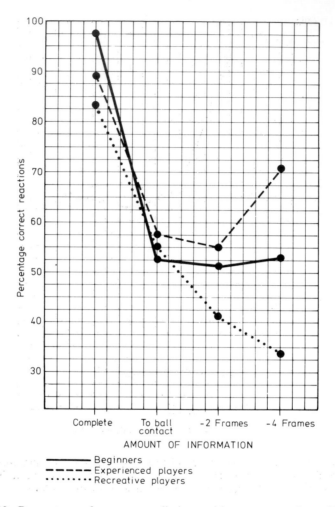

Percentage correct reactions (y-axis); AMOUNT OF INFORMATION: Complete, To ball contact, -2 Frames, -4 Frames (x-axis)

——— Beginners
– – – Experienced players
·········· Recreative players

Figure 6.10. Percentage of correct predictions with respect to the calibre of the player under the four viewing conditions. From Souliere & Salmela (1979); reprinted with permission of the authors.

techniques of the players by recording their eye movements during the presentation of the film. While this does not answer the above criticism, since *looking* does not necessarily imply *seeing*, it is a step in the right direction. Bard, Fleury, Carriere & Halle (1980) utilised this kind of approach in an analysis of gymnastic judges' visual search patterns. The problem for such judges is that they are presented with a gymnastic event which occupies a comparatively short interval of time. It is a 'one-off' event, and on the basis of the information they are able to pick up from that event they have

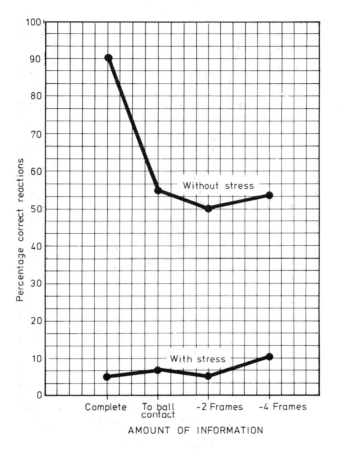

Figure 6.11. Percentage of correct predictions for the four viewing conditions irrespective of the calibre of the player and under a stress or no-stress condition. From Souliere & Salmela (1979); reprinted with permission of the authors.

to make a decision about the extent to which it deviates from some established model as well as making a qualitative judgement. The problem facing Bard *et al* (1980) was whether 'the structural limitation for information processing might not allow them to solve problems according to established requirements'. Obviously, under the time restrictions implicit in judging gymnastic events, it pays to know where to look for the pertinent information.

In their study Bard *et al* used a sample of seven gymnastic judges—four national (experienced) and three local (novice). Judges were required to evaluate from film 'clips', two Olympic Games compulsory balance beam routines and two optional routines performed by two national-level gymnasts. Sixteen-millimetre colour films were used, taken three metres from the centre and perpendicular to the balance beam simulating the position of the chief judge. The baseline for errors was derived from an evaluation of the four routines, undertaken by an expert judge prior to the experiment.

Judges' eye movement patterns were traced by means of a NAC Eye-movement Recorder linked to a videotape camera. This allowed the routine being evaluated and judges' eye fixations to be recorded simultaneously. An eye fixation was defined as a discrete look between eye displacements, lasting at least 100 to 125 ms. Three measures were recorded:

1. the total number of eye fixations for each routine,
2. the location of each eye fixation,
3. the number of errors made.

The number of eye fixations for the two groups of judges are given in Table 6.7. Although expert judges had 27% less fixations than novice judges, the differences were not significant (due in part to the excessive variance between the novice judges). More fixations were made by both groups of judges for the optional routines. Table 6.8, however, expresses the location of fixations by routine and level of experience. Significant differences between the judges are apparent for body parts. Experts had more fixations on the upper part of the gymnast's body while novices concentrated their attention on the legs. While novice judges detected only half the number of errors detected by the experts, the difference was not significant. Once again, this was the result of large variability between the novice judges.

The fact that all the judges made more fixations for the optional routines gives credence to Bard *et al*'s contention that the predictability of the sequence of movements favours the selectivity of the search pattern. Uncertainty seems to be a major factor affecting the decision-making of the judges. The extent to which more experienced people are able to operate in sophisticated pattern recognition is an important consideration in this respect.

Table 6.7. Number of eye fixations (mean and standard deviation) by level of expertise and type of routine.

	Compulsory	Optional	Combined
Expert judges			
Mean	69.44	94.65	82.05
Standard deviation	22.28	19.38	
Novice judges			
Mean	94.65	129.41	111.66
Standard deviation	16.45	52.33	

From Bard, Fleury, Carriere & Halle (1980); reprinted with permission of the American Alliance for Health, Physical Education, Recreation and Dance.

Table 6.8. Location of eye fixations by routine and level of experience (in percentages).

Type of routine	Expert judges	Novice judges
Compulsory routines		
Head and arms	31.5	14
Trunk	29	30.2
Hips	23.9	24.5
Legs	15.6	31.2
Optional routines		
Head and arms	26.3	23.3
Trunk	32.5	27.3
Hips	23.8	21.9
Legs	17.4	27.5

From Bard, Fleury, Carrière & Halle (1980); reprinted with permission of the American Alliance for Health, Physical Education, Recreation and Dance.

It will receive further attention in the Abernethy & Russell (1987) study, which will be discussed in more detail later.

The preference of novice judges for information from the legs rather than the upper body is difficult to interpret, although as Bard *et al* suggest, they normally evaluate less expert gymnasts in whom foot and leg placement constitutes a major problem.

Two interpretations of the differences in error detection between experts and novices given by Bard *et al* are of interest. In the first place novices are less familiar with refined discriminations, i.e. they may not appreciate the subtlety of some of the information which constitutes an error. In the second place their greater number of fixations brings with it an increase in the number of inter-fixation intervals — periods of time in which detailed information cannot be picked up.

While the studies cited so far are informative, and point in the same general direction, there remains a further interpretive problem. It has to be asked whether the stimulus film 'clips' for different target areas (particularly in the ice-hockey goal-tending experiment) are 'equivalent' just because the same time occlusion intervals are used for all targets. This is a question which intrigued Tyldesley & Bootsma (1981) and precipitated their research on perceptual information picked up by soccer goalkeepers. Initial experiments to be described here focused on some issues of this general theme.

The basic paradigm used in these experiments was that of presenting to football players of varying levels of experience, slides depicting head-on views of a penalty kick action recorded from the goalkeeper's position and with the ball on the penalty spot. Subjects were made aware that the slides presented depicted action 'stills' in which the penalty-taker can direct his kick in one of only four directions (high/low; left/right). Subjects were presented with a central 'start' key and a choice of four response keys on a board in front of them, reflecting the four possible directions of the shots — top left, top right, bottom left, bottom right. Two basic questions were addressed:

1. Do experts extract different information from a display than less expert players?
2. Do they process this information faster?

With respect to the latter question, Tyldesley & Bootsma (Tyldesley, 1981) were able to show that even using slide presentations (as compared to film 'clips') a group of experienced players demonstrated faster reaction times than inexperienced players when using either compatible or incompatible displays (Figure 6.12). Two interpretations of this data seem plausible. Firstly, that through extensive learning experiences the relevant information sources become very familiar and/or the irrelevant features are better filtered out. Thus, there may be — along the lines already suggested with respect to the experiments of Chase & Chi (1980) (page 163) — more elaborate pattern recognition procedures which can more quickly be put into operation by the expert. The alternative proposal, already suggested, is that the same information is picked up and/or processed by both groups of players but that the expert picks up or processes at a higher rate.

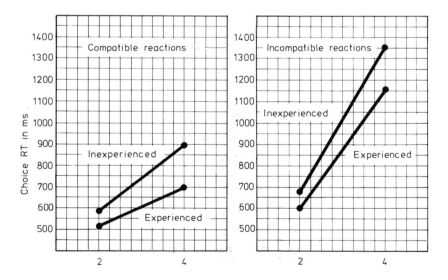

Figure 6.12. Differences in choice reaction time to football displays with compatible and incompatible S−R configurations for inexperienced and experienced players. From Tyldesley (1981); reprinted with permission of the author.

These suggestions give rise to a number of possible experimental paradigms. However, Tyldesley & Bootsma (1981) for a follow-up experiment chose to focus attention on the question already addressed by Bard *et al* (1980) as to whether experts and non-experts pick up qualitatively different information. To make this kind of determination, players of different experience levels were put into an experimental paradigm similar to that of the previous experiment but with the addition of eye-movement monitoring apparatus in order to determine their scanning behaviour. Figure 6.13 shows typical scanning behaviour of experienced players. In the paradigms used, slides were presented and subjects were required to verbally report the outcome of the situation as quickly as possible. Averaged over 60 trials the non-experienced player was shown to have a longer fixation time (22.6 ms). His eyes were fixated on parts of the display for longer than the more experienced — suggesting that he had more difficulty picking up information from these centres.

If the first ten saccades of the trials are analysed then the trained player seems to scan more systematically, his eyes moving gradually up and down the right side of the opponent's body. Indeed, since in kicking a football the opponent pivots around a relatively stable left leg, the variability of body locations on the left side varies little from one shot to the next. It is a reasonable — although as yet an untested assumption — that for right footed

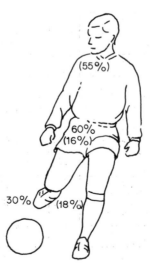

Figure 6.13. Scanning patterns of an experienced player. Frequencies of first and second (between brackets) fixations during the four-choice reaction time task. From Tyldesley & Bootsma (1981); reprinted with permission of the authors.

players most information comes from the knee, hip and shoulder on the right side of the body, regarding where he intends to aim the ball.

In contrast, the non-experienced player was shown to saccade more irregularly and also from side to side across the opponent's body (e.g. left hip—right foot—left knee). If a global assumption is made that the right side of the display presents relevant and useful information, then over nine fixations the expert spent 100% of the time (128 ms) viewing 'relevant' details. The non-experienced player, on the other hand, spent 95% of his total fixation time (184 ms) viewing 'less relevant' parts of the display. Saccade times between subjects did not differ significantly (10—20 ms).

These findings obviously require elaboration and replication with a more representative group of subjects. They do, however, open up interesting methodological approaches to problems which stand central with respect to information pick-up in sport.

The work of Abernethy has extended the earlier studies on perceptual prediction identifying the source of the information used by badminton players to predict the final position of the shuttle. But even here, as Buckolz, Prapavesis & Fairs (1988) have stated, this study has nothing to say about the specific cues within these sources that enable such predictions to be made. These authors maintain that such information is useful to the athlete only when the specific cues in these locations have been identified and their predictive value pointed out.

This is precisely what Buckolz *et al* (1988) attempted to do in their study on tennis. More specifically, an attempt was made to delineate the *specific* advance cues tennis players report they use to predict their opponents' passing shots (i.e. forehand and backhand; cross-court, down-the-line, and lob). Additionally, these research workers examined possible differences between players of advanced and intermediate levels of ability with a view to determining whether their skills were due to some extent to a comparatively greater efficiency in identifying and using telegraphic cues from their opponent's body.

In their study, 44 subjects (25 male, 19 female, 15—16 years of age) possessing either intermediate ($N=23$) or advanced ($N=21$) tennis ability on the basis of criteria stemming from their membership of the All-Canadian Tennis Academy in London, Ontario, took part. Three of the forty-four subjects were randomly selected and filmed in a competitive match against another player from the Academy. Successfully executed down-the-line (DL), cross-court (XC) and lob passing shots from both the forehand and the backhand were retained. Filming was at two different speeds (24 or 48 frames per second). Five film strips were constructed for each of the six possible passing shots. Each strip was appropriately ordered to allow the subjects a progressively greater amount of information. To accomplish this, the film strips all began 12 frames prior to racquet-ball contact. Each differed, however, as to its termination point, ending at one of five possible locations (i.e. -4 or -2 frames before racquet-ball contact, at contact (0 frame) or $+2$ and $+4$ frames post-contact).

Subjects for the perceptual study were required to provide written responses to questions about a series of such films covering the six examples of passing-shot types:

(a) What is the passing shot being attempted?
(b) What cue(s) did you employ as a basis for your prediction?

In summary, three main factors were examined:
1. Skill level (intermediate vs advanced).
2. Passing-shot type (forehand and backhand lob, cross-court, and down-the-line shots).
3. Information extent.

The dependent variables of interest were:

(a) The correct prediction percentages, calculated as a function of the levels of the three main factors.
(b) The prediction accuracy—associated with cues declared as having served as the bases for predictions.

From the results, Buckolz *et al* (1988) were able to demonstrate the existence of advance 'body-language' cues that allow accurate forecasting of passing-shot location (particularly for the forehand). Generally, advanced players predicted passing-shot type more accurately than intermediate-level players. In some instances this difference in accuracy could be attributed to the fact that the intermediate players were unaware of what the telegraphic cues were (e.g. backhand shots) while in other situations, the difference in prediction ability was primarily due to the intermediate players' more frequent failure to detect the presence of known telegraphic cues (i.e. forehand shots).

6.5.1. INDIVIDUAL DIFFERENCES

It is interesting from the point of view of individual differences in decision-making to reconsider an earlier experiment of Whiting & Hutt (1972) on the effects of personality and ability on speed of decisions regarding the directional aspects of ball flight. This study was concerned with individual differences in information sampling time, their significance for sport, in this case table-tennis, and possible sources of explanation of such differences. In seeking possible sources of explanation Whiting and Hutt were attracted by the work to Eysenck (1947, 1967) and Broadbent (1956). Eysenck had accumulated evidence to suggest that, in tasks which provide a speed—accuracy trade-off, extraverts tend to choose speed in preference to accuracy and introverts to choose accuracy in preference to speed. Possible explanations proposed by Eysenck are: (1) the tendency for extraverts to have more involuntary rest pauses because of a greater rate of accumulation of reactive inhibition which would lead to more errors; (2) cortical excitation leading to a greater control over risk-taking behaviour being greater in introverted persons; and (3) in a culture where there is a tendency for social pressure on accuracy, the ease of conditioning exhibited by subjects towards the introverted end of the continuum making them more cautious. In view of the earlier discussion of risk-taking behaviour, these kinds of interpretation have an intrinsic appeal.

Broadbent (1956), on the other hand, prefers an alternative explanation not involving the concept of inhibition. He proposes individual differences in sampling strategies. The more introverted person, on this explanation, would be a 'long-time sampler' and the more extraverted a 'short-time sampler'.

For an experimental investigation of these possibilities, the apparatus shown in Figure 6.14 was constructed. A table-tennis ball machine projected balls onto a table-tennis table, the impact point being directly in the centre of an aperture (3 x 3.75 inches) of a black screen which hid the equipment from the subject's view. By altering the projection angle of the wheels, which was not detectable by the subjects, balls could be projected with or without side-spin so that on striking the table they would travel either directly towards the subject or deviate to his right or left by $10°$. The time of projection was recorded by means of photocells and the speed of response by the difference between time of projection and time of pressing of response button by the subject.

In addition to the task of detecting as quickly as possible the direction in which the ball was projected, subjects were also required to perform a three-choice reaction-time task in the same situation.

As it happened no significant effects of personality on speed of decision-making in this table-tennis situation were found. However, reclassifying the subjects into three ability groups did produce some interesting findings (Table 6.9).

Analysis of variance of the decision times and the choice reaction times showed significant differences to be present. The decision times and choice reaction times of the high-ability and average table-tennis players were significantly different from the non-players ($p<0.01$) but not significantly different from each other. There was no significant difference in errors made between the three groups of subjects. Thus the argument that differences in decision time and choice reaction time could be accounted for in terms of frequency of error was not tenable.

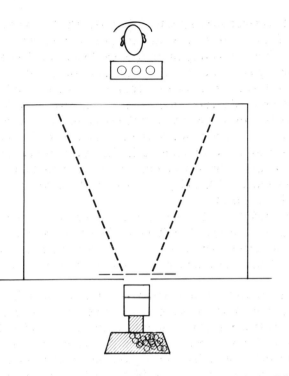

Figure 6.14. Ball projection machine and apparatus set-up. From Whiting & Hutt (1972); reprinted with permission of the Helen Dwight Reid Educational Foundation. Published by Heldref Publications, 4000 Albermark St, NW, Washington, DC 20016. Copyright 1972.

Table 6.9. Mean decision times and standard deviations for the parameter of ball flight direction (B F D) and choice reaction time (C R T) for the three ability groups.

Ability group	BFD mean (ms)	Standard deviation	CRT mean (ms)	Standard deviation
High ability	431.1	23.65	329.5	20.59
Average ability	438.5	28.63	323.7	23.93
Non-games players	467.1	32.91	365.1	29.86

From Whiting & Hutt (1972); reprinted with permission of the Helen Dwight Read Educational Foundation. (Published by Heldref Publications, 4000 Albermark St, NW, Washington, DC 20016; copyright 1972.)

The possibility that decision times were merely reflections of a more complex choice reaction-time situation was tested by computing correlations between decision times and choice reaction times for the three ability groups:

$r = 0.41$ ($p>0.05$) high ability group
$r = 0.67$ ($p<0.01$) average-ability group
$r = 0.83$ ($p<0.01$) non-players

Thus, while for the average-ability group and the non-players correlations were significant and high, for the high-ability group the correlation was not significant. The suggestion is that for the high-ability group another kind of information is being used in the decision task than in the choice reaction-time task, whereas for the other two groups of players both tasks are in fact similar. On being questioned the high-ability players maintained that in the decision task they could detect the spin of the ball. There was no way of checking this contention. A further significant finding was the faster choice reaction times of the players in comparison with the non-players. The full significance of this has not yet been elaborated upon, but it received attention in the work of Tyldesley and Bootsma peviously discussed.

The reaction and decision times reported in this study are interesting in the light of the more recent study of McLeod (1987) on visual reaction time in high-speed ball games, namely cricket. In this study the cricket batsman faced a bowling machine on a wicket covered with Recticel matting. Under the matting, and not visible to the batsman, were a number of 1 cm cross-section half-round dowel rods, 1.5 m long, spaced a few centimetres apart and laid parallel to the line of flight of the ball. Thus, any ball landing between the dowels would come straight through to the batsman without changing direction. If, however, the ball should strike the mat in the vicinity of a dowel it would change direction unpredictably to the left or right and by an unpredictable amount. The change appeared to be more exaggerated than a top-class batsman would meet most of the time. Subjects used in this study were three international cricket batsmen. An analysis of high-speed film of these batsmen showed reaction times of around 200 ms—similar to those found in traditional laboratory studies. More specifically, no evidence could be provided of any adjustment of stroke in less than about 190 ms after the bounce of the ball.

There are two constraints on the validity of this study, however, which need to be borne in mind. In the first place the analysis of reaction times was based on the assumption that the information that the ball has changed direction is available to the batsman *as soon as* the ball has left the ground (McLeod does, however, allow the possibility of a delay of 10—20 ms before the direction becomes clearly apparent). That this assumption is not necessarily valid is suggested by the decision times reported in Table 6.9 with respect to changing direction of the flight path of a table-tennis ball. This statement must also be qualified, since the considerable extra weight of the cricket ball would probably make any directional change more immediate and more obvious — nevertheless, the situation sketched by McLeod represents a choice and not a simple reaction time paradigm, the ball adopting one of three possible directions: left, right or straight on. Reaction times of 200 ms to a *three-choice condition* might then be considered to be extremely fast! Compare those reported in Table 6.9 (329.5−365.1).

Secondly, as McLeod suggests, the response — movement of the bat — involves considerable inertia. It may therefore be slower to become apparent to the observer (data analyst) than, say, a simple arm movement. Thus, the actual *initiation* of a change in the direction of the movement may be somewhat earlier than the movement of the bat itself might suggest.

A second experiment by McLeod (1987), the results of which run counter to some of those discussed earlier in this chapter, was addressed to the perceptual abilities of professional cricketers. A film was made, from a position at head height behind the batsman, of the approach and delivery of a cricket ball by an international fast bowler. The run-up of the bowler was about 20 paces and the ball was about 700−800 ms in flight. The film used in the experiment comprised the approach of the bowler and a variable amount of the initial flight of the ball. The film was occluded either at the frame where the ball left the bowler's hand or, 80, 160 or 240 ms later. A film which contained two examples of each length (short, good or overpitched) at each of the four exposure durations was prepared. These were arranged in random order with blank film between them. Subjects viewed the film and for each clip they made a forced-choice judgement of 'length' by ticking one of three shots labelled 'short', 'good length' and 'overpitched' on a piece of paper. Three international players and 22 non-expert subjects took part in the experiment.

The results are given in Table 6.10. When the ball is in the bowler's hand neither group does better than chance. In this respect McLeod makes the following observation:

> In a similar study, Abernethy & Russell (1984) found that when skilled batsmen watched only the run-up of bowlers (that is, they watched a film which terminated at the delivery frame) they were able to predict ball flight parameters at better than chance. It is possible that the difference between that result and the one found here is that Abernethy & Russell stopped all film clips at the moment of delivery. This would force the viewer to concentrate on any cues which were available in the run-up. In my films, where such deliveries were mixed in with clips showing ball flight information, there was less incentive to concentrate on the run-up and so, perhaps, less information was picked up.

On the basis of this study, McLeod concludes that professional cricketers take roughly as long as recreational players to pick up ball flight information from films of bowlers. This is, of course, contrary to the expert/novice

Table 6.10. The percentage of correct judgements of length (short, good length, or overpitched) as a function of the amount of ball flight viewed.

	Experts: viewing time (ms)				Non-experts: viewing time (ms)			
	0	80	160	240	0	80	160	240
Short	17	0	33	100	29	25	36	100
Good length	83	66	100	100	54	54	93	100
Overpitched	0	100	100	100	11	93	93	100

Chance performance = 33%; ball flight viewed varies from 0 ms, where the film stops just as the ball leaves the bowlers' hand, to 240 ms.
From McLeod (1987); reprinted with permission of the publisher.

distinctions discussed in the latter part of this chapter. A possible interpretation, perhaps, needs to be sought in the determination of the amount of experience that is necessary to be able to make quick perceptual decisions within a particular sport. For example, in the tennis experiment of Jones & Miles (1978), discussed above, top-level trainers did not differ significantly from ordinary trainers in terms of their perceptual judgements but both were superior to novices. In a similar way, in the experiment discussed in this section, top-level table-tennis players did not differ significantly from average table-tennis players in their decision and reaction times, but both groups differed significantly from novices. Thus the McLeod finding has to be seen in this light. Overall, these joint findings raise the interesting question as to how much experience is necessary within a particular sport for optimal perceptual functioning?

In a more recent extension of the methodology being discussed in the greater part of this section, i.e. prediction of the events from film clips, Abernethy & Russell (1987) carried out a comparative study of 'expert' (national standard) and 'novice' badminton players. In a laboratory paradigm they presented players with the display of an opposing player filmed from an on-court perspective. The display was manipulated by either varying the time course of information provided (temporal occlusion, as, for example in the Jones and Miles study) or by maintaining a constant time-course of information and masking visibility to selected display features (event occlusion). Temporal occlusion varied from 167 ms prior to racquet−shuttle contact to 83 ms subsequent to contact. Event occlusion involved masking of the player's racquet but not the arm; occluding player's face and head; occluding player's lower body, and a control condition in which irrelevant background features were occluded. Eye-movement recording of the players' visual search patterns was also made.

Under the temporal occlusion conditions, expert players were shown to make significantly fewer prediction errors under all conditions except the 167 ms condition. The experts' superiority lies somewhere in the region of the time interval 167 to 83 ms prior to racquet—shuttle contact. Under the spatial occlusion condition both racquet and arm were shown to be significant sources of anticipatory information for the expert players, whereas only the racquet was significant for the novices.

The question to which these findings give rise is whether these differences between experts and novices can be attributed to visual search strategies. Evidence in this respect is provided by the eye-movement analyses. No differences were shown between experts and novices with respect to their initial preparatory strategy, i.e. both groups of players fixated the screen centre followed by, on the appearance of the film display, a general orientation to gross regions of the opponents' body — trunk, head or lower body. These initial fixations, as Abernethy & Russell suggest, seem to be concerned with picking up early visual information about the opponents' direction of movement and the kind of shot he is likely to play (forehand, backhand, etc.) — reminiscent of the Alain & Proteau studies reported earlier. As soon as the opponents' stroke execution commenced, attention switched to the racquet head and/or arm — the expert being more able to utilise advance information from the arm action. These differences, however, do not reflect differences in the eye-fixation distributions. Both experts and novices fixated for equal periods of time upon the racquet and supporting arm but, it would appear, only the experts had the necessary prior knowledge to extract usable features from the arm. Once again, 'looking' does not necessarily imply 'seeing' (Tables 6.11 and 6.12). This finding has to be seen as contrary to that of Tyldesley's & Bootsma's earlier reported finding, using static displays of footballers where novices were shown to have longer fixation times. This may reflect an inherent difference in static and dynamic displays.

Abernethy & Russell make the further salient point that experimental studies of this kind that use a dynamic display task may act to restrict the search orders which are possible. In this sense the use of static displays is artificial in that all aspects of the display are, at all times, available, whereas in a dynamic display informativeness is restricted primarily to those spatial regions which contain features changing as a function of time.

6.6. Perception—action coupling

One of the criticisms that might be levelled at all the studies in Section 6.5 is that they focus on perception to the exclusion of action, whereas in real-life sport it is precisely the subtlety of the perception—action coupling which is crucial to success. While some concession was made to this issue in the Souliere & Salmela (1979) study, since they required their volleyball players to dive to the appropriate simulated target position, a degree of artificiality is still apparent. In addition, these studies are restricted to one aspect of decision-making in sport, namely, spatial positioning. In this respect, den

Table 6.11. Mean percentage of trial time allocated to each fixation location expressed as a function of both temporal occlusion and expertise.

Fixation location	Temporal occlusion conditions				
	t1	t2	t3	t4	t5
Racquet (%r)					
Experts	67.48	65.75	68.74	68.28	69.92
Novices	60.87	61.01	64.85	66.93	60.58
Shuttle outflight (%s)					
Experts	0.00	0.00	0.06	0.18	6.25
Novices	0.00	0.00	0.00	0.02	10.23
Trunk (%t)					
Experts	5.36	5.41	4.87	5.36	3.27
Novices	8.20	8.58	7.68	6.76	6.90
Head (%h)					
Experts	6.64	7.88	6.45	6.98	5.21
Novices	11.91	11.73	10.95	9.35	9.00
Feet (%f)					
Experts	1.29	1.67	2.39	1.94	1.62
Novices	3.94	4.04	3.00	3.40	2.68
Screen centre (%x)					
Experts	12.61	12.06	11.60	10.39	8.71
Novices	11.39	10.46	9.50	8.90	7.50
Not determinable (%n)					
Experts	6.78	7.55	6.89	6.86	5.03
Novices	4.08	4.34	4.02	4.63	3.15

[a] Anticipatory saccades for shuttle outflight.
From Abernethy & Russell (1987); reprinted with permission of Elsevier Science Publishers BV, Amsterdam.

Brinker, Stabler, van Wieringen & Whiting (1986) have pointed out the limitation of using one-dimensional tasks in learning studies given the fact that success in many everyday skills is usually indexed by both temporal and spatial criteria. This is confirmed in the high-speed cine analysis of Alderson, Sully & Sully (1974) of one-handed catching. They demonstrate the need (early in the flight-path of the ball) to position the hand in the general region of the flight-path followed, some 50 ms later, by a more precise 'fine-tuning' of this position. The timing (grasping) of the catching action which follows on was shown to have a tolerance band of approximately 30 ms for success. Not only do such typical sport actions involve both spatial and temporal constraints, but they would also appear to involve a series of sequential decisions. However, some caution must be exercised in relation to the latter since questioning, of expert catchers at least, will indicate that introspection on their part will provide very little insight into how they are able to do what they do! They are aware that they have caught the ball but not of consciously making decisions. The catch is, as it were, the decision!

Table 6.12. Mean percentage of trial time allocated to each fixation location expressed as a function of both event occlusion and expertise.

Fixation location	Event occlusion conditions					
	e1	e2	e3	e4	e5	t3
Racquet (%r)						
Experts	65.46	66.13	66.13	66.41	68.52	68.74
Novices	63.24	64.26	66.35	65.23	65.41	64.85
Shuttle outflight (%s)						
Experts	0.00	0.00	0.00	0.00	0.00	0.06
Novices	0.00	0.00	0.00	0.00	0.00	0.00
Trunk (%t)						
Experts	4.81	3.79	4.77	3.24	3.34	4.87
Novices	6.38	6.58	5.55	6.14	6.40	7.68
Head (%h)						
Experts	5.06	5.26	4.20	7.66	4.86	6.45
Novices	10.18	10.28	9.22	9.68	8.09	10.95
Feet (%f)						
Experts	1.39	1.29	0.55	0.89	1.07	2.39
Novices	0.98	0.60	1.09	0.45	0.99	3.00
Screen centre (%x)						
Experts	19.00	17.53	18.11	17.57	17.42	11.60
Novices	17.42	15.62	15.57	18.04	16.37	9.50
Not determinable (%n)						
Experts	4.61	6.24	6.94	5.69	6.06	5.89
Novices	1.80	2.80	2.48	2.50	2.73	4.02

From Abernethy & Russell (1987); reprinted with permission of Elsevier Science Publishers BV, Amsterdam.

While, in situations in which the objective is to catch a ball, the criterion will be 'caught' or 'not caught', there are other situations—for example teaching and coaching—in which interest will focus on the reasons for not catching. In such cases the separation out of spatial and temporal decision faults may well be important. Thus, while in earlier studies of Whiting and his co-workers (Sharp & Whiting, 1974, 1975; Whiting & Sharp, 1973; Whiting, Alderson & Sanderson, 1973; Whiting, Gill & Stephenson, 1970) players were shown, on occasions, to be capable of highly successful catching when only able to see the ball for approximately 100 ms early in its flight, it was unclear what errors were made under such circumstances when balls were not caught.

Smyth & Marriott (1982) faced this issue in addressing the question as to whether it is necessary, for success, to view the catching arm and hand when making one-handed catches. The rationale for needing to look at the arm/hand was their contention that articular proprioception is, in itself, not sufficient to provide accurate information about limb position, particularly

Table 6.13 Means and standard deviations for successful catches in each condition and frequencies for positions and grasp errors in each condition.

	Opaque screen[a]	Transparent screen[b]	No screen[b]
Mean number of catches out of 20 trials	9.21	15.04	17.50
S.D.	3.78	3.65	3.16
Total number of position errors	183	48	18
Total number of grasp errors	76	71	42

[a] Hand not visible.
[b] Hand visible.
From Smyth & Marriott (1982); reprinted with permission of the publisher.

in those ball skills in which the eyes are thought to be occupied with tracking the ball. Smyth and Marriott (Table 6.13) demonstrated more position errors when the arm/hand could not be seen (the catching arm/hand being occluded by a screen attached to the side of catcher's head).

However, some qualifications to this finding were deemed necessary following a study of Whiting, Savelsbergh & Faber (1988) in which persistently 'good' and persistently 'poor' catchers were used. While occlusion of the catching arm and hand resulted in a significant increase in position errors for the 'poor' catchers it had no significant effect on the positional errors of the 'good' catchers (Table 6.14). The information used by 'good' catchers in positioning their catching arm/hand would appear to differ from that used by 'poor' catchers. While occlusion of the catching arm/hand had no significant effect on the number of grasp (timing) errors for either category of catchers, significant differences could be demonstrated for both categories of catchers when the information available was further reduced by allowing a luminous ball, or ball and catching hand only, to be seen in an otherwise completely dark room.

This study underwrites the findings from the perceptual studies, reported earlier in the chapter, confirming differences in the information used by 'experts' and 'novices' in fitting their actions to environmental contingencies.

6.7. Conclusion

It will be appreciated that, in the context of the wide domain of decision-making in sport, the experimental work reported here is only a drop in the ocean. Nevertheless, much of the work is directed at sport-relevant questions

Table 6.14 Means and S.D. of number of position errors for 'good' and 'poor' catchers under various conditions.

Condition[a]	Good ($N=15$)		Poor ($N=14$)	
	X	S.D.	X	S.D.
Test	0.06	0.25	4.42	3.10
TS	0.80	0.94	6.21	4.62
BS	1.20	1.56	8.28	4.14
UVBH	3.00	3.50	12.57	5.47
UVB	4.13	3.99	15.50	4.76

[a] Test = full light; TS = transparent screen, hand visible; BS = opaque screen, hand not visible; UVBH = ball and hand illuminated with ultraviolet light in an otherwise dask room; UVB = ball only illuminated by ultraviolet light.
From Whiting, Savelsbergh & Faber (1988); reprinted with permission of the authors.

and at a collection of related problems such that a body of integrated knowledge is beginning to be assembled. Too much of this work is still restricted to laboratory simulation, but this may be a necessary step in formulating the right kind of question to ask, and determining the important parameters.

The work of Alain and his co-workers with respect to racquet games marks a significant step forward in methodology, since it recognises the important factor that sport involves other competitors and that information from such competitors — particularly in team games — is an important factor in decision-making. Moreover such analyses as they used were based upon observation of 'real' games. It seems rational to propose that further developments of this kind of thinking and approach are likely to lead to the acquisition of information that may be more meaningful to coaches and teachers. Eventually, it will be necessary to come to terms with prediction in relation to sequences of actions, since players may be basing their strategies and decision-making on events three or more shots ahead.

As far as movement observation plays an essential role both for player and spectator, the developments reported in this area are of particular interest. The methodological problems are, however, complex and this is one explanation of why only a limited number of studies in more natural settings have been carried out. In future experimental work it is to be expected that questions and methodologies developed from more limited laboratory approaches will lead themselves to more ecologically valid approaches.

References

Abernethy, B., & Russell, D.G. (1984). Advance cue utilisation by skilled cricket batsman. *American Journal of Science and Medicine in Sport*, **16**(2), 2–10.

Abernethy, B., & Russell, D.G. (1987). The relationship between expertise and visual search strategy in a racquet sport. *Human Movement Science*, **6**, 283−320.

Alain, C., & Girardin, Y. (1978). The use of uncertainty in racquetball competition. *Canadian Journal of Applied Sport Sciences*, **3**, 240−244.

Alain, C., & Proteau, L. (1978). Etude des variables relatives au traitement de l'information en sports de raquette (Study of variables related to information processing in racquet sports). *Journal Canadién des Sciences Appliquées aux Sports*, **3**, 27−35.

Alderson, G.J.K., Sully, D.J., & Sully, H.G. (1974). An operational analysis of a one-handed catching task using high speed photography. *Journal of Motor Behavior*, **6**, 217−226.

Aspin, D.N. (1977). Kinds of knowledge, physical education and the curriculum. *Journal of Human Movement Studies*, **2**, 21−37.

Bard, C., Fleury, M., Carriere, L., & Halle, M. (1980). Analysis of gymnastics judges' visual search. *Research Quarterly for Exercise and Sport*, **51**, 267−273.

Brinker, B.P.L.M. den, Stabler, J.R.L.W., Wieringen, P.C.W. van, & Whiting, H.T.A. (1986). The effect of manipulating knowledge of results on the learning of slalom-type ski movements. *Ergonomics*, **29**. 31−40.

Broadbent, D.E. (1956). *Perception and Communication*. London: Pergamon.

Broadbent, D.E. (1971). *Decision and Stress*. London: Academic Press.

Buckolz, E., Prapavesis, H., & Fairs, J. (1988). Advance cues and their use in predicting tennis passing shots. *Canadian Journal of Sport Sciences*, **13**, 20−30.

Carr, D. (1980). The language of action, ability and skill: Part II − the language of ability and skill. *Journal of Human Movement Studies*, **6**, 111−126.

Chase, W.G., & Chi, M.T.H. (1980). Cognitive skill: Implications for spatial skill in large scale environments. In J. Harvey (Ed.), *Cognition, Social Behavior and the Environment*. Potomac, M.D.: Erlbaum.

Chase, W.G., & Simon, H.A. (1973). Perception in chess. *Cognitive Psychology*, **4**, 55−81.

Cohen, J. (1975). Psychological aspects of sport with particular reference to variation in performance. In H.T.A. Whiting (Ed.), *Readings in Sports Psychology*, Vol. 2. London: Lepus.

Cohen, J., & Christensen, J.P. (1970). *Information and Choice*. Edinburgh: Oliver & Boyd.

Cohen, J., & Dearnaley, E.J. (1962). Skill and judgement of footballers in attempting to score goals. *British Journal of Psychology*, **53**. 71−88.

Coombs, C.H., Dawes, R.M., & Tversky, A. (1970). *Mathematical psychology: An elementary introduction*. Englewood Cliffs, NJ: Prentice-Hall.

Cratty, B.J. (1975). *Psychology in Contemporary Sport*. Englewood Cliffs, NJ: Prentice-Hall.

Drouin, D., & Salmela, J.H. (1975). Le gardien de but: le temps de reaction en le concept de 'reflexes' (The goal-keeper: reaction times and the concept of reflexes). *Mouvement*, Actes du Symposium.

Edwards, J. (1979). The home-field advantage. In J.H. Goldstein (Ed.), *Sports, Games and Play: Social and Psychological Viewpoints*. New York: Wiley.

Edwards, W. (1954). The theory of decision-making. *Psychological Bulletin*, **51**, 380−417.

Edwards, W., & Tversky, A. (Eds) (1967). *Decision Making*. Harmondsworth: Penguin Books.

Eysenck, H.J. (1947). *Dimensions of Personality*. London: Routledge & Kegan Paul.

Eysenck, H.J. (1966). Personality and experimental psychology. *Bulletin of the British Psychological Society*, **19**, 1−28.

Gibson, J.J. (1979). *The Ecological Approach to Visual Perception*. Boston, MA: Houghton Mifflin.

Goldstein, J.H. (1979). Outcomes in professional team sports, skill and situational factors. In J.H. Goldstein (Ed.), *Sports, Games and Play: Social and Psychological Viewpoints*. New York: Wiley.

Groot, A. de (1965). *Thought and Choice in Chess*. The Hague: Mouton.

Groot, A. de (1966). Perception and memory versus thought: some old ideas and recent findings. In B. Kleinmuntz (Ed.), *Problem Solving*. New York: Wiley.

Hueting, J.E. (1977). Het waarnemen van risico's (The perception of risks). *Geneeskunde en Sport*, 1, 26−34.

Jones, C.M., & Miles, T.R. (1978). Use of advance cues in predicting the flight of a lawn tennis ball. *Journal of Human Movement Studies*, 4, 231−235.

Luce, R.D. (1963). Detection and recognition of human observers. In R.D. Luce, R.R. Bush and E. Galanter (Eds), *Handbook of Mathematical Psychology*, Vol. I. New York: Wiley.

Marteniuk, R.G. (1976). *Information Processing in Motor Skills*. New York: Holt, Rinehart & Winston.

McLeod, P. (1987). Visual reaction time and high-speed ball games. *Perception*, 16, 49−59.

Meredith, G.P. (1966). *Instruments of Communication*. London: Pergamon.

Moray, N., & Fitter, M. (1973). A theory and the measurement of attention. In S. Kornblum (Ed.), *Attention and Performance*, Vol IV. London: Academic Press.

Polanyi, M. (1958). *Personal Knowledge: Towards a Post-critical Philosophy*. London: Routledge & Kegan Paul.

Salmela, J.H., & Fiorito, P. (1979). Visual cues in ice-hockey goal tending. *Canadian Journal of Applied Sport Sciences*, 4, 56−59.

Sharp, R.H., & Whiting, H.T.A. (1974). Exposure and occluded duration effects in a ball-catching skill. *Journal of Motor Behavior*, 3, 139−147.

Sharp, R.H., & Whiting, H.T.A. (1975). Information-processing and eye-movement behaviour in a ball catching skill. *Journal of Motor Behavior*, 4, 124−131.

Smyth, M.M., & Marriott, A.M. (1982). Vision and proprioception in simple catching. *Journal of Motor Behavior*, 14, 143−152.

Souliere, D., & Salmela, J.H. (1979). Visual cues and motor performance in volleyball. *Proceedings of the French-Canadian Association for the Advancement of Science, Quebec*.

Tanner, W.P., & Swets, J.A.A. (1954). A decision-making theory of visual detection. *Psychological Review*, 61, 401−409.

Tyldesley, D.A. (1981). Motion prediction and movement control in sport. Paper presented at International Congress of the Hockey Federation, Amsterdam.

Tyldesley, D.A., & Bootsma, R.J. (1981). The place and role of perceptual-motor experience in sport oriented reaction-time task. Internal paper, Department of Psychology, Faculty of Human Movement Sciences, Free University, Amsterdam.

Welford, A.T. (1968). *Fundamentals of Skill*. London: Methuen.

Whitfield, D.C. (1967). Human skill as a determinant of allocation of function. In W.J. Singleton, R.S. Easterby and D.C. Whitfield (Eds), *The Human Operator in Complex Systems*. London: Taylor & Francis.

Whiting, H.T.A. (1969). *Acquiring Ball Skill − a Psychological Interpretation*. London: Bell.

Whiting, H.T.A. (1984). The concepts of 'adaptation' and 'attunement' in skill learning. In M.A. Arbib, E.L. Rissland and O. Selfridge (Eds), Adaptive Control of Ill-defined Systems. New York: Plenum.

Whiting, H.T.A., & Hutt, J.W.R. (1972). The effects of personality and ability on speed of decisions regarding the directional aspects of ball flight. *Journal of Motor Behavior*, **4**, 89–97.

Whiting, H.T.A., & Sharp, R.H. (1973). Visual occlusion factors in a discrete ball-catching task. *Journal of Motor Behavior*, **5**, 11–16.

Whiting, H.T.A., Gill, B., & Stephenson, J. (1970). Critical time intervals for taking in flight information in a ball-catching task. *Ergonomics*, **13**, 265–272.

Whiting, H.T.A., Alderson, G.J.K., & Sanderson, F.H. (1973). Critical time intervals for viewing and individual differences in performance of a ball-catching task. *International Journal of Sport Psychology*, **4**, 155–156.

Whiting, H.T.A., Savelsbergh, G.J.P., & Faber, C.M. (1988). Catch questions and incomplete answers. In Ann M. Colley and J.R. Beech (Eds), *Cognition and Action in Skilled Behaviour*. Amsterdam: North-Holland.

Wilberg, R.B. (1973). Criteria for the definition of a field. *Proceedings of the Third International Congress of Sport Psychology, Madrid*.

Wilberg, R.B. (1975). An analysis and application of game and human performance theory to sport and competition. In H.T.A. Whiting (Ed.), *Readings in Sports Psychology*, Vol. 2. London: Kimpton.

7 SPORT PSYCHOLOGY AND PRACTICE

7.1. Introduction

From the previous chapters it would seem that a gulf exists between theory and practice, between conclusions from experimental research and inferences that are relevant to practice. In the chapter devoted to decision-making the gap between the various decision models and the application possibilities was repeatedly signalled. Another example was provided by laboratory studies addressed to the influence of spectators on the achievement of the sports performer (see, for example, page 43). Research into the influence of aspects of cognitive style on the catching of tennis balls which could be seen for longer or shorter intervals, may serve as a last illustration of the proposition that theoretically relevant research need not necessarily lead immediately to conclusions which have direct, concrete practical implications.

In addition to the gulf between theory and practice there is another gap, namely that between scientific knowledge and intuitive findings based on experience. Personality would not appear to change as a consequence of participating in sport or, for that matter, top-level sport. Providing rewards for good achievement can, under certain circumstances, have a demotivating effect. The relationship between the number of spectators and the extent to which aggression occurs is also more bogus than real.

In this last chapter we will pay attention to this gap between theory and practice and to the possibility of bringing them closer together. In addition, we will explore the causes of the strained relations between scientific knowledge and intuitive ideas, from which it will become apparent that doubts about the correctness of intuitive appraisals are justified.

The presence of a gulf between theory and practice relates directly to the question of the usefulness of sport psychological knowledge and therewith also to the question of why one would actually want to use this knowledge. Two answers can be provided to the last question.

Knowledge in the area of sport psychology can be used to improve individual or group performances. In this case it concerns insight into processes which underlie achievement and the factors which influence performance, insight which can be useful for improved training, the development of a more efficient way of learning, better preparation, better tactics during competition and so on.

In addition, sport psychological knowledge can also play a role in clarifying the relationship between sport and well-being. In this case the concern is with gaining insight into the circumstances under which sport contributes to a person's well-being, into the effects that sport has on both participant and spectator and, for example, the factors that determine whether or not someone will participate in sport.

Below, we shall address, separately, both these possible uses of sport psychological knowledge.

7.2. Sport psychology and (top-level) performance

Many of the questions by which each of the chapters were introduced had a direct or indirect relationship to the possibility of improving the performance of individual athletes or of teams. How can risks be minimised in decision-making situations? What really is the disadvantage of playing away and how can this disadvantage be overcome? How is it possible that a weaker team, on paper, can win and how can this be prevented — by the stronger team — or exploited — by the weaker team? When does an athlete become optimally motivated and how does one arrive at such a state? Can athletes be selected at an early stage of their careers and, if so, on the basis of which qualities? How can a sport performer learn to manage the tensions that go together with a competition?

As we have seen, the contribution that sport psychology can make to these questions is based on knowledge: in the first place, knowledge about the processes that underlie performance, and sport performance in particular (for example, knowledge about the taking of decisions, about the kinds of information that play a role thereby, about the reasons why experienced players, in general, make better decisions that inexperienced players, about the characteristics of situations in which wrong decisions are easily made and so forth); in the second place, knowledge about factors that influence performance (not only personal factors such as personality characteristics and motivational factors, but also external factors varying from extrinsic rewards to the presence of a (hostilely disposed) public); finally, knowledge about the reactions of athletes in sport situations (for example, aggressive reactions or the experiencing of, and learning to cope with, stress).

In Chapter 1 it was explained that the coach/trainer* plays a central role in the application of this knowledge (see Figure 1.1, page 5). He or she forms the connecting link between all the knowledge bases, including sport psychology and the concrete advice given to an athlete or a team. On the basis of the information available to him the coach decides what the athlete must do during the competition, how he can motivate his team, how the training must be organised, etc. Sport psychology would seem to be pre-eminently suitable for providing information to the coach in order that his instructions might be better founded. Not in the sense of providing a recipe, but of extending his/her possibilities by the provision of data and theoretical frameworks that give access to alternatives, provide suggestions about new approaches and alert him/her to possible causes of success or failure of his athlete or of his team.

To this end, sport psychology must trace, and systematically map out, the factors that have an influence on performance, and make clear how they operate. In addition, an important second task is testing the tenability of existing ideas and opinions. Does amphetamine indeed have the supposed performance-increasing effect? Does the system of premiums for winning matches, in the end, have the desired (motivational) result? Is it sensible to promote a 'healthy mutual rivalry' in teams? (For this reason, Kessler, a Dutch soccer coach, for example, had at his disposal three centre forwards of whom only two would be played in any match.) Are players really so easy to distract (compare, for example, the record of Blitz on page 45)? Because existing ideas and opinions are so persistent (also often incorrect, as will be shown at the end of this chapter), sport psychology has an extremely prac-tically relevant task.

In carrying out this task, sport psychology provides sound, applied knowl-edge, albeit not cut-and-dried recipes: the translation of theory into practice remains a task for the coach although it is not realistic to leave this translation entirely to him. The researcher must allocate a portion of his inventiveness to making apparent the possibilities that theory and experiment can have for everyday situations.

Further, it is not to be denied that in the application of scientific knowl-edge — thus, also sport psychological knowledge — a number of problems arise. It is important that these be signalled. By so doing they will not be solved, but it is thereby possible to ensure that knowledge is not uncritically — and therefore wrongly — translated into practice. In this connection, four such problems will be discussed.

---

* To avoid misunderstanding it should be stated that the athlete can be his own coach/trainer.

Figure 7.1. In the application of sport psychological knowledge the coach plays a central role.

7.2.1. THE PROBLEM OF GENERALISATION

The first problem relates to the question of how far results are also valid outside the experiment in which they were obtained. For answering this question the distinction already made in the first chapter between recipient and generated knowledge (page 3) is important. Linked with this distinction is the difference between more fundamental as opposed to more applied research. Nevertheless, both recognise their shortcomings when it has to do with the generalisation of results, albeit that in the first case the origin is different from that of the second. This will be illustrated by means of two pieces of research related to the influence of amphetamine on performance.

The first of these is taken from a series of experiments of Deboeck, Hueting, Michels & Soetens (1983). From this series we focus on the study in which the influence of amphetamine on the running performance (1500 metres) of second- and third-year students was investigated, and in which it appeared that this expedient had no effect at all on their maximum performance. The time required to run the 1500 metres was, after taking amphetamine, on average one second less than after taking a placebo; a negligible difference.

The second investigation was carried out by Frowein (1983) and was concerned with the performance of a choice reaction time task. Now, such a task can be separated into three components, namely:

1. The perception and interpretation of the stimulus.
2. Taking the decision as to which response belonges by which stimulus.
3. Making the movement.

From the results it seemed that amphetamine affected only the last of these. The first two components relate to cognitive processing while the last component is the motor part of the task which was carried out faster under the influence of amphetamine.

The research of Deboeck et al generated knowledge specific to sport psychology while the experiment of Frowein might be seen to reflect Wilberg's (1973) concept of recipient knowledge from the parent discipline of psychology It is clear that in the latter case the applications are limited. The results of Frowein's experiment require speculations to be made about the relative contributions of cognitive processes, respectively motor processes in those sports for which one wishes to make statements about the effect of amphetamine on performance. Further, it is probable that the relationship between cognitive processing and motor processes for the same sport task differs considerably depending on whether experienced or inexperienced athletes carry out the task (see Chapter 5). A difference that can, indeed, mediate the effect of amphetamine.

Even if the approach of Frowein can be designated as more fundamental, and that of Deboeck *et al* as more applied, the latter still has its limitations. It is not known, for example, if the results also hold for top-level athletes. It is also not known if this result is typical for the middle-distance event or if it holds, for example, for long-distance runners.

In the first case generalisation is limited by the extrapolation that must be made from fundamental processes to everyday situations; in the second case generalisation of findings is limited by the fact that the sample on which the results were based is far from representative of all the other interesting groups.

7.2.2. THE PROBLEM OF SUITABLE SUBJECTS

Particularly when one is interested in the performance of top-level athletes, and in the factors that influence their performance, finding the right subjects to participate in the research poses a difficult problem. On the one hand it is clear that variables such as the number of hours spent in training per week, motivation, movement experience, etc. are so specific for top-level sport performers that only the sport performer himself is suitable as subject. It is unwarranted, therefore, to suppose that such variables for less skilled or mediocre athletes will operate in the same way as for top-level athletes. On the other hand, no athletes will make himself available for research just before or during a competition if this in any way might have an influence on what he is used to doing. However, it is just at these moments that the variables in question have their unique effect. Sport psychological research is, therefore, generally speaking forced to compromise by choosing situations that deviate from the really important events or by using subjects other than top-level sport performers. These limitations do, indeed, have consequences for the application of such research.

7.2.3. THE PROBLEM OF THE SMALL MARGINS

In top-level sport, in particular, the margins that make the difference between winning and losing are extremely small. The difference between a first place that attracts everyone's attention and a fourth place that quickly passes into oblivion is often a question of seconds or fractions thereof. Showing effects within this margin is extremely difficult on account of the — by definition — limited range. Moreover, it is out of the question that all the relevant variables can be brought strictly under control, even if one is working with top-level athletes, so that possible significant effects are easily overshadowed by the influence of variables other than those experimentally chosen. The problems signalled here, however, also hold when particular research findings become applied to the practice of top-level sport. Here also, the effect of a particular action, assignment, method and so forth can be nullified by the many other factors that play a role.

7.2.4. THE PROBABILISTIC NATURE OF (SPORT) PSYCHOLOGICAL PRONOUNCEMENTS

The last problem to be pointed to here has to do with the probabilistic nature of many (sport) psychological pronouncements. The underlying reason lies in the fact that: (1) a phenomenon cannot be sufficiently well explained — school success for example, is related to intelligence, but also to a large number of other variables; as long as those are not known in any detail, the importance of intelligence per se can never be exactly stated. Or (2) it is a fact that the phenomenon itself fluctuates and at one moment has more chance of making its effect felt than at another (see, for example, the explanation in Chapter 6 of signal-detection theory and fluctuations in the perception of signal and noise). One of the consequences of this is that predictions referring to groups may be much less appropriate when applied to a single individual of that group. To choose one example by way of illustration: giving a reward would seem to have a negative effect on intrinsic motivation of children performing a balance task (see page 23). Nevertheless, from the research of Orlick & Mosher (1978) it seemed possible in their experimental group to point to children who had a higher intrinsic motivation score than children in the control group. Put in other words; what holds in general, does not necessarily hold for a specific person or for a specific moment in time. The limitations that go together with this statement have already been referred to in connection with the relationship between extraversion and top-level performance. In spite of the significant differences on this personality dimension between athletes and non-athletes it is apparent that the selection of athletes on the basis of this attribute would run into many serious problems.

7.3. Sport, psychology and well-being

In Chapter 1, Nisbet was quoted as follows: 'in as far as sport contributes to personal health and social interaction it offers powerful possibilities'. The possibilities of sport can, rightly, be termed powerful. Sport, within the framework of physical education, has a firm position in education (in contrast to, for example, ballet or dance). Excellent media-connections exist, so that sport is highly visible. The sport world in general is well organised and has an extensive group of professional appointees and volunteers at its disposal. The practice of sport takes place in all age groups and at all levels of society. Finally, sport has the aura of being a healthy activity.

The question can, however, be put as to whether sport really contributes

Figure 7.2. Sport, within the framework of physical education, has a firm position in education.

to personal health, social interaction or, in short, the well-being of the sport performer. Sport psychology can make a contribution to the answer to this question from a number of different angles. The following points can be mentioned:

1. Testing of common-sense ideas about the relationship between sport and well-being. The number of presuppositions about the influence of 'sport' are legion. To mention some of these: the practice of sport can lead to all kinds of personality changes, to healthier daily habits and, related to this, less chance of cardiac and circulatory problems, for example. Sport practice can provide good possibilities for expressing aggression in a socially acceptable and institutionalised form and can thereby prevent the expression of uncontrolled aggression. Taking part in sport will prevent undesirable antisocial behaviour. But it can also lead to social isolation, to reduced chances of developing one's talents, to dependence on coaches and parents, to physical overload and irreversible bodily damage. The investigation of the validity of these and similar statements provides the

first possible contribution of sport psychology to the discussion around sport and well-being.

2. A description and explanation of the way in which sport performances are produced and the factors that have an influence thereon, so that the possible positive or negative consequences of sport practice become clear, is a second possible contribution. Insight into the reasons why people are prepared to take risks as, for example, in parachute-jumping, mountain-eering and car racing provides the possibility of reducing such risks and of estimating their true value. Knowledge about the effects of amphe-tamine — for example, on increased reactive aggression (Ekkers, 1980) — can be used to promote the well-being of the athlete involved. The same holds for knowledge about the effects of fatigue, the probability of wrong decisions, the reactions of athletes to stressful events and so on.

3. Research into phenomena which clearly do not make a contribution to the well-being of the athlete is a third possible contribution. Research into the aggression of players and public is an example (see Chapter 4). Research into the effects of doping is another (see for example Hueting, 1988, who demonstrated that the ACTH-hormone, a probably frequently used expedient amongst cyclists, had no effect on the maximum cycling performance of professional cyclists. However, the expedient had several other, unfavourable physiological and psychological effects).

The investigations of Kranenborg (1980, 1983), the subject of which was the practice of sport and injuries that ensue, can serve to illustrate this point further. Kranenborg researched, amongst other topics, the frequency with which injuries — in The Netherlands — appear, and the differences in their frequency of occurrence related to the nature of the sport and the manner of sport practice (competitive or recreative). The author estimated that yearly injuries to active sport participants between the ages of 16 and 45 years amount to 1.2 million. Field contact sports (e.g. soccer and hockey) account, in both an absolute and a relative sense (thus, taking account of the actual number of participants), for by far the greatest proportion of these. Further, it seems that the number of injuries that occur in competitive sport is, in an absolute sense, twice as many as in recreative sport. If account is taken of the number of participants in both categories the difference amounts to a factor of four. Such figures represent a beginning in attempts to trace possible causes of, or the prevention of, injuries.

4. In tracing the determinants of participation in sport lies a further con-tribution that sport psychology can make in terms of the relationship between sport and well-being. By this means the possibility exists to exert an influence on people or on circumstances that stimulate or detract from sport participation.

The three last-named points have been sufficiently addressed in the preceding chapters—it is not necessary to give them more attention here. The first point will be expanded in the following section on the basis of a number of recent investigations.

7.4. Sport, well-being and prejudice

With regard to the relationship between sport and well-being, there is no lack of opinions. With respect to both the (putative) promotion of well-being as a consequence of participation in sport as the disadvantageous influences thereof, there exists a multitude of ideas and opinions. In general these are almost never founded on empirical data, and what is also noteworthy is that research into this issue is scarce. The range of subjects that can be addressed in this connection is, indeed, extremely wide-ranging. We restrict ourselves here to two themes which enjoy a certain popularity. The first has to do with the consequences of participating in top-level sport at a very young age. Thereafter, attention will be paid to the health-promoting effects that the practice of sport can have.

In a thesis about top-level sport at an early age (Fahlbusch-Wendler, 1982), it was clearly illustrated that there was no dearth of opinions about the influence of top-level sport on the well-being of the children concerned. The author presented an inventory of the dangers that were named in the discussion about top-level sport for youth*. She used, in this respect, divisions into risks of a physical, psychical, pedagogical and social nature from which it is worthy of note that with respect to the last three categories there is little empirical data from which these dangers could really be made apparent. Nevertheless, the list is impressive. Without wishing to be complete, the following can be named: loss of naivety; reduced independence, subordination to the trainer; exposure to the assertiveness of parents and trainers; weighed down by diverse forms of stress (for example, as a consequence of selection, appearing in public, attention of the press); mental overload; one-sided personality development; paucity of social contacts; general problems of socialisation.

The vague formulations are an indication of the empirical quality of the assertions, which also holds for the sources from which they were obtained—mainly opinionated magazines and lectures.

---

* It is remarkable that the negative picture of top-level sport (and especially top-level sport for young people) in the West is far stronger than it is, for example, in eastern Europe and the Soviet Union. This not only illustrates our departure point that sport forms an integrated part of our culture pattern whereby esteem for the phenomenon of sport will be extremely diverse in the different cultures; it also justifies a certain scepticism with respect to the validity of this picture (see for example, van den Heuvel, 1978).

Kaminski and Ruoff are among the few authors who relate material factors about young people and sport (Kaminski & Ruoff, 1979a,b; Ruoff, 1979a,b; Kaminski, Mayer & Ruoff, 1984; Ruoff & Kaminski, 1980). Their findings give clear reasons for reservation with respect to the psychological dangers of youth sport. These authors compare children in the age range 10−14 years belonging to the top national level in figure skating, gymnastics and swimming with children who practise music intensively and with a group of 'normal' children. An overview of the numbers of subjects is given in Table 7.1.

Data were collected about, among other things, timetable, school achievement and school (non)-attendance, free-time activities; about social, emotional, motivational and psychosomatic variables and biographical aspects. The children completed a series of questionnaires, interviews were held and tests taken. Moreover, the parents, teachers, classmates and trainers were interviewed and they also filled in questionnaires and assessment scales. This is not the place to go into all the available results of this large-scale research programme. A few of the interesting results will, however, be reported here.

As might be expected, the young top-level sport performers spend a great deal of their time in training — averaged over the three sports, three to four hours per day. The time spent by practitioners of music lags behind, although they also spend two to three hours per day studying. In Table 7.2 the time spent on training or studying by the different groups is reproduced in detail. From these data it would seem that, in spite of the obvious differences, the situation of the young top-level sport performer in comparison to children who excel in music is less exceptional than might seem at first sight.

In addition, it can be noted that, with their choice of figure-skating, gymnastics and swimming, Ruoff and Kaminski have invoked the — at least in Germany — most training-intensive sports, as is clear from Table 7.3.

In spite of the extensive training times, Ruoff and Kaminski found, in general, no difference or very little difference between the top-level sport

Table 7.1. Numbers of subjects in the different groups researched by Ruoff and Kaminski.

	Top-level sport performers					
	Figure skaters	Swimmers	Gymnasts	Practitioners of Music	Control group	Total
Number of subjects	28	37	33	30	50	178

From Ruoff & Kaminski (1980); reprinted with permission of Karl Hofmann Verlag, Schorndorf.

Table 7.2. Time spent on training by young top athletes, and on music lessons by music practitioners, respectively, in minutes.

	Figure skaters	Swimmers	Gymnasts	Total top-level sport performers	Music practitioners
Time spent on training/lessons on the most intensive day of the week					
Total	317	227	237	254	179
Of which:					
Training/lessons	207	153	160	171	138
Preparation (undressing, showering, waiting, etc.)	52	25	20	31	9
Travelling time	53	43	50	47	30
Other	5	6	7	5	2
Time spent on training/lessons on Sunday					
Total	339	169	64	180	116
Of which:					
Training, lessons	227	107	45	120	97
Preparation	40	11	2	15	—
Travelling time	66	38	9	36	4
Other	6	13	8	9	15

Adapted from Kaminski & Ruoff (1979b).

Table 7.3. Average number of training hours and training sessions per week for male and female amateur top-level sport performers in Germany.

Male	Hours	Training sessions	Female	Hours	Training sessions
Rowing	17	8	Figure-skating	23	6
Figure-skating	17	6	Gymnastics	17	5
Gymnastics	17	6	Swimming	13	7
Swimming	15	7	Skiing	12	4
Boxing	15	6	Diving	10	5
Judo	14	5	Speed skating	8	4
Speed skating	10	5	Volleyball	7	3
Skiing	8	4			
Volleyball	7	3			
Diving	7	4			

Adapted from Fahlbusch-Wendler (1982); adapted with permission of the publisher.

performers, the practitioners of music and the control groups. With respect to personality differences, the authors remark, for example, that:

> *these differences seem to be much smaller than one might suppose given all the variety of insubstantiated opinions. Only for a few personality variables are there significant differences between the groups. Moreover, these differences have to do with variables that hang narrowly together with occupations and circumstances that are specific to top-level sport, such as, for example, attitude with respect to the achievement principle, 'equal chances and rivalry', 'achievement pressure' or 'respect for own physical possibilities and bodily functioning'. On these, the young top-level sports performer clearly scores higher* (Ruoff & Kaminski, 1980, p. 180).

This finding, for that matter, is completely in line with the results of the research discussed in Chapter 3. Differences in personality between sport performers and non-sport performers do not seem to be as large as was once thought, while changes in personality as a consequence of sport participation seem to be non-apparent.

Also, in other areas, top-level sport performers would appear to differ little from the two control groups. Their social position in class does not deviate from that of other children, they do not sleep longer (or less), they do not have more (or less) friends than the others and their school achievements are not below those of the music group or the 'normal' group. In as far as there is talk of differences, this often has to do with rather obvious things. Top-sporting children spend, for example, on average, only $6\frac{1}{2}$ hours per day on school work compared to $7\frac{1}{2}$ hours by children in the control group—a difference that is primarily the result of the fact that they are regularly, for a few days, absent from school for competitions or training. That, in spite of this, their grades are not worse, is probably related to the fact that the young top-level sport performers clearly had a higher level of intelligence than the control group subjects. Further, it seems that the top-level sport performers spend less time on leisure activities (assuming training not to be included therein) and in general are less burdened by household chores.

All in all, the differences are not very sensational. Bakker (1988) arrives at the same conclusions with respect to leisure activities, interests and hobbies of young ballet dancers, spending about 15 hours weekly on ballet education. In this study, however, differences between dancers and 'normal' children were found on several personality traits—among other things, achievement motivation, self-esteem and introversion/extraversion. The research of Ruoff & Kaminski and Bakker can contribute to the idea that in the discussion about the disadvantages of top-level sport for young people *facts* and *opinions* can better be separated.

This last comment is, indeed, also desirable when talking about the promotion of well-being through sport.

The figure of 1.2 million injuries per year, noted by Kranenborg, may in itself give rise to a qualification of the statement, but also shows that empirical evidence is urgently needed if the discussion is to reach any level. An investigation by Deurenberg (1983) into some of the living and eating habits of sport performers and non-sport performers shows that sport performers rarely have healthier eating habits than non-sport performers. Also, the average body weight of sporting men and women deviates very little from that of non-sport performers. For his comparison, Deurenberg makes use of data from almost 4000 men between the ages of 20 and 30 years. They reacted to a request addressed to, in total, more than 11 000 people to take part in an investigation into overweight, and reported to a research institute where height and weight were measured. There, they also handed in a questionnaire they had been required to complete in which, amongst other questions, the following information was requested: number of hours spent on sport per month, eating, drinking and smoking habits. People who spent five or less hours per month on sport ('non-sport performers') were compared to people who spent 10 or more hours per month ('sport performers'). The male sport performers appeared to consume just as much alcohol as the non-sport performers. They missed breakfast just as often, they ate just as many snacks, and they ate brown or white bread to a similar extent. In contrast to their lesser consumption of coffee, sport performers consumed more tea and mineral waters. For women, with respect to these eating and drinking habits there was sometimes a difference between sport performers and non-sport performers, although the extent of the differences was not great. For the sake of completeness it must be said that sporting men and women on the whole ate more fruit and took fewer painkillers than non-sport performers and they also smoked less.

Indeed, from an investigation such as that of Deurenberg, no conclusions about causes and effects can be drawn. Nevertheless, the differences between sport performers and non-sport performers with respect to a number of living and eating habits are so low that the statement that sport and a healthy way of life are inseparably related to each other must be looked at with at least some reserve.

This investigation also produced results on the basis of which speculations can be made about the origin of the idea that sport and health are so closely related. The questionnaire asked to what extent people felt that they themselves lived a healthy life and whether they felt themselves to be in good health. In Table 7.4 the answers to such questions by different groups are given in percentages.

There seem to be many more sport performers who feel themselves to live a healthy life than non-sport performers. This is most noticeable for males:

Table 7.4. Answers (in percentages) of sport performers and non-sport performers to the question to what extent they themselves find that they eat and live in a healthy way or feel themselves to be in good health.

	Male		Female	
	Non-sport performers (5 hours or less/month)	Sport performers (10 hours or more/month)	Non-sport performers (5 hours or less/month)	Sport performers (10 hours or more/month)
Healthy eating	65.9	73.7	75.0	79.6
Unhealthy eating	15.8	14.0	14.1	12.4
Healthy living	49.1	75.5	56.7	76.6
Unhealthy living	34.0	15.6	29.4	14.4
Feel healthy	86.6	92.6	78.2	87.1
Do not always feel in good health	1.7	0.4	1.5	0.5

From Deurenberg (1983); reprinted with permission of the publisher.

three-quarters of the sporting men said that they lived a healthy life compared to only half of the non-sport performers. It is probable that the idea that sports are healthy is, to an important degree, responsible for this difference.

It is precisely in the testing of the validity of such ideas — so positive, such as here, or negative such as in the case of top-level sport for young people — that there lies an important task for sport psychology or, to put it in a more general framework, sport scientific research.

There is, finally, a striking point that demands further elucidation, namely, the noticeable gap — especially in this section — between scientific knowledge and intuition.

7.5. Maintaining prejudices

Decisions are often not made by people conceived as completely informed, rational beings (see Chapter 6). In addition people are not usually intuitive statisticians. This is elaborated in our opinion-forming about a whole number of issues. Vroon, in the *People's Paper* (Netherlands) of 30 April 1983, expressed it in this way: 'Our intellectual capacity relies on the law of keeping things simple.' Because the coach/trainer in taking decisions cannot always dispose of this law, it is worthwhile in finishing to indicate on just what this law is based.

From an overview article of Einhorn & Hogarth (1978) into the taking of decisions and the estimating of chances it seems that people make at least three kinds of mistake.

In the first place people look mainly, and perhaps exclusively, to the *frequency* with which an event arises and not to the *chance* that a particular event will occur. If, in the first round of the European Cup Tournament, eight soccer players were sent off, that would seem much worse than two sent off in the quarter-finals of the three tournaments. Nevertheless, the latter is at least as noteworthy since, in that case, only 12 matches were played as against 64 in the first round.

Secondly it would seem that there is a stronger inclination to pay special attention to information that confirms an already taken standpoint than to information that is in conflict with one's own ideas. Put in another way: confirmatory evidence is looked for and not non-confirmatory. Opponents of top-level sport for young people are more prone to cite examples from which the negative effects of top-level sport can be deduced than examples in which the opposite is the case. Moreover, these are better remembered.

Thirdly, it would seem that confirmatory evidence in general has more chance of catching one's attention than disconfirmatory arguments. To stay with this example: in particular, when something goes wrong with the young top-level sport performer, it will come to the attention of the media. When there is nothing to report, the phenomenon is not interesting. In the light of the shortcomings of intuition listed above, the arising of prejudice with respect to such a frequently described phenomenon as sport, and its maintenance, is not particularly surprising.

Conclusions are often drawn on the basis of information which people accidentally possess, whereby the most accessible information then plays a role out of all proportion. Sport psychology can make a contribution to breaking down this pattern of thinking — we hope to have made this apparent in the foregoing chapters. By this means not only can prejudices be combated, but the decisions of coaches and trainers also improve in quality. If the latter becomes realised this would indeed mean an important application of scientific knowledge to practice.

References

Bakker, F.C. (1988). Personality differences between young dancers and non-dancers. *Personality and Individual Differences*, **9**, 121–131.

Deboeck, M., Hueting, J.E., Michels, L., & Soetens, E. (1983). Drukproeven met amfetamine (Effects of amphetamine on performance under stress). In J.E. Hueting and H. van der Brug (Eds), *Sport Wetenschappelijk Onderzocht (Research in Sport)*. Haarlem: De Vrieseborch.

Deurenberg, P. (1983). Sporten: enkele leef- en eetgewoonten (Sport and living and eating habits. *Voeding*, **44**, 278–281.

Einhorn, H.J., & Hogarth, R.M. (1978). Confidence in judgment: persistence of the illusion of validity. *Psychological Review*, **85**, 395–416.

Ekkers, C.L. (1980). Emotionerende en activerende invloeden op agressie in de sportsituatie (Effects of emotion and activation on aggression in sport). *Geneeskunde en Sport*, **13**, 85−86.

Fahlbusch-Wendler, C. (1982). *Kinderhochleistungssport. Die Zulässigkeit der staatlichen Förderung des Kinderhochleistungssports in der BRD (Top-level Sports for Children. The Admissibility of Public Encouragement of Top-level Sports for Children)*. Ahrensburg: Czwalina.

Frowein, H.W. (1983). Amfetamine beïnvloedt de prestatie wel, maar niet in alle taken (Amphetamine has an effect on performance, but not in all tasks). In J.E. Hueting and H. van der Brug (Eds), *Sport Wetenschappelijk Onderzocht (Research in Sport)*. Haarlem: De Vrieseborch.

Heuvel, M. van den (1978). *Sport in de Sovjet-Unie (Sport in the Soviet Union)*. Haarlem: De Vrieseborch.

Hueting, J.E. (1988). *Invloed van Hormonen (ACTH) op de Maximale Prestaties van Beroepsrenners (Effects of Hormones (ACTH) on Maximal Performance of Professional Cyclists)*. Haarlem: De Vrieseborch.

Kaminski, G., & Ruoff, B.A. (1979a). Auswirkungen der Hochleistungssports bei Kindern und Jugendlichen. Konzeptuelle Grundlagen und Fragestellungen einer empirischen Untersuchung an Eiskunstläufern, Kunstturnern und Schwimmern (Influence of top-level sports on children. Conceptual basis and questions of an empirical investigation in figure skating, gymnastics and swimming). *Sportwissenschaft*, **9**, 200−217.

Kaminski, G., & Ruoff, B.A. (1979b). Kinder im Hochleistungssport (Children in top-level sports). In H. Gabler (Ed.), *Praxis der Psychologie im Leistungssport (Psychology in Competitive Sport)*. Berlin: Verlag Bartels & Wernitz.

Kaminski, G., Mayer, R., & Ruoff, B.A. (1984). *Kinder und Jugendliche im Hochleistungssport (Children and Adolescents in Top-level Sports)*. Schorndorf: Karl Hofmann.

Kranenborg, N. (1980). Sportbeoefening en blessures (Sport practice and injuries). *Geneeskunde en Sport*, **13**, 89−93.

Kranenborg, N. (1983). Blessures in Nederland (Sport injuries in The Netherlands). In J.E. Hueting and H. van der Brug (Eds), *Sport Wetenschappelijk Onderzocht (Research in Sport)*. Haarlem: De Vrieseborch.

Orlick, T.D., & Mosher, R. (1978). Extrinsic awards and participant motivation in a sport related task. *International Journal of Sport Psychology*, **9**, 27−39.

Ruoff, B.A. (1979a). Die soziale Position des Hochleistungssportlers in seiner Schulklasse (The social position of top-level sport performers at school). In G. Bäumler, E. Hahn and R. Nitsch (Eds), *Aktuelle Probleme des Sportpsychologie (Current Questions in Sport Psychology)*. Schorndorf: Karl Hofmann.

Ruoff, B.A. (1979b). Zum Tagesablauf zehn bis 14 jahriger Hochleistungssportler (Daily schedules of 10 to 14 year-old children in top-level sport). Paper presented at FEPSAC Congress, Varna.

Ruoff, B.A., & Kaminski, G. (1980). Auswirkungen des Hochleistungssports bei Kindern und Jugendlichen (Eiskunstläufer, Kunstturner, Schwimmer) (Influence of top-level sports on children and adolescents (Figure skaters, gymnasts, swimmers)). *Sportwissenschaft*, **10**, 169−184.

Wilberg, R.B. (1973). Criteria for the definition of a field. Paper presented at the IIIrd International Symposium on Sports Psychology, Madrid, Spain.

AUTHOR INDEX

Abernethy, B. 179, 182, 187, 188, 189, 191, 193
Abrams, L. 25, 26, 48
Adam, J.J.M.E. 74, 78
Alain, C. 170, 171, 172, 189, 193, 194
Alberts, R.V.J. 40, 47
Alderman, R.B. 9, 16, 20, 47
Alderson, G.J.K. 190, 191, 194, 196
Allison, M.G. 139, 151
Allport, G.W. 57, 60, 78
Apter, M.J. 38, 47
Arbuthnot, J. 71, 78
Arms, R.L. 101, 105, 106, 124
Arnold, R.K. 146, 152
Artus, H.G. 16, 47
Aspin, D.N. 154, 194
Atkinson, J.W. 9, 47
Atkinson, R.C. 14, 34, 49
Atkinson, R.L. 14, 34, 49
Ayllon, T. 139, 151
Azrin, N.H. 134, 135, 136, 137, 151, 152

Bakker, F.C. 64, 72, 74, 78, 129, 146, 151, 209, 212
Bandura, A. 83, 84, 85, 86, 100, 123, 137, 138, 151
Bannister, R. 4, 7
Barber, P.J. 145, 152
Bard, C. 176, 177, 178, 179, 181, 194
Barnett, F.T. 136, 152
Bauer, R.S. 43, 50
Bergen, T.C.M. 40, 47

Berkowitz, L. 83, 86, 100, 123
Betley, G. 25, 26, 48
Biddle, S.J.H. 39, 47
Bielefeld, J. 16, 20, 47
Bierhoff-Alfermann, D. 40, 47
Bijlard, M.J. 139, 153
Birch, D. 14, 47
Birch, J.S. 96, 126
Blitz, P. 45, 47, 199
Block, J. 59, 78
Bloss, H. 16, 20, 47
Blumer, H. 109, 123
Bootsma, R.J. 147, 151, 179, 180, 181, 186, 189, 195
Brackhane, R. 15, 16, 32, 48, 74, 80
Brannigan, A. 27, 48
Brawley, L.R. 39, 51
Brinker, B.P.L.M. den 139, 147, 151, 153, 190, 194
Broadbent, D.E. 160, 161, 183, 184, 194
Broadhurst, P.L. 34, 35, 36, 48
Brug, H.J.H. van der 106, 107, 108, 112, 115, 116, 117, 118, 119, 123
Buckolz, E. 182, 183, 194
Bullen, B.A. 29, 49
Burwitz, L. 138, 151
Buss, A.H. 101, 123
Butt, D.S. 18, 19, 48

Carr, D. 154, 194
Carriere, L. 176, 178, 179, 194
Carroll, W.R. 138, 151

215

Casady, M. 22, 23, 48
Cattell, R.B. 14, 48, 57, 63, 78
Chase, W.G. 163, 180, 194
Chi, M.T.H. 163, 180, 194
Child, D. 14, 48
Christensen, J.P. 160, 161, 194
Clarke, J. 88, 89, 123
Cohen, J. 160, 161, 163, 165, 167, 168, 194
Colt, E.W.D. 29, 48
Coombs, C.H. 159, 162, 194
Cox, D.N. 64, 78
Cox, P.W. 71, 80
Cratty, B.J. 155, 194
Critcher, C. 88, 89, 123
Crossman, E.R.F.W. 130, 151
Crum, B.J. 16, 48

Dalton, J.E. 42, 48
Dawes, R.M. 159, 162, 194
Dearnaley, E.J. 163, 167, 168, 194
Deboeck, M. 201, 202, 212
De Charms, R. 22, 48
Deci, E.L. 9, 11, 12, 13, 14, 15, 19, 21, 22, 25, 26, 48
Dellen, T.J. van 16, 48
De Soto, C.B. 59, 79
Deurenberg, P. 210, 211, 212
Deutsch, M. 110, 123
Dickinson, J.A. 135, 151
Dodson, J.D. 34, 35, 52
Dollard, J. 83, 123
Doob, L.W. 83, 123
Drouin, D. 175, 194
Dunleavy, A.O. 17, 48
Dunning, E. 112, 123
Durkee, A. 101, 123

Easterbrook, J.A. 37, 45, 48
Eber, H.W. 63, 78
Edwards, J. 166, 194
Edwards, W. 158, 194
Einhorn, H.J. 211, 212
Ekkers, C.L. 83, 86, 90, 111, 124, 205, 212
Elias, N. 86, 87, 119, 124
Elliot, D.L. 29, 48
Emmen, H.H. 147, 151
Endler, N.S. 60, 79
Epstein, S. 31, 48, 56, 57, 60, 75, 76, 78

Ewel, W. 84, 125
Eysenck, H.J. 64, 66, 67, 68, 69, 71, 73, 76, 78, 183, 184, 194

Faber, C.M. 192, 196
Fahlbusch-Wendler, C. 206, 208, 213
Fairs, J. 182, 194
Feij, J.A. 59, 78
Feltz, D.L. 43, 50, 148, 149, 151
Fenz, W.D. 75, 76, 78
Ferguson, E.D. 34, 48
Ferracutti, F. 84, 126
Fiegenbaum, T. 68, 69, 79
Filter, M. 162, 195
Fiorito, P. 174, 175, 195
Fischhold, R. 15, 16, 32, 48
Fisher, A.C. 60, 79
Fleury, M. 176, 178, 179, 194
Fodero, J.M. 17, 48
Folkins, C.H. 64, 79
Fowler, C.A. 146, 151
Frantz, A.G. 29, 48
Freud, S. 82, 100, 124
Frieze, I. 38, 40, 48, 52
Frogner, E. 99, 124
Frowein, H.W. 201, 202, 213

Gabler, H. 16, 19, 48, 49, 63, 64, 79
Galen, W.C.C. van 94, 124
Gange, J.J. 43, 49
Gaskell, G. 91, 124
Gaul, M. 74, 79
Geen, R.G. 43, 49, 84, 100, 123, 124
Gibson, J.J. 145, 151, 154, 155, 162, 163, 195
Gill, B. 191, 196
Girardin, Y. 170, 172, 194
Goldberg, L. 29, 48
Goldfoot, D.A. 27, 49
Goldstein, A. 29, 30, 49
Goldstein, J.H. 101, 105, 106, 124, 166, 195
Goodenough, D.R. 71, 80
Gorsuch, H.R. 17, 49
Gould, D.R. 138, 151
Gowan, G.R. 4, 7
Groot, A. de 163, 195
Grossman, A. 29, 49
Guilford, J.P. 56, 57, 58, 79
Guttmann, A. 103, 124

Hahmann, H.   16, 49
Halle, M.   176, 178, 179, 194
Halliwell, W.R.   21, 22, 49
Hardley, M.E.   29, 49
Hardy, L.   38, 49
Harré, R.   89, 125
Harvey, O.   111, 125
Harzem, P.   133, 152
Heckhausen, H.   11, 14, 19, 39, 41, 49
Heider, R.   22, 49
Heinilä, K.   99, 124
Hendry, L.B.   1, 7
Hermans, H.J.M.   11, 49
Heuvel, M. van den   206, 213
Hilgard, E.R.   14, 34, 49
Hinton, E.R.   29, 51
Hirschi, T.   117, 124
Hoefnagels, G.P.   86, 124
Hogan, R.   59, 79
Hogarth, R.M.   211, 212
Holding, D.H.   141, 152
Holz, W.C.   134, 135, 151
Hood, W.   111, 125
Horsfall, J.S.   60, 79
Hosek, V.   17, 52, 54, 80
Howlett, T.A.   29, 49
Hueting, J.E.   169, 195, 201, 205, 212, 213
Hunt, V.V.   73, 74, 80
Hutt, J.W.R.   183, 185, 196
Hyrcaiko, D.   140, 152

Ismail, A.H.   30, 50

Jackson, A.   26, 52
Jones, C.M.   173, 175, 188, 195
Jones, J.G.   38, 49
Jordan, F.R.   138, 152
Junger-Tas, J.   118, 124

Kagan, J.   71, 79
Kahle, J.   25, 26, 48
Kahneman, D.   37, 49
Kaminski, G.   207, 209, 213
Kane, J.E.   55, 79
Kanfer, F.H.   27, 49
Kelley, H.H.   22, 50
Kerr, J.H.   38, 50
Killian, L.M.   110, 125
Kingsmore, J.M.   100, 101, 124
Klapp, O.E.   83, 124

Klavora, P.   36, 50
Kogan, N.   71, 79
Komaki, J.   136, 152
Koop, S.   139, 140, 152
Kozan, B.   44, 50
Kranenborg, N.   205, 210, 213
Kugler, P.N.   146, 152
Kuhla, A.   39, 52

Landers, D.M.   36, 43, 44, 50, 148, 149, 151
Lang, G.E.   83, 124
Lang, K.   83, 124
Latham, G.P.   41, 42, 50
Lefebre, L.   96, 124
Lefebvre, L.M.   33, 40, 41, 50
Legge, D.   145, 152
Leibowitz, G.   101, 124
Leith, L.M.   101, 124
Lewis, J.M.   103, 124
Lobstein, D.D.   30, 50
Locke, E.A.   41, 42, 50
Lorenz, K.   82, 89, 100, 125
Lovaas, O.J.   84, 125
Luce, R.D.   162, 195

MacGillivary, W.W.   72, 79
Machin, V.J.   29, 51
Maddi, S.R.   56, 79
Magnusson, D.   60, 79
Maguire, J.   112, 123
Mahoney, M.J.   138, 152
Maier, R.A.   42, 48
Malmo, R.B.   36, 50
Manders, T.G.W.M.   16, 17, 18, 50
Mangillo, B.M.   81, [125]
Marriott, A.M.   191, 192, 195
Marseille, N.   112, 115, 116, 123
Marsh, P.   85, 88, 89, 114, 115, 116, 121, 125
Marteniuk, R.G.   142, 152, 163, 195
Martens, R.   36, 43, 50, 54, 60, 79, 152
Martin, G.L.   139, 140, 152
Martin, W.S.   68, 69, 79
Mayer, R.   207, 213
McArthur, J.W.   29, 49
McClelland, D.C.   15, 50
McCloy-Layman, E.   64, 65, 79
McDougall, A.A.   27, 48
McGuinness, D.   36, 51
McLeod, P.   186, 188, 195

Shaw, K.N. 41, 50
Sherif, C. 111, 125
Sherif, M. 111, 125
Shiffrin, R.M. 142, 153
Sime, W.E. 64, 79
Simon, H.A. 163, 194
Simons, D. 74, 80
Singer, R.N. 81, 125
Skinner, B.F. 132, 133, 137, 138, 153
Skrinar, G.S. 29, 49
Slaby, R.G. 84, 125
Slepicka, P. 54, 80
Smith, M.D. 98, 99, 125
Smyth, M.M. 191, 192, 195
Soetens, E. 201, 212
Solano, C. 59, 78
Solomon, R.L. 31, 32, 33, 46, 51
Soulierc, D. 175, 176, 177, 189, 195
Span, P. 71, 80
Spielberger, C.D. 73, 80
Stabler, J.R.L.W. 148, 151, 190, 194
Stephenson, J. 191, 196
Stevenson, C.L. 64, 65, 80
Streng, J. 43, 51
Suinn, R.M. 148, 149, 153
Sully, D.J. 190, 194
Sully, H.G. 190, 194
Summers, J.J. 29, 51
Sutton, J.R. 29, 49
Swets, J.A.A. 159, 195

Tannenbaum, P.H. 83, 125
Tanner, W.P. 159, 195
Taylor, I.R. 88, 89, 112, 114, 125
Thomas, A. 74, 80
Tomlin, S. 29, 49
Turner, E.T. 100, 125
Turner, R.H. 110, 125
Turvey, M.T. 146, 151, 152
Tutko, T.A. 17, 51, 55, 80
Tversky, A. 158, 159, 162, 194
Twitmyer, E.B. 131, 153
Tyldesley, D.A. 3, 7, 74, 80, 153, 179, 180, 181, 186, 189, 195

Ungerer, D. 144, 153

Vanek, M. 17, 52, 54, 55, 80

Vaz, E.E. 98, 99, 125
Veroff, J. 14, 47
Vinnai, G. 83, 100, 101, 125
Voigt, H.F. 40, 51, 92, 96, 125
Volkamer, M. 91, 93, 94, 96, 126
Volpert, W. 145, 153
Vroon 211

Wade, M.G. 146, 153
Walter, C.B. 146, 152
Walters, R.H. 84, 123
Wardlaw, S.L. 29, 48
Watts, W.J. 29, 48
Weber, R. 100, 105, 106, 125
Weinberg, R.S. 26, 52, 73, 74, 80
Weiner, B. 39, 40, 48, 52
Welford, A.T. 37, 52, 141, 153, 159, 195
Wesseling, L.G. 147, 151
White, B. 111, 125
Whitfield, D.C. 162, 163, 195
Whiting, H.T.A. 3, 7, 73, 74, 80, 132, 139, 146, 147, 148, 151, 153, 155, 162, 183, 185, 190, 191, 192, 194, 195, 196
Widmeyer, W.N. 96, 126
Wieringen, P.C.W. van 74, 78, 147, 148, 151, 190, 194
Wiggins, J.S. 56, 80
Wilberg, R.B. 3, 7, 157, 161, 196, 201, 213
Williams, J. 112, 123
Willis, D. 144, 153
Winkler, T. 91, 126
Witkin, H.A. 71, 72, 80
Wolf, P.G. 93, 126
Wolfgang, N.E. 84, 126
Wolpe, J. 138, 153
Wood, N.L. 16, 47

Yerkes, R.M. 34, 35, 52
Young, I. 17, 51

Zajonc, R.B. 43, 52
Ziegler, S. 140, 153
Zillmann, D. 83, 125
Zimbardo, P.G. 86, 109, 126
Zuckerman, M. 68, 80

SUBJECT INDEX

achievement 9
  motivation (*see* motivation)
  orientation 65, 66, 69
ACTH-hormone 205
actions
  complex 154
  simple 154
activation 35, 36, 37, 38, 43, 44, 45,
  83, 87, 101
addiction 28, 29
  running 29
affective contrast 31
affective reaction 31
  primary 31
  secondary 31
affordance(s) 155, 156, 162, 172
aggression 9, 18, 19, 81–126
  definition of 82
  instrumental 87, 90, 98, 99, 115, 116
  physical 84
  reactive 87, 90, 98, 115, 116, 205
  ritualisation of 82, 89, 115
  verbal 84
aggressive behaviour 81–126
aggressive
  behavioural disposition 86
  drive 82, 83
  modelling 86
  signals 84, 86, 101
  subculture 85, 88, 99, 111
aggro 89
amphetamine 199, 201, 205
anticipation 157

anxiety 36, 37, 38, 64, 65, 66, 68, 71,
  73, 75, 132, 138
  state 73, 74, 75
  trait 73
applied behaviour analysis 135
aptitudes 56, 57
arousal 36, 37, 38, 43, 44, 68
athletes (*see* sport performers)
attention 37, 41, 45, 130, 145
  and activation (arousal) 148, 149
attentional processes 74
attitudes 56, 57
attribution 39, 40
  pattern 42, 43
  process 41, 47
  theory 22
audience (*see* spectators)
automation 130

behavioural
  disposition 56
  packages 137, 139
  traits 57
behaviourism 131
beta-endorphins 29, 30
Buss–Durkee Inventory 101, 105

catastrophe curve 38
catharsis 82, 100, 121
classical conditioning 131, 132, 135
cognitive restructuring 86
cognitive style 71, 72, 197
combat sports 90, 92

competence (feelings of) 16, 21, 22, 25
configuration theory 119
contact sports 84, 90, 92
contagion 110
contagion theory 109
contingencies of reinforcement 133
contingency management 133
cortical arousal 67
coach 3, 136, 137, 139, 146, 193, 199
competence 12, 13
competition 18, 25, 26
consistency 59, 60
cooperation 9, 18
criterion 169, 170
cue-function of violent stimuli 101
cue utilisation theory 45

d' 159, 169
decision processes 130
de-individuation 86, 109, 110
discounting principle 22, 23
disinhibition (of aggression) 86
disposition 57, 58, 73
drive(s) 10, 12, 13, 31

ecological validity 43
effector processes 140, 141
emotion(s) 83, 87, 90, 109
emotional
  arousal 109
  lability 68
endogenous opioide peptides 29
extraversion 63, 65, 66, 68, 69, 71, 75, 203, 209
extravert 61, 66, 67, 68, 69, 184

false-negatives 160
false-positives 160
fault analysing strategy 150
fear 73
  of failure 40
feedback 19, 20, 127, 139, 140, 141, 146, 147, 173
  external (visual and auditory) 141, 142
  extrinsic 141, 142
  informational 136, 137
  internal (proprioceptive) 141, 142
  intrinsic 141, 142
field dependence 71, 72

field independence 71, 72
Fisher, Bobby 18
Frasier, Joe 101
frustration 82, 83, 87, 104, 106, 107, 108
frustration–aggression hypothesis 94, 105, 106

gang (in relation to violence) 84
generalisation 201, 202
goal 10, 11, 13, 19, 41, 42, 47
  -oriented behaviour 83
  -setting 20, 41

habit (aggressive) 81, 85
habituation 31
home-field advantage 166
hostility 81

imitation 127
impulsivity 71
incidental learning 129
individual differences 56, 59
  in decision-making 183
information-processing 140, 142, 143, 145, 177
  approach to motor learning 127
  capacity 45
  processes 74
  system 162
instinct 82
instinctive energy 82
instrumental behaviour 133
interests 56, 57
introversion 63, 65, 66, 71, 209
introvert 61, 66, 67, 68, 69, 184
intuition 211
invariances 163
inverted-U hypothesis 36, 37, 38, 46

Kessler 199
knowledge
  body of 2
  generated 3, 157, 201
  of performance 141, 142, 146
  of results 141, 142, 146
  recipient 3, 157, 201
  tacit 163

learning
  by imitation 137
  curve 129
  strategies 71, 150
level of aspiration 19, 42, 43
limbic system 67
Liston, Sonny 18
locus of control 40

medical/paramedical team 5
memory processes 140, 141
mental
  practice 127
  training 127, 148, 149
Merritt, Jeff 28, 143
Michels, Rinus 120
modelling (see observational learning)
moment strategy 150
momentary approach 72
morphological characteristics 56
morphology 57
motivation 10, 35, 40
  achievement 40, 61, 209
  and achievement 33, 46, 47
  intrinsic 11, 12, 21, 23, 25, 26, 27,
    46, 203
  optimal level of 34
  psychology 8, 9
  and sport 9
motivational
  traits 56
motive(s) 9, 10, 12, 14, 17, 31, 33, 35
  achievement 10, 11, 15, 17, 46
  affiliation 10, 11, 15, 46
  competence 12, 13
  development of 11, 19
  development of sport 20
  exploration 10
  for participation in sport 14, 16, 18,
    46
  health 15, 46
  power 10
motor coordination 130
motor learning 70, 71, 72, 76, 127
mountaineering 27
Muhammad Ali 28, 50, 101, 143, 152
muscular excitation 148

need(s) 10, 56, 57
  biological 13, 14
  for acceptance 12

for achievement 12
for affection 12
for approval 12
for competence 11, 12, 15, 18, 30,
    33
for knowledge 12
for novelty 12
for power 12
for skill mastery 12
psychological 14
neurotic conflict 18, 19
neuroticism 63, 65, 66, 69
noise 159, 160, 203

observational learning 137, 138, 139,
    145
operant
  behaviour 133
  conditioning 127, 131, 132, 133,
    134, 135, 136, 137, 138, 139
opponent-process theory 31

parachute jumping 27
pay-off analysis 90
perception–action coupling 189
personality 55
  changes in 61, 62, 64, 65
  characteristics 55, 56, 58
  and decision-making 184
  differences in 62, 65, 69
  psychology 55, 56, 57
  and sport 53, 70, 75, 77
  stability 56, 64, 65
  traits 54, 55, 56, 57, 58, 59, 60, 65,
    73, 75, 76, 77, 81, 209
physical aggression (see aggression)
physiological
  activation 83, 101
  characteristics 56
physiology 57
prejudice 206, 212
probability 158
psychoanalysis 82
psychological
  decision theory 161
  refractory period 141
psychology
  of motivation (see motivation
    psychology)

Psychology (*cont.*)
  of personality (*see* personality
    psychology)
  of sport (*see* sport psychology)
psychoticism 69
punishment 134, 135, 136, 139

reactive aggression (*see* aggression)
receptor processes 140, 141
reflexivity 71
reinforcer 132
  primary 134, 137
  secondary 135, 137
reinforcement 82, 84, 134, 139, 140
  contingencies 140
  differential 132
  extrinsic 26
  selective 132
reminiscence 128
response
  acquisition 84
  conditioned 131
  criterion 160
  establishment 84
  unconditioned 131
reticular formation 36, 67
reversal theory 38
rewards
  extrinsic 21, 22, 23, 46, 199
risk 157, 159, 161, 162
  perceived 160, 162

second order factors 63, 66, 73
  extraversion–introversion 66
  neuroticism–stability 66, 73
  psychoticism–strength of super-ego
    66
secondary conditioning 134
selection hypothesis 65
self-concept 64, 75
self-esteem 209
sensation-seeking 67, 68, 69
sensory-motor quotient 144
shaping 135, 136, 137
signal
  detection theory 159, 160, 203
  plus noise 159, 160
single-channel hypothesis 141, 145
skiing 27
skill 154, 156
skinheads 88

Skinner-box 132
soccer
  hooliganism 88, 112, 117, 118, 119,
    120, 121
  war 81
sociability 58
social
  facilitation 43, 155
  control theory 117
  critical theory of sport 83
  learning theory 82, 84, 85, 127, 137
socialisation processes 98, 99
Spasski, Boris 164
spectators 43, 44, 45, 99, 100, 101,
    103, 104, 106, 108, 109, 110, 112,
    114, 115, 116, 123
sport
  competitive 17, 18, 61, 65, 205
  individual 65
  recreative 17, 18, 61, 65, 205
  selection 61, 62, 69
  team 65
sport participation 16
  reasons for 17
sport performers
  recreational 16, 18
  competitive 16, 18
sport psychologist
  role of 3
sport psychology
  as a research field 2
sport scientist 4
stability 67, 69
statistical decision theory 159
stimulus
  conditioned 131
  constellation 87
  discrimination 132
  discriminative 137
  generalisation 84, 132
  unconditioned· 131
stimulus–response compatibility 142,
    143
stress 71
  and performance 38
  reactions 30
structural functionalism 82
structuring tendency 72
subjective probability 161, 162, 167,
    169, 170, 171
  uncertainty 143

sublimation 82, 114
symbolic learning 148

temperament 57
temperamental characteristics
  57
Thematic Apperception Test (TAT)
  15, 100
trait(s) 58
  inidicators 58, 59, 60
  psychology 54
  specific to sport 60
translatory processes 140, 141

uncertainty 171, 172, 178
utility 158
  value 162

verbal aggression (see aggression)
viewpoints/controversy
  credulous 54, 55, 77, 78
  sceptical 54, 55, 59, 77
violence 89–126
violent role model 98

well-being 203, 204, 205, 206, 210

youth sport 207